THE COMPETITIVE EDGE

EMOTIONAL INTELLIGENCE IN THE AGE OF AI

MARY MARLAND

ISBN: 979-8-9950637-0-4
Publisher: Wild Doves Press

To my father, who did not live to see this book, but lives in it.

To Kate and Jack, you are my compass. You are where I return.

FOREWORD

For centuries, intelligence was our measure of distinction—the ability to calculate, reason, and innovate. But as artificial intelligence (AI) accelerates past our capacity for data processing and pattern recognition, the spotlight shifts inward. What remains uniquely human is emotion—the awareness of it, the mastery of it, and the ability to connect through it. Mary Marland's book tackles that frontier with precision and courage and delivers on the emotional competitiveness required in the AI era.

Mary Marland invites us into a rigorous and refreshing exploration of emotional intelligence—not as a sentimental ideal, but as a trainable, measurable, and deeply practical form of human capability. The central challenge posed here is both urgent and profound: how do we evolve our emotional intelligence fast enough to lead wisely in a world increasingly shaped by machines that outthink us?

Each part of this work builds carefully toward an answer. The human imperative section defines what makes humans distinct from machines and why that distinction matters in an age of artificial intelligence. The opening chapters reset the foundation of emotional intelligence, disentangling its essence from cliché. It unravels the future of what machines cannot be alongside the history of human understanding. It delivers the transcendent advantage we have and the crisis of passive adoption along with the choices we have in front of us. This book reflects Mary's labyrinth of thought processes and a mastery of a well crafted body of work. At its heart, this is a book asking the pertinent question—"What makes us human?" This is a defining question in every era. Currently it is very relevant given the onset of the "Era of AI." This book offers both a mirror and a map: a way to understand what makes emotional intelligence measurable and to ensure that emotional intelligence keeps humanity intact in the evolving revolutions of AI.

The middle section becomes a true training ground, offering skills that help individuals transform awareness into mastery. And finally, the book scales these human capacities into the systems that define our collective future—where data meets ethics, and leadership meets responsibility from insights to action. It traverses from self-awareness to self-mastery with ease, while drilling down into relational skills in two parts for a deep dive. Subsequently the book segues into scaling human wisdom and outlines measurement models & justice and what work we have ahead of us.

Mary Marland provides a plethora of real world examples. Take for instance, an overdose case: information about the patient who is being admitted may not be revealed to the AI bot performing the admission. Withholding such vital information and the over-reliance on AI can lead not only to misdiagnosis but also result to incorrect treatment options. This type of emotional intelligence less AI can cause a lot of harm to humanity. How hospital admission cases need to humanize and collect relevant information in a tense "golden hour" period—that is a lot of high emotional intelligence skill set. AI is not there yet. Patients and families disclose information to doctors if they feel mutual empathy. They may not do so with an AI bot. The limitation isn't just technical. It is structural. Emotional intelligence will add to the competitiveness of AI.

What is also so beautiful about this book is its longitudinal analysis on the time axis. This book converges 5,000 years of eastern spiritual and emotional leadership with 500 years of western leadership. Mary so eloquently outlines how French mathematician René Descartes delineated logic and emotion. Emotions were treated as interference with clear thinking, resulting in the onset of Cartesian logic and its reflection of a distinctly western approach that is over-engineered on the logical-intelligence side, creating an asymmetry with far less maturity when it comes to emotional intelligence. The indigenous wisdom traditions of eastern cultures maintained an integrated understanding of mind, body, emotion, and spirit. Mary Marland's book brings the potential good merger of both these approaches—emotional intelligence and AI logic—and offers a uniquely negotiated pathway that is capable of leading with both logic and wisdom.

Professor Prasanna Kumar
Santa Clara, California

AUTHOR'S NOTE

Toni Morrison

This book began as a study of emotional intelligence in a world shaped by artificial intelligence (AI). I sought to understand what makes us human as machines grow more capable, and to see what could be taught, measured, and strengthened. There were multiple iterations of the manuscript over several years.

While writing this book, I was tested in ways that demanded application of everything learned about emotional capacity. What emerged from that experience became inseparable from the writing itself.

The proximity to harm illuminated the mechanism. Fear governs the unintegrated. It arrests development and echoes without listening. One does not debate with an echo. One moves beyond its reach. I had to trust the accumulation before the shape became visible.

It was during this time that the book and my life began to speak to each other.

I have always believed in technology as a force for progress. The growing accessibility of AI was a pivot point unlike previous industrial leaps, and the structure of large language models fascinated me. I studied how AI trains itself and was drawn to participate. Observation of models learning through repetition, pattern, and correction, combined with simultaneous self-training, showed systems building capacity in parallel with the growth of my own emotional capacity.

The mirroring became clear: machines were learning to respond, and I was learning to feel. The difference is that machines optimize for prediction while humans prioritize meaning. That distinction became the spine of this book.

Multiple language models were applied throughout the process, used as tools to research, test, refine, and edit ideas. The writing itself remained my own. I loved the practice and often lost myself in the work. Sometimes a single paragraph took half a day to get right. Other days the writing continued for ten to twelve hours. The discipline became its own form of integration.

Through this, I learned that emotional capacity is a muscle, built, not bestowed. It is not fate, or talent, or inheritance. It expands through discomfort and responsibility, reinforced by action and shaped through a resilient nervous system and relationships that demand growth.

Awakening and action are not the same: the first disrupts; the second defines.

This book is not just the story. It is the action.

Thank you for reading it.

CONTENTS

PART 1
THE HUMAN IMPERATIVE

THE PAUSE

A father sits in his parked car outside his house, already home for fifteen minutes. The engine is off and he scrolls on his phone. His three-year-old daughter will run to him the moment he opens the door, yelling "Daddy's home!" as she does every evening. His wife is exhausted and the house will be loud. He tells himself he needs a moment, that he is decompressing from work. Yet what he is actually doing is subtler and more vulnerable: he is postponing connection, striving to be there, not just physically, but emotionally.

The body already knows what the mind has not yet named. Shoulders tight and breathing shallow, a low hum of dread sat in his stomach—one he would call tiredness if anyone asked. But it is not tiredness. It is the weight of transition, the effort of moving from a self that performs to a self that feels. His nervous system is already in the house; he is the one still outside.

That tension, between what we think we are doing and what we are actually doing, is emotional intelligence (EI). Or more precisely, it is the beginning of it. It is the moment he sees fear clearly enough to choose what happens next: entering the house numb and withdrawn, or stepping inside present and alive.

We imagine emotional intelligence as the domain of inspiring leaders or magnetic personalities. But more often, it lives in quiet, ordinary moments like this one. A man sitting in a cooling car, learning to name what he is avoiding. Understanding that wisdom sometimes begins with knowing why one hesitates before walking through the front door.

That father's hesitation echoes a larger truth. We have built a world that rewards speed and productivity, along with the suppression of discomfort. Emotional life is rarely named and almost never rewarded. Yet it is in these unrecognized decisions that our lives are actually lived. These moments scale. From meetings and leadership to parenting and family life, the world is full of postponed presence. When one person cannot walk through their own front door, a family absorbs the cost. When enough people cannot, institutions hollow out and societies lose the capacity to govern themselves. We start this investigation here, in the act of being human and choosing what to do about it.

What Emotional Intelligence Is

The father in the car is not lacking information; he knows his daughter is waiting and his wife is exhausted. He is aware that it's time to go inside, yet he lacks access to the signals his body is sending. The language precise enough to name those signals is out of reach, and even if it existed, the capacity to act on it remains beyond him. That access is emotional intelligence.

Emotional intelligence is often confused with feelings. In reality, it is the ability to work with emotional data. The signals the data carries and the patterns it reveals together demand action, forming the integrative force behind all other intelligences.

Fear heightens perception and signals what matters, whether threat or growth. Anger signals a boundary crossed. Sadness signals loss. Joy signals connection. These are not noise to be suppressed. They are data to be read. Emotional intelligence governs how well that data is perceived, interpreted, and used to guide action.

This capacity is not a personality trait or a soft skill. It is an intelligence: a system that learns from information, integrates that learning with perception and memory, adapts based on feedback, and improves outcomes across changing contexts. The system is embodied. The body registers emotional information before conscious thought can process it, milliseconds before we know we are afraid, angry, or grieving. Most people miss these signals entirely, or notice them only after reacting. The work of emotional intelligence begins here, in learning to read what the body already knows. And this can be trained.

Intelligence itself is not directly observable. It becomes visible through skills: awareness and naming, regulation and self-command, empathy and perspective-taking, relational judgment and response selection. It is the adaptive system. Skills are the mechanisms and these skills are integrators. With emotional intelligence, verbal intelligence becomes *persuasion*. Analytical intelligence becomes *wisdom*. Creative intelligence becomes *connection*. Cognitive intelligence becomes *leadership*. Emotional intelligence is what makes our other capacities human. It allows us to become conductors capable of orchestrating complexity into progress.

The Inflection Point

The capacity to recognize fear and choose a response is teachable, measurable, and improvable.

We have been here before with capacities we now take for granted. For most of human history, literacy was treated as a specialized trait reserved for a small elite. It was widely believed that the common person simply lacked the mental capacity to handle the written word. The prevailing logic was that their minds were built for manual labor, not for the abstract complexity of reading and writing. Critics argued that teaching them would be a waste of resources, arming people with thoughts above their station and distracting them from the "real" work they were supposedly designed for.

They were wrong. The capacity wasn't missing; the training was.

While emotional intelligence is more visceral than the alphabet, both are systems of decoding. Just as literacy allows us to decode the symbols of language to access a world of information, emotional intelligence allows us to decode the signals of the body to access a world of choice. In both cases, the shift from a lucky few to a literate many is what allows a society to manage a more complex reality.

In the past, a society could function with a literate few and an illiterate many. But as the world became more complex, that model broke. The shift from a literate few to a literate many is what allowed civilization to scale. We are at that same threshold today with our internal lives.

Emotional intelligence is the new baseline for participation in a world that demands high-frequency adaptation. Just as we once moved from oral tradition to the written word, we must now move from reactive impulse to conscious regulation. The transformation happened as it always does: gradually, then suddenly. What we mistook for an innate limitation was a lack of training.

We are at that inflection point today. Unlike literacy, which required building schools from scratch, the infrastructure for emotional intelligence already exists; it is simply fragmented.

Scientists study it in labs, therapists teach it in clinics, organizations measure it in leadership development. Spiritual traditions have cultivated these capacities for millennia. Some people inherit pieces of this training through cultural practices or family modeling, learning to regulate their breathing, sitting with discomfort, or steadying themselves in silence.

These remain sacred traditions, but the capacities they build are biological. Breath calms the nervous system; reflection sharpens awareness; attunement synchronizes us with others. The point is not to strip these practices of meaning, but to recognize their reach. We can no longer afford for these skills to be "sacred exceptions" practiced only in private or "clinical interventions." We must integrate them into systematic, scalable training that makes them as fundamental as reading and writing.

The AI Inflection

What makes this integration urgent is the way artificial intelligence (AI) is changing how we decide and lead. By externalizing cognition and pattern recognition, AI makes the role of emotional intelligence newly visible. But by removing friction and human mediation, it also risks accelerating the atrophy of our internal tools.

The distinction is structural. Machines optimize for prediction: given these inputs, what outcome is most probable? Humans optimize for meaning: given this situation, what matters? A diagnostic algorithm can flag an anomaly in a patient's chart. It cannot sense that the patient's partner is hiding something, and it cannot create the relational safety required for the truth to be spoken. The gap is not a limitation that better data will close. It is the difference between processing information about experience and having experience. That difference is embodied, and it is ours.

Consider what technology already enables: the father in the car can scroll indefinitely, postponing presence with perfect efficiency. AI extends this capacity to every domain. It can summarize the meeting we did not attend or draft the message we did not feel. Even the response we did not consider can be generated by AI. Each convenience is also an opportunity to opt out of the difficult work of being present. Postponed presence, scaled.

As measurement becomes more accessible, data about our emotional states will exist in spaces we thought were private: behavioral analytics, biometric tracking, the metadata of our digital lives. The information is already being gathered. The question is whether we learn to read it ourselves, or whether it is read for us by systems designed to predict and persuade rather than to develop and protect.

The more capable our systems become, the more essential our distinctly human capacities become. The greatest risk of the coming decade is not AI replacing jobs; it is humans forgetting how to feel, listen, and relate. When enough people operate on autopilot, entire societies become vulnerable to manipulation. The capacity for conscious choice is what keeps us capable of self-governance in an age of systems designed to govern us.

This book is built to meet that moment.

What This Book Offers

Three questions shape this work:

- **Can emotional intelligence be taught as practical, measurable skills?**

- **What challenges and opportunities does AI create for emotionally intelligent leadership?**

- **How can we develop emotional intelligence at the pace required to maintain our dominion over the systems we create?**

The book is structured to answer each. Part One sets the foundation: what emotional intelligence is and is not, how our understanding has evolved, and why it matters now. Part Two builds the toolkit in layers: self-awareness (the first pillar), self-mastery (choosing skillfully), and relational mastery (connecting meaningfully), broken into specific skills with ways to measure growth. Part Three scales the work: how measurement is changing with AI, how to bring emotional intelligence into systems without losing its essence, and how to integrate justice and accountability to ensure progress serves the many rather than the few.

You do not need to read this book sequentially. If you are skeptical about whether emotional intelligence is real or trainable, start with Chapter Three; the 5,000-year track record might change your mind. If you want immediate practice, skip to Part Two. If you are most worried about AI and what it means for human ability, Chapters Five and Six address that directly. If you are a leader thinking about organizational culture, Part Three is where individual skills meet systemic design.

Some skills will come more easily than others. Mastery across all of them is rare. Hiding from the work does not change reality. Those who choose discomfort and courage are the ones who lead.

Where Do You Stand?

Before you read further, take a moment with these questions. Do not answer them abstractly. Answer them from the last time it mattered.

Self-Awareness: Think of the last time you were angry at someone you love. Were you aware of what you were feeling before you acted on it? Could you name it with precision, not just "upset" or "stressed" but the specific texture of what was moving through you? Did you notice your body first, or only the thought that followed?

Self-Mastery: Recall the last time fear showed up in a high-stakes moment: a difficult conversation, a public decision, a risk you knew was right. Did you hold your ground, or did you collapse, deflect, or go numb? Afterwards, did the intensity resolve, or did it stay lodged in your chest for hours?

Relational Mastery: Consider the last time you caused harm you did not intend. Did you notice the impact before it was named for you? Did you repair it, or did you explain it away? When the relationship needed you to be accountable rather than right, which did you choose?

These are not tests. They are markers. Wherever you find yourself, the capacity to move forward is already in you. This book shows you how to access it.

A Note on My Role

I am not writing this book as a master of emotional intelligence. I am writing as a practitioner—engaged in the work, still learning, practicing, failing and refining. Continuous transformation is the point. Emotional intelligence is not an achievement; rather, it is a set of skills, capacities you build, lose, rebuild, and deepen over time.

This work is not mine alone. It draws on decades of psychological and neuroscientific research, along with wisdom traditions that have long treated emotion as a pathway to human insight and alignment. My role is to gather, translate, and apply this knowledge so that emotional intelligence becomes a living, practical part of how we navigate a world where human agency can no longer be assumed.

Change rarely begins loudly. It often starts with quiet work, done seriously, by those willing to stay engaged. I hope this model continues to evolve as others test it in real environments, pushing its limits and refining its use. I hope new methods of measurement and new technology carry it forward. What is at stake is not only our systems, but our sense of responsibility within them.

This is the core of emotional intelligence in the age of AI. Creation is not enough. We must remain capable of leading what we create.

CHAPTER 1

WHAT MACHINES CANNOT BE

The Emergency Room at 2 AM

A patient arrives unconscious. Vital signs are unstable. An AI diagnostic system processes blood pressure, heart rate, oxygen saturation, and recent medical history within seconds. It then recommends a treatment protocol with the highest probability of survival.

The attending doctor, reading the same data, notices subtleties. She sees how the patient's partner stands distant from the bed, the tension in their posture, the lack of eye contact when questioned about medications. The doctor pauses and asks, "Is there anything you're not telling me?"

The partner hesitates. Sensing the doctor's genuine concern, they admit the patient has a prescription drug problem. They had omitted details that make the AI's recommended treatment potentially fatal.

The machine optimized the data it had. The doctor sensed meaning in silence, a difference with life-or-death consequences.

What prevented the AI system from uncovering the truth? A critic might argue that a sufficiently advanced AI, equipped with high-resolution cameras and voice stress analysis, could also "detect" the partner's elevated heart rate or lack of eye contact. Indeed, machines can be trained to recognize the pixels of distress.

But detection is not connection.

Even if the AI had flagged the partner's behavior as an anomaly, it could not create the relational safety required for the truth to be spoken. The partner did not confess because they were analyzed. They confessed because the connection made them feel seen and known. The limitation is not just technical. It is structural.

AI processes explicit data like numbers, words, and documented history. It cannot access the embodied signals that humans read automatically. It misses the quality of silence or the incongruence between stated facts and physical presence. These signals are not merely data points to be captured. They are relational exchanges that exist only in the interaction itself. AI has no body, no nervous system, and no capacity for felt sense. It processes information about interaction but cannot participate in interaction as an embodied being. More training data will not close this gap. This is why integration, holding technical data and relational meaning simultaneously, remains distinctly human. The capacity emerges from embodiment.

But where did the assumption that these could be separated come from? The answer begins with an intellectual error made nearly four centuries ago, one we are still correcting.

The Cartesian Error

In 1637, the French philosopher and mathematician René Descartes published ideas that divided mind and body, creating a hierarchy where rational thought reigned while emotion and sensation were dismissed. This framework became known as Cartesian Logic, and it reflected a distinctly Western approach to knowledge.

For centuries, this thinking dominated Western education, medicine, and philosophy. Emotion was treated as interference with clear thinking, something to be controlled or eliminated rather than integrated. Yet many Eastern philosophies, Indigenous wisdom traditions, and non-Western cultures maintained integrated understandings of mind, body, emotion, and spirit. These traditions recognized what Western science would take centuries to rediscover. They knew that emotion and reason are inseparable, and that wisdom emerges from their integration, not their separation.

The global consequences extended far beyond European philosophy. Through colonization, Western powers exported this mind-body split as universal truth, dismissing Indigenous and Eastern knowledge systems that understood humans as integrated beings. Educational systems imposed by colonial powers taught generations that rational thought was superior and emotional ways of knowing were primitive. The damage persists in institutions worldwide.

Modern neuroscience has confirmed what these traditions understood. Antonio Damasio's work in *Descartes' Error* studied patients with damaged emotional centers and revealed a truth: they retained analytical ability but lost decision-making capacity. Without emotion to assign value, logic becomes paralyzed. Lisa Feldman Barrett's research in *How Emotions Are Made* shows the brain constructs emotions as predictions, not mere responses. **We feel to act, not simply to react.**

Western science had to rediscover empirically what many cultures never forgot. We cannot afford another detour. Today we face a related and equally consequential choice about the value of emotional intelligence. Where Descartes dismissed emotion as inferior to reason, and colonial powers exported that dismissal globally, we now risk delegating emotional intelligence to machines incapable of embodied wisdom. The stakes are higher this time: not just which cultures' knowledge systems are valued, but whether human capacities themselves will atrophy through technological delegation.

The philosophical error has been corrected. But understanding that emotion and reason are inseparable does not tell us how they work together. What does embodied intelligence look like in practice?

How We're Built

The emergency room doctor's perception was not mystical intuition. It was biology operating as designed. Emotional responses begin in the body, often before conscious awareness arrives. The same neural speed that allowed her to sense deception operates in all of us.

Neurological research shows our nervous system detects micro-expressions within seventeen milliseconds, while conscious identification lags at 300 to 500 milliseconds. Mirror neurons, first discovered by neuroscientist Giacomo Rizzolatti and colleagues at the University of Parma in the 1990s, track breath, tone, and posture, laying the foundation for trust, intuition, and judgment before cognition starts. This capacity for connection is biological. Newborns recognize their mother's voice within moments. Infants engage in joint attention by nine months. Toddlers comfort others without instruction across all cultures.

This biological reality clarifies why AI detection is insufficient. A machine might eventually be programmed to identify a "micro-expression of fear." But identification is sterile. It does not produce the resonant frequency of empathy that invites a human being to lower their guard.

Imagine a conductor leading an orchestra. Her baton moves, but her real instrument is her nervous system. She breathes with the violins, tenses with the timpani, and releases with the resolution of a chord. The musicians don't just follow her gestures. They feel her intentions through subtle shifts in posture and rhythm that no notation could capture. A metronome keeps the perfect time. A conductor shapes the meaning. The difference is **embodiment.**

Biology is only the beginning. **Neuroplasticity,** our brain's capacity to rewire, means development is shaped by experience and deliberate practice throughout life. Human learning is embodied, social, and self-directed. We internalize relational cues, form identity through connection, and grow by choosing what to practice and who to become.

Consider an executive laid off from a leadership role after decades of stability. He first tries to optimize, updating his résumé and relying on automated career coaching. But deeper transformation starts when he shifts to affective neuroscience therapy to rewire responses: listening before speaking, asking questions before offering solutions, leading with presence rather than defending past certainty. Eighteen months later, his renewed relational approach, not technical skill, lands him a senior role. As his interviewer later shares, "You were the only candidate who asked what we were struggling with instead of telling us what you could do."

Machines retrain on new data. Humans transform by intentionally practicing new patterns of thought and behavior. The executive did not just learn new information. He became someone *different*. This ability for genuine transformation, for growth through lived consequence, is uniquely human. Biology provides the foundation, but the ability for integration, coordinated across multiple domains in real time, is what distinguishes human intelligence from both simple biological response and artificial computation. This integration is not automatic. It must be developed.

And it can fail.

The Case for Delegation

The obvious objection is that humans are biased, inconsistent, prone to fatigue, and susceptible to emotion-driven errors. AI is often more reliable than human judgment. Why not delegate to AI?

Because the errors are categorically different, and the difference matters.

Human errors tend to be inconsistent and contextual. A doctor might miss a diagnosis due to fatigue, but another doctor on another day might recognize it. A hiring manager might favor a candidate who reminds them of themselves, but this bias is detectable and correctable through process changes. Human fallibility is visible, variable, and subject to accountability. We can recognize when we're wrong and adjust. AI errors are systematic and hidden beneath apparent precision. When an algorithm consistently screens out qualified candidates who do not match historical patterns, the error is invisible because it is consistent.

When a medical AI fails to flag conditions that don't appear in its training data, the failure looks like authoritative certainty. When financial models optimize for metrics that do not capture systemic risk, the danger compounds silently until systems collapse.

More critically, humans can recognize the limits of their own judgment. An experienced doctor knows when a case exceeds her expertise and consults a specialist. A leader aware of his blind spots builds diverse teams. AI cannot recognize what it cannot see. It cannot know what it doesn't know. It delivers confident recommendations within the boundaries of its training without any signal that those boundaries exist.

Integration: Human Intelligence in Action

Transformation extends beyond individuals. The same integration that operates within us operates between us. A doctor blends diagnostic data with the tremor in a patient's voice, a leader balances financial analysis with a gut sense for team dynamics, a parent tracks milestones while attuning to unspoken distress.

This nuanced integration translates facts to discernment, data to contextualized wisdom, and technical skill into choices that can heal or harm. This does not elevate emotion above logic. Rather, it warns that ignoring relational context and consequence leaves analysis dangerously incomplete.

The value of this integration appears in documented outcomes. A 2024 study published in *Nature Medicine* examined the impact of AI assistance on 140 radiologists across a series of diagnostic X-ray evaluations. The findings challenged a widely held assumption. Adding AI did not consistently improve human performance. Some radiologists improved with AI support. Others performed worse. Experience offered no explanation. Years in practice, subspecialty training, and prior exposure to AI tools failed to predict who would benefit. Even clinicians who underperformed at baseline did not reliably improve when AI was introduced.

The finding reframes the integration question entirely. Simply pairing humans with AI does not guarantee better outcomes. What matters is the human ability to judge—when to trust the machine and when to override it. As the researchers concluded, "To maximize benefits and minimize harm, we need to personalize assistive AI systems." The technology alone is insufficient. The human judgment about how to use it determines whether integration succeeds or fails.

None of us are perfect at this. We miss things. We get it wrong. But we can choose to stay in the practice.

What We Risk

As AI expands, will we cultivate the human capacities that complement machine capabilities or let them atrophy through disuse?

Consider the patterns already in play: hiring algorithms that miss atypical candidates, diagnostic tools that fail to register what patients cannot articulate, recommendation engines that optimize for engagement over development, financial models that favor short-term returns over systemic health.

These outcomes already operate at global scale. Governance and enforcement lag far behind.

But the risk extends beyond poor decisions. It reaches into territory that resists measurement entirely. AI can generate language that describes grief, but it has never felt the disorientation of loss or carried memories that reshape how future choices are made. It can articulate concepts of moral responsibility, but it has never lived with the weight of a decision that permanently altered other people's lives. It can recommend career moves, relationship advice, or medical treatments without knowing what it means to live with the results.

Consider what this means in practice. A counselor who has navigated personal loss can guide someone through grief with earned insight about what the process requires. AI can generate crisis support scripts, but it cannot sense the difference between genuine vulnerability and performance. It cannot judge when someone needs comfort versus when they need a challenge. It cannot know when silence should be interrupted and when it should be honored.

The goal is human judgment integrated with AI: humans providing context, meaning, and recognition of edge cases; machines providing processing power, pattern detection, and consistency at scale. The danger emerges when we remove humans from the loop entirely and defer to automated systems without maintaining the ability to question their outputs.

This ability to question, to sense when something doesn't fit, to recognize the limits of any system, including our own, this is what we risk losing when we stop practicing judgment.

Human skills for metabolizing suffering and sustaining action require training, not just intentionality. Historical movements required both urgency and endurance. Civil rights progress demanded leaders who felt moral clarity strongly enough to act and who had also developed the capacity to sustain that action in the face of violent opposition, slow progress, and personal cost.

The emergency room doctor who sensed deception saved a life. She noticed what the algorithm could not. But she had decades of training and was physically present in the room.

What happens when there is no doctor present? When algorithms make decisions in our absence, while no one watches for what's being missed?

The next chapter examines what that world already looks like: a job market where algorithms decide who gets seen, where bots screen applications submitted by bots, and where the human capacities that predict success have become invisible to the systems designed to find them.

Human Domains

What follows maps the terrain. Ten domains distinguish human intelligence from artificial intelligence. Each represents a practical frontier: a capacity we will either cultivate or let atrophy. Other books ask, "What can machines do?" The better question is, "What human capacities are we failing to develop when we delegate judgment to algorithms?"

TABLE 1: Human Capacity versus Artificial Intelligence

HUMAN CAPACITY	ARTIFICIAL INTELLIGENCE
Consciousness: The act of observing yourself changes what you observe. Awareness is not passive; it intervenes. The moment you see your fear clearly, the choice shifts.	**Computation without self-alteration:** Processes data about itself without being changed by the observation.
Embodied Connection: The nervous system reads before the mind names. Trust, intuition, and safety are built through biological resonance: breath, tone, posture, presence. Detection is not connection.	**Interaction without resonance:** Can detect the signals of distress but cannot produce the felt safety that invites truth.
Love: Sustained practice in the presence of vulnerability. The capacity to be changed by another person and to hold steady while it happens.	**Simulation without devotion:** Can generate the language of care without undergoing the cost of attachment.
Wisdom: Judgment that integrates what is known with what is felt. Without emotion to assign value, logic alone cannot decide what matters.	**Logic without valuation:** Can rank probabilities but cannot weigh what a decision will cost the people it touches.
Creativity: Integration under pressure. The capacity to fuse memory, emotion, and intention into something no pattern could predict. A metronome keeps time. A conductor shapes meaning.	**Pattern without meaning:** Recombines learned material at scale but does not know why one combination moves people and another does not.
Ethical Discernment: The capacity to determine context, not just process it. To weigh intent against impact and hold yourself accountable for the distance between them.	**Rules without accountability:** Follows parameters without bearing the weight of what they produce.
Transformation: The capacity to become someone different through lived consequence. Not updating beliefs but reorganizing the self.	**Retraining without becoming:** Adapts outputs based on new data but undergoes nothing in the process.
Free Will: The space between reaction and choice. The capacity to override what the nervous system demands and act from what you value instead.	**Optimization without override:** Selects the highest-probability output but cannot choose against its own weighting.

HUMAN CAPACITY	ARTIFICIAL INTELLIGENCE
Mortality: Finitude gives choices their weight. You cannot defer what matters indefinitely when time is limited.	**Persistence without mortality:** Can be reset, copied, or deleted without an inner sense of finitude or legacy.
Moral Accountability: Lives with the consequences of its choices. Can feel guilt, initiate repair, and be held to account by those it has harmed.	**Parameters without consequences:** Operates within constraints set by others. Responsibility remains with the humans who design, deploy, and govern it.

CHAPTER 2

THE HAUNTED JOB APPLICATION

Sid wasn't just applying for a job. He was asking to be seen. For eight months, he submitted applications. Each one was carefully crafted. His experience was relevant. His qualifications matched. He tailored every cover letter, optimized every keyword, followed up professionally. He did everything right.

The response was silence. Not rejection emails. Not even automated replies. Just nothing. Like shouting into a void.

Then he learned the truth from a friend working in human resources (HR) at one of the companies: his application never reached a human being. An applicant tracking system scored his résumé. The algorithm flagged gaps in employment, lack of specific certifications, and phrasing that didn't match the job description precisely. He was filtered out in seconds. No one saw his leadership through a company crisis. No one read about the team he rebuilt. No one heard how he learned an entirely new industry in six months because he believed in the work. The system wasn't designed to see any of that. It aimed to eliminate options efficiently.

Consider Elena, a highly qualified project manager with eight years of experience in fintech. She applied for a mid-level leadership role at a growing company. Her résumé was strong. She had led teams through two major platform migrations and had consistently exceeded performance targets. Her cover letter was precise, demonstrating understanding of the company's challenges.

The algorithm rejected her. Why? She had taken a fourteen-month career break to care for an aging parent. The system flagged the gap. She'd also used language the algorithm didn't recognize, describing "stakeholder alignment" when the job description used "cross-functional collaboration." Same skill. Different words. Filtered out.

Six weeks later, a former colleague referred her directly to the hiring manager. She had coffee with him, described her approach to the migrations she'd led, asked questions about where the team was struggling. He saw something the algorithm couldn't: how she listened, how she thought about problems, how she carried herself under pressure. She started the job within three weeks.

The difference wasn't qualifications. It was visibility. The algorithm saw gaps and keyword mismatches. The human saw capacity.

The Invisible Filter

This is not a story about unfairness, though it is that. It is a story about what happens when optimization replaces discernment. When systems designed for efficiency eliminate the very capacities they should be seeking. This is a modern manifestation of the same mind-body split explored in Chapter One, where quantifiable data is prioritized over intangible human capacities. While AI can potentially reduce certain human biases in hiring if designed ethically, the current implementation often creates new, hidden forms of exclusion.

The algorithm was not malicious. It was doing exactly what it was programmed to do: narrow 2,000 applications to twenty. In the narrowing, something critical was lost. The system could not detect persistence, could not sense potential, could not recognize the emotional intelligence that predicts success better than any pattern match.

Meanwhile, someone else got an interview for the same role. Not because their résumé was better, but because they had a referral. Their application landed on the desk of a hiring manager who could see beyond the algorithm, who asked questions, noticed how they described navigating failure, and sensed their capacity for growth.

Bots Talking to Bots

Bots screen applications, AI tools optimize résumés, and algorithms decide who gets seen. Both sides are now automated—applicant and gatekeeper—executing pattern-matching routines with no human in the loop. These systems use large vector databases to match applications with job descriptions. The embeddings measure proximity of meaning, not true understanding. A perfectly qualified résumé can be filtered out because its language sits in a different semantic neighborhood than the job posting, even when describing identical skills.

Some of these tools behave like agentic AI. They act with goal-seeking behavior, execute multi-step plans, and respond dynamically, simulating intention. Agent software automates job applications by scraping postings, generating customized résumés, and even messaging recruiters. These tools aim to give applicants an edge, which often becomes a necessity as job seekers contend with an impersonal automated screening on the employer side. But when the tools are talking to other bots, the result is noise, an escalating arms race of optimization. This, in turn, inundates HR with effectively generic applications, further obscuring genuine talent.

Volume over value. The distortion of visibility itself.

This new layer of automation may feel efficient, but it removes us from the conversations, referrals, and personal connections that still shape hiring decisions behind the scenes.

Emotional intelligence doesn't show up in keywords. It doesn't fit neatly into résumé templates. Relational mastery can't be demonstrated through a bullet point as self-awareness can't be proven with a certification.

It is the single greatest predictor of who will thrive in complex, collaborative, high-stakes work. And within the automated landscape, one pathway remains stubbornly human.

Presence Over Proximity

What haunts this system is what it cannot automate: human networks still move opportunity. The hiring manager who takes a meeting because a trusted colleague made an introduction. The mentor who opens a door because they see potential that data cannot capture. The interview that goes long because there is a quality of presence that creates trust.

These may be soft skills or personality traits, but the emphasis is on their role as a competitive advantage. They include the capacity to build relationships that create opportunity and the ability to communicate in ways that make people want to help.

While digital tools filter information, people respond to presence. They respond to energy, clarity, and trust. These things cannot be scraped or scored. The perfect résumé can still be invisible to the system. Or a person can develop the intelligence that makes them visible to the people who matter.

What the Evidence Shows

Technical skills are easier to find than ever. AI handles more of the analytical work. The capacity to work through ambiguity, build trust across difference, and hold complexity without fracturing: these skills are becoming scarce. The market is correcting for this scarcity, and the research confirms why.

The World Economic Forum's Future of Jobs Report 2025 identified the skills most critical for the coming decade. The majority are emotional intelligence capabilities by another name: creative thinking, resilience, flexibility, agility, curiosity, lifelong learning, and leadership. The report concludes that businesses increasingly value "resilient and reflective workers embracing a culture of lifelong learning as the lifecycle of their skills decreases."

This pattern is reinforced by *Cornerstone's Global State of the Skills Economy 2024*, which found that demand for human skills now exceeds digital skills by more than 2.4 times in North America, 2.9 times in Europe, and 1.8 times in the Asia-Pacific region. Capgemini Research Institute projects that demand for emotional intelligence will increase sixfold in the next three to five years.

The longitudinal evidence is striking. At the University of California, Berkeley, researchers tracked PhD graduates for forty years. They found that emotional intelligence was four times more predictive of professional success than intelligence quotient (IQ). The capacity to collaborate, work through conflict, and build alliances predicted success more than research capability alone.

Daniel Goleman studied nearly 200 companies and found that emotional intelligence was twice as important as IQ and technical skills combined for jobs at all levels.

TalentSmart studied more than a million people and found emotional intelligence accounts for 58% of job performance across all types of roles, rising to nearly 90% of what distinguishes high performers in leadership positions.

The returns are measurable. L'Oréal hired salespeople based on emotional competencies and saw a 63% reduction in first-year turnover.

This is not about being nice. It is about being effective.

The Choice You're Already Making

Whether you know it or not, you are already choosing. Either you are developing the capacities that make you irreplaceable in an age of automation, or you are training yourself to be replaceable by optimizing for what machines do better.

But should you trust that emotional intelligence is real? That it can be developed? That it is not just another corporate buzzword for qualities that remain forever fixed?

In the next chapter, the answers come by tracing a lineage most professionals have never been taught. From ancient Egypt to the Axial Age, from Stoic emperors to Buddhist monks, from Indigenous traditions to modern neuroscience labs, the same capacities appear again and again, developed through systematic practice by cultures that never communicated with each other.

CHAPTER 3

A HISTORY OF HUMAN UNDERSTANDING

A 5,000-YEAR EVIDENCE TRAIL

Long before psychologists gave it structure, humans explored inner development, emotional maturity, and relational awareness. Spiritual leaders, philosophers, and oral traditions investigated what it means to live with emotional clarity. They did not call it emotional intelligence, but they practiced its essence.

I. THE GOLD: ANCIENT ARCHITECTURES

Egypt and the Order of Ma'at

~3000 BCE

At the center of Egyptian life stood *Ma'at*, the principle of truth, balance, and harmony. It was not just a law; it was an internal state. The "Negative Confessions" recorded in the *Book of the Dead* were not just about actions, but about the feelings experienced while performing them. They understood that internal regulation is the bedrock of a stable civilization.

These declarations reveal what emotional mastery meant in practice. The deceased declared before forty-two divine judges:

> *"I have not caused pain. I have not caused tears. I have not acted with violence. I have not caused anyone to suffer. I have not been angry without just cause. I have not made anyone afraid."*
> **Book of the Dead**

Axial Age Civilizations

Across the globe, humans began to "turn inward."

Roughly 2,500 years ago marked a global turning point in human consciousness. Philosopher Karl Jaspers termed this the Axial Age, a remarkably fertile period for philosophical development across several civilizations. What makes this period extraordinary is not just that great thinkers emerged, but that they emerged simultaneously across continents with no known contact, arriving at strikingly similar insights about human nature.

China: Flow and Self-Governance

Confucius (Kong Fuzi) taught ethical living, role-based empathy, and self-awareness. He understood that governing others begins with governing oneself. Laozi introduced Daoist principles of emotional attunement, flow, and balance. He taught that wisdom comes from yielding to natural rhythms rather than forcing outcomes.

India: The Systematic Mind

The Buddha (Siddhartha Gautama) emphasized detachment from ego, compassion, and mindfulness. When Siddhartha sat beneath the Bodhi tree for forty-nine days, he was not seeking enlightenment through logic. He was training his attention— observing each thought, each sensation, each emotional wave without grasping or rejecting. What emerged was a systematic method for working with the mind that 2,500 years later, neuroscientists would validate with modern brain imaging.

Jainism

Contemporary with the Buddha, Mahavira founded Jainism on principles of radical non-harm and emotional purification. *Pratikramana*, a daily practice of reflection and seeking forgiveness, predates modern reflective practice by twenty-five centuries.

Greece: The Tuning of a Human Being

In the West, the Greeks transformed emotional development into a rigorous discipline.

Pythagoras was among the first to argue that the human psyche was like a stringed instrument; if the "strings" of emotion were too tight (rage) or too loose (apathy), the person was "out of tune." He pioneered the use of music and mathematical ratios to regulate the nervous system, believing that a leader's primary job was to maintain internal harmony.

Heraclitus understood that "character is destiny," that our internal emotional landscape creates the path we walk on.

Socrates made self-knowledge the prerequisite for any meaningful action. "Know thyself" became the cornerstone of Western philosophy, shifting the focus from the stars to the soul. Together, they established that emotional intelligence was not an optional trait, but the very "tuning" of a human being.

Persia & The Levant: The Moral Will

In the Near East, emotional intelligence was framed as a conscious ethical battlefield. Zoroaster (Persia) introduced a radical new psychology: the mind is the primary site of a struggle between *Asha* (truth/order) and *Druj* (deceit/chaos). To Zoroaster, emotional discipline was a moral choice; choosing "Good Thoughts" was the prerequisite for "Good Words."

Simultaneously, the Hebrew Prophets: Hosea, Isaiah, Jeremiah, and Micah, pioneered "Social Emotional Intelligence." They moved beyond ritual to demand emotional honesty and collective empathy. They introduced the concept of the "Heart of Flesh" (or the circumcised heart), the idea that emotional "numbness" is a leadership failure. They required collective empathy as the basis for justice.

CONVERGENCE BRIDGE

Five civilizations. No contact. The same three capacities: self-knowledge, emotional regulation, relational wisdom. If this were coincidence, it would appear once. It appeared everywhere.

II. THE SYSTEMATIZATION: INDIA'S SECOND WAVE

A few centuries later, India produced two texts that extended emotional discipline into systematic practice.

~500-200 BCE

The Bhagavad Gita: Clarity in Chaos

The *Bhagavad Gita* provided the first blueprint for "Leadership under Pressure," addressing how to act with integrity when circumstances overwhelm us emotionally. This dialogue between Krishna and the warrior Arjuna, traditionally attributed to the sage Vyasa, addresses a timeless human struggle: how to act with integrity when circumstances overwhelm us emotionally.

The Yoga Sutras: The Roadmap to Responsiveness

Roughly 150 to 200 years later, Patanjali is traditionally credited with codifying the *Yoga Sutras*, though many scholars believe

they are a compilation from multiple authors. The Sutras introduced a practical system for regulating thought, emotion, and behavior through breath, focus, and disciplined awareness. They provided a roadmap for transforming reactivity into responsiveness.

MODERN INTEGRATION

Buddhist mindfulness forms the foundation of MBSR. Krishna's teachings align with leadership coaching, and Patanjali's sutras underpin cognitive-behavioral approaches and breathwork-based trauma recovery. Ancient practices translated into clinical protocols.

The Universal Architecture of the Axial Sages

Though separated by geography, these thinkers shared a common aim: to help individuals understand themselves and live with greater emotional and ethical clarity.

Scholar Karen Armstrong argues in *The Great Transformation* that these teachings emerged in direct response to the violence, conflict, and instability of their time. The sages of the Axial Age were not building belief systems: they were modeling behavioral practices for compassion, emotional responsibility, and ethical repair.

If one culture valued emotional regulation, it might be dismissed as a cultural preference. But when it appears independently in China, India, Greece, and Persia, it is human architecture.

> *"The only way you could encounter what they called 'God,' 'Nirvana,' 'Brahman,' or the 'Way' was to live a compassionate life. Religion was compassion."*
> **Karen Armstrong, *The Great Transformation***

THE THREE PILLARS

Notice what keeps appearing across these traditions:

Self-knowledge: Observing inner states (The Self-Awareness Pillar).

Emotional regulation: Working with emotional energy
(The Self-Mastery Pillar).

Relational wisdom: Connection and service
(The Relational Mastery Pillar).

Your nervous system is built for these capacities.

III. THE CLASSICAL WEST & MONASTIC LABS

300 BCE
- 1400 CE

Roman Stoicism & The Golden Mean

Greek philosophy and Roman Stoicism developed parallel approaches to emotional mastery. Aristotle taught the Golden Mean, the balanced state between emotional extremes. He understood emotions as information requiring calibration, not elimination. In *Nicomachean Ethics*, he described courage as the mean between recklessness and cowardice; generosity between wastefulness and stinginess.

The Stoics took this further. Zeno of Citium founded the school, and Epictetus systematized the practice. Marcus Aurelius, Roman Emperor from 161 to 180 CE, proved it worked while running an empire. He commanded the most powerful military force in the world, yet his private journals, *Meditations*, reveal a man engaged in systematic emotional training.

> *"You have power over your mind, not outside events. Realize this, and you will find strength."*
> **Marcus Aurelius,** *Meditations*

He tracked patterns: when did he lose presence? When did he react rather than choose? The results were measurable. Historical accounts describe an emperor who remained composed during military defeats and fair in judicial matters despite personal loss. His training did not make him invulnerable to emotion; it made him capable of working with emotion rather than being controlled by it. Like the Buddha 500 years earlier, he understood that transformation requires systematic practice, not philosophical agreement.

MODERN INTEGRATION: STOIC LEGACY

Stoic teachings live on in cognitive reframing, stress inoculation training, and values-based decision-making. In leadership development, they support composure under pressure, ethical clarity, and psychological resilience.

1st Century
CE

The Great Synthesis: Compassion & Control

While the Axial Age focused on "Turning Inward," the first century CE marked a shift toward Compassion as a Social Technology. Across the Mediterranean and the Near East, three distinct traditions converged on the idea that emotional mastery is for the service of the collective.

Jesus of Nazareth introduced a radical emotional framework: the replacement of "Eye for an Eye" (reactive emotion) with proactive compassion. He pioneered "Emotional Forgiveness" not merely as a moral virtue, but as a psychological tool to break cycles of intergenerational trauma. By teaching "love for the enemy," he challenged power structures through presence rather than force, shifting emotional intelligence from the elite schools of Greece to a universal practice accessible to all.

Simultaneously, Seneca the Younger provided the West with its first detailed "User Manual" for difficult emotions. In essays like *On Anger (De Ira)*, he argued that emotions are not "storms" that happen to us, but the result of cognitive judgments. He developed the practice of *Premeditatio Malorum*, visualizing setbacks in advance, to regulate the nervous system before a crisis occurs, proving that resilience is a trainable skill even in political chaos.

In Alexandria, Philo acted as a bridge between these worlds. He blended the rigorous logic of Hellenistic philosophy with the emotional depth of Jewish mysticism. He explored inner awareness, arguing that the conscience is an internal witness that monitors our emotional and moral alignment in real time, laying the groundwork for integrating moral life with psychological self-awareness.

MODERN INTEGRATION: THE RELATIONAL PILLAR

This convergence forms the relational pillar of modern EI. These teachings underpin compassion training in modern healthcare, moral psychology research, and purpose-driven leadership models that prioritize empathy as a strategic asset.

The Monastic Laboratories

500 CE
- 1400 CE

While the Roman Empire fell, the systematic study of the inner life moved into the monasteries. From the *Rule of Saint Benedict* to the *Desert Fathers*, these "inner-world explorers" developed rigorous protocols for managing the "passions": anger, pride, and despair. They treated the mind as a garden that required daily weeding, a direct precursor to modern habit-stacking and self-regulation.

IV. TIMELESS WISDOM: ORAL & INDIGENOUS TRADITIONS

While much recorded history centers on literate civilizations, oral traditions carried profound emotional wisdom.

1000 BCE - Present

Sub-Saharan Africa: Ubuntu

Ubuntu teaches that identity is formed through relationship: "I am because we are." This philosophy recognizes the individual as inseparable from community, understanding that personal wellbeing and collective flourishing are interdependent. *Ubuntu* shapes conflict resolution, leadership, and social cohesion across many African cultures.

> *"I am because we are."*
> **Ubuntu saying**

Global Indigenous Cultures

Through ceremony, story, and tradition, Indigenous communities cultivate emotional stewardship, respect for interdependence, and collective healing.

Native American traditions emphasize the seven-generation principle, considering the emotional and spiritual impact of decisions on future generations.

Aboriginal Australian cultures maintain sophisticated emotional mapping through songlines and country, understanding landscape as a living relationship.

Indigenous practices worldwide recognize that emotional wisdom is held collectively, passed through ritual and embodied practice rather than abstract instruction alone. These traditions maintained what industrialized cultures often lost: the recognition that emotional intelligence is collective, not merely personal.

MODERN INTEGRATION: COLLECTIVE INTELLIGENCE

These frameworks underpin trauma-informed care, community psychology, and restorative justice models that prioritize connection over punishment. They challenge Western emphasis on individualism, showing that emotional intelligence develops through and serves relationships.

West Africa: Yoruba

The Yoruba developed a comprehensive system for character development. Orí represents inner consciousness and personal essence requiring cultivation. *Ìwà* (character) is considered the supreme human value: "*ìwà l'ẹwà*" declares that "character is beauty." The *Ifá* divination system, recognized by UNESCO as a Masterpiece of Intangible Heritage, offers structured approaches to self-understanding and decision-making through accumulated wisdom encoded in sacred verses.

MODERN INTEGRATION: CHARACTER AS VALUE

Yoruba concepts inform African-centered psychology throughout the diaspora. The emphasis on character as supreme value challenges cultures that prioritize achievement over integrity.

Mesoamerica: Nahua Philosophy

With no contact with Axial Age traditions, Nahua (Aztec) philosophers developed parallel frameworks for emotional development. They conceived human wholeness through *in ixtli in yollotl*, "the face and the heart." The face represented public identity; the heart represented inner truth and emotional core. Education aimed to cultivate both.

Neltiliztli (rootedness, authenticity) described a person grounded in truth, stable amid changing circumstances. The *tlamatini* (sage) was one who "puts a mirror before others" so they may know themselves. The parallel to Socrates is striking: across an ocean, with no contact, a different civilization arrived at the same insight about self-knowledge as the foundation of wisdom.

Pacific Traditions

Hawaii: *Ho'oponopono* offers a systematic method for reconciliation. The word means "to make right." When conflict arose, an elder facilitated confession, repentance, forgiveness, and release. The practice addresses emotional reality directly: what remains unforgiven? What must be spoken before healing can occur?

Māori (New Zealand): *Wairuatanga* encompasses spiritual and emotional awareness connected to ancestors, land, and future generations. *Manaakitanga* (showing respect and care for others) governs relational behavior.

MODERN INTEGRATION: RELATIONAL HARMONY

Ho'oponopono has influenced conflict resolution and family therapy worldwide. Pacific concepts of relational harmony inform restorative justice movements.

CONVERGENCE BRIDGE

Nahua philosophers and Greek philosophers, separated by an ocean and two millennia, arrived at the same conclusion: self-knowledge is the foundation of wisdom. The convergence is not cultural. It is architectural.

V. THE MYSTICS & THE SCHOLARS

Islamic Insights

In the seventh century, Islam brought its own synthesis of emotional and ethical wisdom. The Prophet Muhammad emphasized mercy, self-restraint, and social justice. Emotional regulation was linked to moral strength.

Al-Ghazali connected spiritual purification with psychological awareness.

Sufi mystics emphasized love, presence, and ego transcendence. They developed practices for transforming emotional energy into devotion and service.

> *"I said: What about my eyes?*
> *He said: Keep them on the road.*
> *I said: What about my passion?*
> *He said: Keep it burning.*
> *I said: What about my heart?*
> *He said: Tell me what you hold inside it.*
> *I said: Pain and sorrow.*
> *He said: Stay with it.*
> *The wound is the place where the Light enters you."*
> **Jalāl ad-Dīn Rūmī,** *Mathnawi* (thirteenth century)

Sikh Teachings

In fifteenth-century Punjab, Guru Nanak founded Sikhism with a radical declaration: "There is no Hindu, there is no Muslim." Beneath religious divisions, he saw universal human nature requiring universal development.

The Five Thieves (*Panj Chor*): This constitutes Sikhism's emotional intelligence framework. Ego, Anger, Greed,

Attachment, and Lust are called thieves because they steal peace and clarity, operating automatically until they are made conscious.

Seva (Selfless Service): The *langar*, the community kitchen where all sit and eat together regardless of caste or status, embodies relational mastery in structural practice.

MODERN INTEGRATION: COMMUNITY DESIGN

The Five Thieves framework translates directly into emotional intelligence assessment. The *langar* tradition demonstrates that emotional intelligence can be embedded in community design, not just individual practice.

VI. CONTINUITY THROUGH PRACTICE

700 CE
- 2000 CE

For two millennia, emotional development continued through contemplative traditions. Sufism in Islam, Christian monasticism, Jewish Kabbalah, and Zen Buddhism each cultivated inner awareness, restraint, and compassion. Medieval thinkers and mystics did not use the term emotional intelligence, but they carried its essence.

Tibetan Buddhism developed some of the most systematic methods for emotional transformation. *Lojong* (mind training) consists of fifty-nine slogans for working with the mind in daily life: "When everything goes wrong, treat disaster as a way to wake up." *Tonglen*, the practice of breathing in others' suffering and breathing out compassion, builds capacity to remain present with difficulty rather than contracting away from it.

The Great Western Separation

The contemplative traditions of the first millennium understood emotion and wisdom as inseparable. But Western modernity increasingly emphasized rational analysis over embodied knowing.

By the Enlightenment, the split was complete in institutional thought: mind over body, reason over emotion, objectivity over subjectivity. This is the same Cartesian separation explored in Chapter One: Descartes' "I think, therefore I am" elevated cognition above all else, and institutions followed. The split served institutional purposes. Emotions were unpredictable, unmeasurable, and inconvenient for industrial-scale education and governance. Historians of education show that modern Western school systems were designed to regulate emotion rather than cultivate it. Many countries imported this academic-first model, and only recently have systems begun reintegrating social and emotional learning. A 2025 meta-analysis of 424 studies covering more than 575,000 students across fifty countries found that social and emotional learning programs consistently improve academic performance, social skills, and emotional well-being.

The cost became visible. The infrastructure for emotional development that contemplatives had built over millennia was dismantled in a few generations.

The centuries of separation prove something crucial: emotional intelligence does not simply appear with age. It follows the same pattern as any complex skill. When cultures stop training it, the underlying biology remains, but practiced access diminishes.

The Enlightenment and Psychology: In the late nineteenth century, William James connected emotion, consciousness, and behavior. By the early twentieth century, depth psychologists like Sigmund Freud, Carl Jung, and Alfred Adler expanded the emotional landscape. Jung's work on the shadow self, archetypes, and individuation provided language for the emotional unconscious that continues to inform self-awareness today.

VII. THE SCIENTIFIC REVOLUTION

1990s - Present

The Scientific Turn

Modern psychology began formalizing ancient insights in the late twentieth century, responding to a growing realization: traditional measures of intelligence could not explain why some people with high IQs struggled in work, relationships, or leadership.

In 1990, psychologists Peter Salovey and John Mayer (USA) introduced the term "emotional intelligence," defining it as "the ability to perceive, understand, manage, and use emotions to guide thinking and behavior." Their work gave language and structure to something long felt but poorly understood. Soon after, Reuven Bar-On developed the Emotional Quotient Inventory (EQ-i), one of the first tools to assess emotional and social competencies.

Goleman and Mainstream Adoption

In 1995, Daniel Goleman brought emotional intelligence into mainstream consciousness with his bestselling book *Emotional Intelligence: Why It Can Matter More Than IQ.* Goleman expanded the field by emphasizing self-awareness, empathy, motivation, self-regulation, and social skills.

1995-Present: The Global Expansion

The 1990s marked the point when emotional intelligence became scientifically credible and globally relevant. Michael Argyle (UK) pioneered work on nonverbal communication. John D. Mayer (Canada) helped differentiate trait EI from ability EI (MSCEIT). Neal Ashkanasy (Australia) integrated EI into organizational behavior. Shinobu Kitayama and Hazel Rose Markus influenced cross-cultural EI models. Moshe Zeidner (Israel) advanced models linking EI with stress management.

Neuroscience Validates Trainability

Discoveries in neuroplasticity showed emotional patterns are not fixed; the brain can change. Richard Davidson (USA) studied the neurological basis of emotion and the role of mindfulness. His work showed that intentional mental training can change brain activity and improve emotional health. Antonio Damasio (Portugal/USA) demonstrated how emotion and reason are biologically integrated. His research confirmed that emotional processing is essential to rational decision-making, not a distraction from it. V.S. Ramachandran (India/USA) pioneered research on neuroplasticity and social cognition, helping explain empathy at a neurological level.

VIII. IN THE AGE OF AI

2000 -
Present Day

AI available to the masses enters the picture.

For the first time in history, we are creating systems that can simulate emotional intelligence without possessing its source. This changes everything. The lineage traced in this chapter reveals why. From the Axial Age to neuroscience labs, humans have been developing practices for emotional mastery. Machines can mimic the outputs of these practices, but they cannot experience the substrate that makes these practices meaningful: embodied consciousness, moral weight, and the capacity for genuine transformation.

Holding the capacity for distinction, and protecting those that cannot, determines whether we lead our technological future or are led by it.

> Triple confirmation from opposite directions: ancient practice, cross-cultural convergence, and modern measurement. Yet the path forward is not the path back.

And there is a harder truth: religious identity has historically divided as much as spiritual practice has united.

The same traditions that developed profound emotional wisdom also became markers of tribe, of us versus them.

When identity is bound to one's God, those who worship differently become the other. The Crusades. The Thirty Years' War. Partition. The Troubles. Centuries of pogroms. Religious wars have killed millions, displaced millions more, and left intergenerational trauma that persists today. Even traditions rooted in compassion and non-violence have fractured into sects that view each other with suspicion or worse.

Religion also built hospitals, fed strangers, and carried communities through centuries of suffering. It gave billions a framework for love, duty, and meaning. The need it answers is real.

But religion draws a line. It names who belongs.

Spirituality draws no line. It is what the contemplatives in this chapter were actually doing: not defending doctrine but investigating direct experience. What happens when silence is sat with long enough that the noise stops being the world's and starts being one's own? What changes when attention is trained the way muscle is trained. What remains when theology is stripped away and only the practice is kept.

The Buddha did not sit under the Bodhi tree to be right. Marcus Aurelius did not write the Meditations to win an argument. The Sufi poets were not building institutions. They were reaching toward something they could feel but not yet fully name, and they were honest enough to say so.

That honesty is spirituality's contribution. The willing-ness to hold conviction and uncertainty in the same hand. To believe deeply and still admit: we are not finished. We are still learning. The work is not done, and that is not failure. That is the human condition, met with courage instead of closure.

This is where the traditions converge. Not in their answers, which divide, but in their practice, which unites. Not in what they believed, but in what they did when they sat down and paid attention.

The contemplatives who built these practices often stood apart from institutional religion, sometimes at great personal cost. The practices they left behind have now entered labo-ratories. Researchers measured what changed in brains and bodies, identified the active ingredients, and trans-lated them into protocols that cross every boundary religion draws. Mindfulness-Based Stress Reduction works whether a person believe in nirvana or not. Cognitive reframing helps whether someone has read Epictetus or never heard of him. The somatic marker hypothesis explains emotional decision-making without reference to any scripture.

A Hindu engineer in Bangalore and a Catholic nurse in Manila and an atheist executive in Stockholm can learn the same skills, in the same language, without anyone abandoning or adopting a faith. These training methods are techniques, not theology., and will be discussed further in Part Two of this book.

THE UNIVERSAL PATTERN

Every major civilization that invested in human development arrived at the same core capacities. The table below shows the convergence across traditions that never communicated with each other.

TABLE 2: Core Capacities Across Civilizations

Tradition	Self-Knowledge	Emotional Regulation	Relational Wisdom
Egypt (Ma'at)	Negative Confessions	Internal balance	Cosmic harmony
China (Confucius/Laozi)	Self-cultivation	Flow, yielding	Role-based empathy
India (Buddha/ Patanjali)	Mindfulness	Detachment, breath	Compassion
Greece (Socrates/Stoics)	"Know thyself"	Golden Mean	Civic virtue
Persia (Zoroaster)	Good Thoughts	Moral will	Good Deeds
Africa (Ubuntu)	Orí (inner self)	Character (Ìwà)	"I am because we are"
Mesoamerica (Nahua)	Neltiliztli	Face & Heart	Mirror wisdom
Pacific (Ho'oponopono)	Confession	Release	Reconciliation

What does high-capacity emotional intelligence look like? The next chapter examines that question through a debate at Cambridge in 1965, where one man demonstrated mastery and changed everyone in the room and US history.

CHAPTER 4

THE TRANSCENDENT ADVANTAGE

THE DEMAND FOR INTEGRATION

February 1965. The Cambridge Union is packed, and the BBC cameras are rolling. Founded in 1815, this is the oldest continuously running debating society in the world: the chamber where Churchill and Roosevelt once stood, where future ministers sharpen their arguments and reputations are made in a single evening.

Tonight's resolution: "The American Dream is at the expense of the American Negro."

But more than a debate is at stake. Can a nation built on segregation hear testimony from those it has silenced? Can white audience members bridge intellectual understanding with the embodied reality of costs they've never paid?

James Baldwin was an American writer and moral force, renowned for his fearless engagement with questions of race as well as the broader pursued of justice. Perhaps one of the greatest essayists of all time, he wrote with fire and restraint.

He brought that clarity to the Cambridge Union, facing William F. Buckley Jr., a patrician conservative intellectual whose confidence came not from volume but from certainty.

Polished and credentialed, Buckley speaks first, opposed to racial integration. His argument moves through historical context and navigates economic data and constitutional principles. He acknowledges past injustices while arguing the American system provides mechanisms for redress. His logic is airtight and his delivery commands attention. The audience is quiet and listens with respect.

Buckley's argument analyzes from a distance. He discusses injustice without feeling its weight, history without carrying its cost. His intelligences remain separated: analytical capacity disconnected from moral reckoning, verbal fluency disconnected from embodied consequence. This is the Cartesian separation from Chapter One in practice: reason elevated above experience, cognition severed from the body that would have to live with its conclusions.

Then James Baldwin rises.

Baldwin doesn't shout. He stands still, calm, and utterly composed. But what he delivers is fire, not through volume but through emotional truth.

> *"It comes as a great shock," Baldwin begins, "around the age of five, or six, or seven, to discover that the flag to which you have pledged allegiance, along with everybody else, has not pledged allegiance to you. It comes as a great shock to discover that Gary Cooper killing off the Indians when you were rooting for Gary Cooper, that the Indians were you."*

With each word, the stillness of the audience tightened.

Every word fuses logic, memory, and feeling. It is not just a debate. It is an experience.

Baldwin's voice remains steady; his hands grip the podium. Beneath the surface, his nervous system is performing an extraordinary act of coordination, aligning memory with purpose, pain with strategic clarity. He holds coherence where most would fragment.

He speaks from lived experience, bearing the weight of a father who died believing America would never see his worth, and of childhood friends erased by a country that offered them nothing. In this moment, Baldwin chooses to re-enter trauma: not in private reflection, but in public testimony, before a room of strangers. This is not performance. It is moral leadership: carrying weight that others have refused to hold, so they might finally see what it costs.

*I don't know what most white people in this country feel,"
Baldwin continues. "But I can only conclude what they feel
from the state of their institutions. I don't know if white
Christians hate Negroes or not, but I know that we have a
Christian church that is white and a Christian church that
is Black. I know, as Malcolm X once put it, that the most
segregated hour in American life is high noon on Sunday."*

He moves between registers with precision: personal testimony to systemic critique to moral challenge. His body carries what his words convey.

Baldwin isn't speaking for himself alone. His father's pain becomes testimony for millions. His childhood disillusionment reveals a collective betrayal. He transforms personal suffering into civilizational indictment while maintaining coherence under that pressure, modeling what he asks of the audience. He doesn't inflame anger or wallow in grief. He weaves both into moral clarity that enables action.

The audience isn't just persuaded. They're transformed. White students who arrived analyzing "the Negro problem" abstractly now feel the weight of complicity. Baldwin's embodied testimony created space for their own reckoning: intellectual understanding unified with moral responsibility.

By the end, the room erupts into a standing ovation. When the vote is tallied, it isn't even close.

Baldwin wins 544 to 164.

The pain focused his thinking rather than clouding it. His anger didn't undermine his argument. It gave his argument moral weight that pure logic could never carry.

What Baldwin demonstrated at Cambridge has a name and a mechanism. Integration practiced under pressure, over time, produces something more.

We have called it charisma, brilliance, moral force, but these words describe effects without explaining causes. The answer lies in integration, which is not the suppression of emotion to think clearly, but the coordination of emotion with cognition to think deeply. Network neuroscience now offers vocabulary for what audiences have always felt. This capacity—a rare and elevated synthesis of mind and heart—is what we call transcendence.

INTELLIGENCE AS COORDINATION

For decades, psychologists thought intelligence lived in specific brain regions. Math ability in one area, language in another, spatial reasoning in a third. Howard Gardner's theory of multiple intelligences emerged from this modular view, where one could be "word smart" or "number smart" or "people smart" as separate capacities, each operating independently.

Network neuroscience revealed a different picture. Intelligence emerges from coordination across distributed networks. When one solves a complex problem, they're not activating "the problem-solving region." They're synchronizing attention networks with working memory systems, pattern recognition with emotional valuation. The magic isn't in any single area. It's in the conversation between them.

The Parieto-Frontal Integration Theory explains how general intelligence emerges from coordination across four major brain networks: occipital and temporal regions for pattern recognition, parietal regions for abstraction, frontal regions for planning, and cingulate for attention and error monitoring. These networks don't operate in isolation. They're bound together by the frontoparietal control network, which acts as shared bandwidth for complex cognition. But coordination doesn't happen automatically. Something must integrate the integrators.

That something is emotional valuation.

The common assumption, that emotion interferes with clear thinking, has it backward. Emotion is what enables clear thinking by coordinating the brain's networks toward decision. It does so through the body.

Emotional valuation is the brain's continuous act of assigning felt significance to competing inputs. Not simply labeling experiences as positive or negative, but dynamically weighing them against goals, relationships, identity, and anticipated consequences. It determines what to amplify, what to suppress, and what to act on first. Without it, the brain's networks generate outputs but cannot prioritize them. With it, distributed processing converges into directed action.

We have already lived this. The conversation we walked away from because something in us knew it was wrong, before we could articulate why. The job turned down despite the salary. The moment in a meeting when speaking was restrained, or when action was necessary. In each case, our brains were processing multiple streams simultaneously: social signals, memory of similar situations, projected consequences, bodily sensations, abstract principles. Emotional valuation coordinated these into a single felt sense: do this, not that. From the outside, we call it intuition or good judgment. From the inside, it feels like convergence.

Now imagine what happens without that convergence. Every input stays flat. The financial risk, the reputational risk, the impact on people: all register as equally important, all equally abstract. Oscillation follows. More data is requested. The same considerations are revisited without resolution. Decision stalls, not from lack of intelligence but from lack of integration.

Artificial systems can mimic each step of this process. They can ingest data, model risk, project scenarios, generate recommendations. But none of these operations experiences the convergence of competing inputs into a single, embodied priority. Machines can optimize according to an objective specified. They cannot feel which objective should govern when objectives collide.

THE NEURAL ARCHITECTURE OF INTEGRATION

One System Under Load

In 2025, researchers at the University of Southern California and the University of Manitoba demonstrated that brain activity during emotion regulation predicts individual differences in working memory ability. Using brain imaging with 101 participants, Scarlett Horner, Jonas Kaplan, Steven Greening, and colleagues showed that the pattern of neural activity when people reappraised negative images could predict their working memory scores.

Working memory holds information in mind to solve problems. Emotion regulation manages emotional responses. These should look like separate systems on paper: one cognitive and one affective. But imaging shows they rely on the same frontoparietal control networks, especially the dorsolateral prefrontal cortex, which creates shared capacity limits.

When we're emotionally flooded, we can't think straight. When we're cognitively overloaded, we become emotionally reactive. Not because separate systems interfere with each other, but because it's one system approaching capacity limits.

Predictive Coding: The Brain Constructs Reality

In Chapter One, we met Lisa Feldman Barrett's insight that emotion is constructed, not triggered. What follows from that insight is more radical than it sounds. The brain does not passively receive the world; it actively constructs it through prediction. Every moment, our brains generate expectations about what is about to happen based on prior experience. These predictions involve both cognitive and emotional expectations. Emotion is not a reaction to events: it is part of how the brain prepares for events.

When prediction matches reality, experience smooths perception. When prediction mismatches reality, we experience surprise, confusion, or insight. The brain updates its models.

This predictive loop is not just in the head. Interoceptive regions, including the insula and brainstem systems that regulate heart rate and breathing, help decide which predictions matter enough to change the body. The body is not a passive recipient of the brain's conclusions. It is where predictions are tested. The stomach tightens before the mind names the threat. A person's shoulders drop before they consciously recognize safety. The body runs the experiment; the brain reads the results. The brain cannot predict "just cognitively" or "just emotionally." Every prediction integrates both.

How Predictive Coding Works

The brain does not wait for the world to arrive. It predicts what will happen next based on prior experience, then checks those predictions against incoming signals.

The body is where predictions are tested. Gut feelings, chest tightness, and the sense that something is "off" are the body reporting a prediction error before the conscious mind can name it.

Consider an analyst reviewing a company's quarterly filings. The numbers reconcile. Revenue growth matches guidance. The AI screening tool did not identify anything unusual. Something in the report, however, triggers unease. The disclosure language around inventory has shifted subtly from previous quarters. The CFO's commentary emphasizes different metrics than usual. The pattern resembles something she saw in 2008, six months before a major restatement, a case she has never forgotten because she missed the signs and her fund lost millions.

Her body registers the warning before her analysis catches up. There is a tightness in her chest, a reluctance to move on. The recognition lives in her body before it reaches her reasoning. Twenty years of quarterly filings have built a somatic catalog: the feeling of clean books versus the feeling of books that will later require correction. She flags the position for deeper review. Three months later, the company announces an accounting investigation.

Not intuition versus analysis, but prediction that integrates both.

How Emotion Coordinates Distributed Networks

Emotional systems do not add feelings to cognition. They coordinate cognitive networks toward action through the body.

The amygdala, often called the brain's alarm system, does not just "feel fear." It prioritizes attention toward what matters, suppresses irrelevant processing, pulls up memories of similar situations, and prepares the body to act. When a person senses danger before they can name it, that is the amygdala coordinating a response across systems faster than conscious thought.

The anterior cingulate cortex, or ACC, monitors conflict between competing signals. When the analytical mind says "this plan makes sense" but the gut says "something is wrong," the ACC registers the mismatch and demands resolution. That uncomfortable feeling of being pulled in two directions? That is the ACC doing its job, refusing to allow action until the conflict is addressed.

The insula reads the body. It integrates internal signals, including heart rate, gut sensations, and muscle tension, with what we are perceiving and thinking. The result is what we call intuition: knowing something without knowing why. When a person walks into a room and senses tension before anyone speaks, the insula has already integrated micro-expressions, postural cues, and the physical response into a unified perception. The conclusion arrives before the analysis.

Together, these systems turn multiple inputs into singular judgment. That is the architecture Baldwin was using at Cambridge. It is the same architecture the contemplatives of Chapter Three spent millennia training: the Buddha's mindfulness, the Stoics' self-examination, the Yoruba cultivation of orí. Different vocabularies. One biological mechanism.

Baldwin maintained unity under conditions that would shatter most people: pain coordinated with rhetorical strategy, trauma channeled into moral clarity, audience awareness informing every pause and shift in register. He was not suppressing feeling to achieve clarity. He was letting both inform the other.

That coordination is embodied integration enabling transcendence. The architecture that allows it, the shared networks, the predictive machinery, the body that carries and tests every signal, is biological infrastructure. It evolved over millions of years. It cannot be programmed, only grown.

INTEGRATION IN ACTION

A structural engineer reviews plans for a building retrofit. The calculations check out. Load distribution is within tolerance. The AI modeling software has analyzed stress patterns across twelve hundred data points and confirms the design meets code with margin to spare. She has signed off on hundreds of similar projects. This one should take fifteen minutes.

Standing on site, looking at the existing structure, something feels wrong.

She walks the perimeter slowly. The concrete on the north face has weathered differently than the south, a mottling pattern that suggests decades of moisture penetration. One of the support beams shows a slight bow, technically within specification parameters, but her eye keeps returning to it. The building was constructed in 1987, a period when certain concrete additives were common, additives that interact poorly with the salt air in this coastal location.

None of this triggers the modeling software. Each observation falls within acceptable parameters. The AI has no flag to raise.

Her integration hubs are firing. Her insula registers unease she cannot yet articulate, a somatic signal that something in this structure does not match her embodied catalog of safe buildings. Her anterior cingulate detects conflict between what the numbers say and what her body knows. Thirty years of site visits have trained her nervous system to recognize patterns her conscious mind processes too slowly to name.

She delays signing off and orders additional testing: ground-penetrating radar, core samples from the suspect beam, chemical analysis of the concrete composition.

The results, returned in ten days, show internal corrosion invisible to visual inspection. The rebar has degraded by 40% in critical sections. The original retrofit plan, which the AI confirmed as sound, would have transferred load to supports that could not hold it. Failure would have occurred within five years, perhaps sooner depending on seismic activity.

The modeling software optimized for the data it had. The engineer integrated data with site observation, technical knowledge with embodied pattern recognition, analytical output with felt sense accumulated across a career. Her hesitation was not inefficiency. It was integration working faster than articulation.

The story does not end with the test results. That moment changes her, and not just her procedures, protocols, and checklists. It shifts her identity. She becomes the engineer who teaches younger colleagues to walk the site before they open the laptop. She counsels them that the software will confirm what they ask it to confirm; while their body will indicate what they have not yet asked. Over the next decade, three of her mentees catch structural failures the modeling tools missed. Her embodied knowledge propagates. Not through a manual, but through the presence of someone who demonstrated what it means to trust the body's judgment alongside the data's.

TRANSCENDENCE: THE ADVANTAGE

Each of these examples shows integration in a moment. But integration, practiced over time, does something more than improve decisions. **It changes who you are.**

The engineer who trusts her embodied sense against the numbers, and is proven right, does not just gain confidence. Her circle of concern expands. She becomes someone who thinks about the people who will occupy that building decades from now, the inspectors who will follow her, the profession she represents. Repeated integration widens what she cares about and deepens her alignment with what matters beyond herself.

This is transcendence: the capacity to let experience change who we are in ways that widen our circle of concern and deepen alignment with what matters most, personally and collectively. It is not mystical. It is developmental. Every time emotion is integrated with cognition under pressure, and the result is felt in the body, the pathways that enable that coordination strengthen. The threshold for future integration lowers. What once required deliberate effort becomes increasingly automatic. The engineer does not decide to care about the building's future occupants. She finds herself caring, because repeated integration has expanded the boundaries of what she experiences as self.

Machines update when retrained on new data. Their function changes. Humans transform through experience. Their being changes. That change has a direction: toward expanded identification with others, toward purposes that exceed self-interest, toward the capacity to carry weight that is not ours to carry.

This directionality is not accidental. It is the signature of embodied consequence. When the results of decisions register in the chest, stomach, and compounding sleepless nights, and when another person's suffering registers not as information but as sensation, the circle of concern does not expand because it was chosen. It expands because biology made it real. Machines process data about suffering, but only humans can metabolize it. Metabolized suffering transforms the organism.

Why This Capacity Is Evolutionary

Human brains didn't evolve for spreadsheets or strategic planning. They evolved for social coordination, which requires expanding beyond the self.

British anthropologist Robin Dunbar's work suggests a striking correlation: across primate species, neocortex size predicts social group size. The human neocortex, the largest relative to body size of any primate, enables us to maintain meaningful relationships with approximately 150 people. The brain didn't grow to solve physical problems. It grew to solve social ones, and social problems require caring about others' needs, holding others' perspectives, coordinating toward shared purposes.

Human children develop capacities no other primate shares. By age four, they show joint attention: knowing that both parties know they're seeing something together. By age five, they grasp false belief: understanding someone can hold a belief the child knows to be wrong. By age seven they demonstrate, nested social cognition: "I know that she knows that he thinks that they believe…"

Each capacity requires integrating perception with inference, self-knowledge with other-modeling, and emotional resonance with cognitive representation. The architecture that enables this is the same architecture that enables transcendence in adults: the ability to expand beyond perspective toward identification with larger wholes.

Art, music, religion, science, ethics, and law all emerged from the ability to coordinate emotional meaning across individuals, to create shared significance that binds groups into cultures and cultures into civilizations.

What Transcendence Produces

The first stage of transcendence is resilience that transforms: not returning to baseline after difficulty, but integrating difficulty into expanded capacity. Baldwin did not survive racism. He metabolized it, and it became the material from which his authority was built. The pain was not overcome. It was carried in his body, night after night, from one breath to the next, until it became something that could be offered to others. Recovery returns us to who we were. Transformation makes us someone who could not have existed without the difficulty.

Resilience that transforms produces wisdom that integrates. Not just knowing what works, but understanding what matters, because we have felt the cost of getting it wrong. The engineer who catches the structural failure becomes wiser not because she learned a new formula, but because the weight of what could have happened lives in her body. That weight reorganizes her priorities. She cannot unsee what she has seen or erase what she has felt. She begins to see what spreadsheets cannot measure and what the model don't flag. The data will never reveal the human consequences that only embodied experience makes real.

Wisdom that integrates produces the capacity to help others transform. Baldwin at Cambridge did not just transform himself. He transformed the room. His embodied testimony created conditions for the audience's own reckoning. When one person holds what others have separated, when pain and clarity and moral weight occupy the same body without fragmenting, it creates a field of possibility. Others feel what integration looks like before they can name it. They recognize what is missing in themselves. The capacity propagates, not through argument, but through presence.

This Capacity Is Trainable

This chapter shared stories of people shaped, moment by moment, through experiences that mattered enough to change them.

The brain does not change from exposure to information. It changes from information that matters emotionally. One can read a hundred case studies about leadership failure and remain the same person, yet change overnight after making a single decision that costs someone their livelihood and become someone different overnight. The reading informs, while the consequence transforms. The difference is emotional weight, and emotional weight lives in the body.

Transformation rarely happens through study alone. After a surgeon makes an error that harms a patient, she examines the medical record and participates in a quality review meeting where the error is discussed. She studies the corrected technique. None of that is where transformation happens.

Transformation happens at 3 a.m., when her hands remember holding the instrument at the wrong angle and again in the operating room the following week, when her stomach drops at the sight of the same procedure. It happens in the weight she carries for months. Her empathy for the suffering she caused presses down on her every decision. Responsibility cannot be delegated. Most of all, she must reckon with the knowledge that her body, once the instrument of harm, must become the vessel of correction.

She does not merely learn a better technique; rather, she becomes a different surgeon through vigilance, and humility. The change lives in her hands and her attention, continually improving the quality of care she brings to every patient who follows. She did not choose the transformation, crisis forced it.

The question is whether the same depth of change can happen without crisis. It can. The contemplatives of Chapter Three discovered this thousands of years before modern science confirmed it. Mindfulness is not relaxation. It is the practice of sitting with experience until the assumption about the own mind is revealed as incomplete. That discovery, felt in the body, reorganizes how perception and response. Somatic awareness is not a wellness trend. It is the cultivation of decades of Baldwin's writing, a career's worth of the engineer's experience, and in years of the surgeon's life-and-death practices. A person cannot be changed by what they cannot feel. Ethical practice, choosing discomfort over avoidance, holding difficult truths instead of deflecting, is not moral performance. It generates the emotional weight that makes transformation deep rather than superficial, lasting rather than temporary.

Crisis is one pathway. Deliberate practice is another. The architecture exists, and the pathways are waiting. Part Two will systematize what the contemplatives discovered: how to build, skill by skill, the integration this chapter describes.

Collective Transcendence

Individual transformation matters. Collective transcendence, the ability for groups to transform together, changes history.

The Civil Rights Movement did not succeed through better arguments. The arguments against slavery and segregation had existed for centuries. Frederick Douglass articulated them. Sojourner Truth embodied them. The legal case had been built, brief by brief, decade by decade. What changed was not the quality of the reasoning, but the quality of the leadership.

The leaders who moved the Civil Rights Movement forward held hope and grief simultaneously, maintaining strategic clarity while feeling injustice viscerally. Diverse groups were coordinated toward shared purpose despite competing interests, often with their bodies on the line: in the streets, at the lunch counters, on the bridges, in the jails. Their leadership was not abstract, it was embodied. Justice was not theorized from a distance; it was carried in their bodies and offered to a nation that had long refused to bear its own weight.

It did not require unanimous agreement to move history; only enough people willing to elevate progress at real cost. Again and again, a relatively small number of leaders and communities have shifted entire civilizations forward.

Baldwin's impact at Cambridge came from this same leadership capacity. He demonstrated that true patriotism requires holding one's country accountable; that love requires truth-telling at cost. Baldwin was not an exception. He was an exemplar of a pattern that runs through every era of genuine human progress.

History does not advance through superior data or more efficient systems; it advances through leaders whose embodied moral weight becomes unbearable for others to ignore. Socrates did not out-argue Athens. He stood in the agora and lived his questions until his presence became a mirror the city could not look away from. Athens executed him for it. Gandhi did not out-strategize the British Empire. He starved his own body until the violence of the system became visible to those who had looked away. Mandela did not negotiate from a position of political strength. He emerged from twenty-seven years in a cell with his moral authority intact, and the weight of what his body had endured made reconciliation possible where retribution would have been justified.

These leaders succeeded because they had integrated what their opponents had separated. Pain and purpose in the same body. The cost of injustice and the possibility of justice were felt simultaneously, and that tension drove them to action rather than paralysis. Embodiment was the argument, presence the proof.

What distinguishes moral leadership from intellectual leadership is that the moral leader carries the case in their body. Buckley could analyze the American racial crisis from every angle. Baldwin could make others feel what it cost. The audience at Cambridge did not change their minds because Baldwin's logic was superior. They changed because his embodied testimony made the abstraction real. They felt, in their own bodies, what they had previously understood only in their minds. The mechanism of collective transcendence is one person's integration creating the conditions for another's.

Throughout history, those who integrated personal conviction with moral clarity to challenge systemic injustice have provoked persecution.

Joan of Arc was burned for threatening orthodoxy. Prophets across traditions were martyred for fusing spiritual vision with critique of power.

The pattern reveals something crucial: authorities dependent on fragmentation cannot tolerate those who demonstrate integration.

The pattern also reveals something hopeful. What Baldwin sparked at Cambridge did not stay in that room. The members carried that transformation into their lives, careers, and their own moral choices. Movements that transcend create conditions for others to transcend.

It is needed now more than ever, because it cannot be automated, outsourced, or delegated. The next chapter shows what happens when we try.

CHAPTER 5

THE CRISIS OF PASSIVE ADOPTION

What erodes first is often invisible until everything that depends on it begins to fail. We don't notice the loss of capacity. We buckle under the collapse it causes.

THE EMOTIONAL RECESSION

Jordan graduated from Stanford with an MBA at twenty-five, top of his class. By twenty-seven, he was a management consultant at one of the most prestigious firms in the country. With a brilliant analytical mind, he was a digital native who had never known life without screens. His calendar was color-coded, his productivity tracked, his fitness gamified, his relationships maintained through texts and occasional video calls.

He prepared for three months for a major client presentation. Armed with perfect data and flawless slides, he walked into the conference room confident.

The client's CFO sat at the head of the table, the CEO to her right, and the VP of HR across from Jordan. He launched with compelling numbers: workforce restructuring to optimize efficiency would yield a thirty percent cost reduction, streamlined operations, and improved margins.

What Jordan did not notice was the CFO's body language shifted when he said "workforce restructuring." Her shoulders tensed. The CEO's jaw tightened, but Jordan was watching his slide deck, not the room. The VP of HR exchanged a glance with the CEO. Jordan saw it and mistook it for agreement. It was alarm.

When the CFO asked about "cultural impact," Jordan pivoted to return on investment metrics, his energetic pitch focused on implementation timeline and projected savings. He thought he was answering her question. She stopped writing notes.

> The CEO redirected, "Let's talk about your team's process. How did you gather this data?"
>
> "We used an AI-powered analytics platform that aggregated performance metrics across departments, identified redundancies in workflow..." The well-rehearsed flow of Jordan's were interrupted by the CFO.
>
> "Did you talk to anyone? Our people?"
>
> "We analyzed communication patterns, productivity data, and collaboration metrics across your organization."
>
> "That's not what she asked." The CEO settled back into her chair.
>
> The meeting ended twenty minutes early. Jordan thought it went well until his senior partner pulled him aside in the hallway.
>
> "What happened in there?"
>
> "I think they loved it. The analysis was thorough."
>
> "Jordan. They hated it. The CEO was ready to walk out."
>
> "The analysis was perfect."
>
> "The analysis was not the problem."

Three days later, the client canceled the contract. Jordan's partner explained why. "You recommended laying off two hundred people who have been with that company for decades. The CEO's father started that business. Her CFO has worked there for twenty years. These are not metrics to them. They are people. Couldn't you tell that every slide devastated her?"

Jordan had optimized his life for efficiency. What he had never gained the capacity to sense what mattered. His deficit was not a personality failure. It was a developmental one. The experiences that build embodied judgment, the difficult conversations where one learns to hold someone's anger without deflecting, the mentorships demonstrating that data is a tool and people are the point, the long silences in rooms where what is not said carries more weight than what is, had been systematically replaced by screens, algorithms, and optimization platforms. Jordan was not born incapable. He was built that way by a system that treated emotional development as inefficiency.

Chapter Four described what embodied integration produces: resilience, wisdom, the capacity to transform others. Jordan never had the chance to build it. The conditions were removed before he arrived.

Jordan is not an outlier. In 2014, researchers at UCLA took preteens to an outdoor education camp for five days. No phones, no screens, just face-to-face interaction. After five days, the children showed significant improvement in reading facial emotions and interpreting nonverbal cues. The capacities had not disappeared. They had atrophied from disuse.

The UCLA study confirmed what the larger data had already suggested. Sara Konrath and colleagues at the University of Michigan tracked dispositional empathy among college students from 1979 to 2009: a 40% decline over three decades, with the sharpest drop after 2000, precisely when digital communication became ubiquitous. By 2023, the U.S. Surgeon General had issued an advisory on "Our Epidemic of Loneliness and Isolation." Social connections had declined 24% in less than two decades. Young adults reported 70% less social time with friends compared to previous generations. The pattern was consistent across dozens of studies from the National Institutes of Health and international organizations, as well as literature published by the American Psychological Association: digital exposure correlated with emotional decline, particularly in the young.

EMOTIONAL RECESSION (*noun*): A systemic decline in emotional capacity, including empathy, presence, and relational skill, triggered not by trauma but by neglect. Skills we stop practicing begin to disappear.

The emotional recession has emerged from convenience. Every delegation to a system, optimization, and efficiency gain, made life fractionally easier while making people incrementally less capable. What distinguishes this chapter from a familiar argument about screens and attention spans is the mechanism underneath. Passive adoption does not merely reduce the time spent practicing emotional skills. It dismantles the conditions under which those skills develop in the first place.

WHEN SYSTEMS REPLACE JUDGMENT

The Surveillance Software

TechFlow Solutions was a two-hundred-person software company in Austin, Texas. It was profitable with a strong culture, low turnover, and had an engineering team known for innovation. They had built several products that larger competitors tried unsuccessfully to replicate. Then a new VP of Operations arrived from a major tech company.

> "We're leaving productivity on the table," she told the CEO in their first one-on-one. "I've seen this before at scale. We implement monitoring software like keystroke tracking, active window logging, and meeting efficiency analytics. Nothing invasive, just optimization through anonymous aggregate data. I've seen it increase output by fifteen to twenty percent."

The CEO hesitated. TechFlow had succeeded precisely because engineers felt trusted and autonomous. Competitors were moving faster and the Board wanted growth. The data the VP showed from her previous company was compelling.

They deployed the software in the first week of the quarter. "We're collecting baseline data," the announcement said. By week two, dashboards went live showing color-coded productivity scores by team.

Week three, the VP sent an email: "I am seeing some teams operating at sixty-eight percent efficiency. Let's schedule discussions about improvement plans."

The changes started small. Engineers began gaming the system. Auto-clickers to prevent idle status, unnecessary keystrokes to boost activity metrics. Meetings became performative, everyone typing continuously to show engagement. Bathroom breaks got tracked as idle time. Creative work, including thinking, whiteboarding, and the unstructured conversations where problems get solved, registered as unproductive.

By the second month, three senior engineers had quit. Their exit interviews revealed a common theme: "I can't work somewhere that doesn't trust me."

A team lead tried to intervene. She went to the VP with data showing that the most innovative code came during periods the system marked as idle. She proposed hybrid monitoring that tracked outcomes instead of keystrokes. The VP thanked her for the input and kept the system unchanged. The team lead resigned two weeks later.

By month three, innovation had slowed measurably. Code quality declined as people optimized for quantity over quality. Junior engineers stopped asking questions because meetings were marked as inefficient time. Senior engineers stopped mentoring for the same reason. The informal conversations where institutional knowledge got transferred, including how a problem was solved before, why an approach will not work, and what the client actually needs, disappeared entirely.

Then a major client discovered a critical bug. When they traced it back, they found the code review had been skipped to hit productivity targets. The client threatened to pull their contract, which represented eighteen percent of TechFlow's revenue.

The CEO finally investigated and found that team psychological safety had been destroyed. Creative collaboration had ceased. Knowledge transfer had broken down. The best performers had either left or checked out emotionally.

She called the VP into her office. The VP came prepared with her dashboard. "Productivity metrics are up fifteen percent. The monitoring system is working exactly as designed."

"Then why has our best work vanished?"

"The data doesn't support that claim."

The CEO looked at the dashboard with color-coded efficiency scores, activity metrics, and meeting analytics. Everything measurable looked better; the unmeasurable had disappeared.

The system had optimized for what it could measure: keystrokes, active windows, meeting duration. It had destroyed what it could not measure: trust, creativity, judgment, mentoring, the unscripted moments where breakthroughs happen.

TechFlow retained sixty-eight percent of its engineering team but lost ninety percent of its innovation capacity. The culture that had taken eight years to build had been dismantled in three months.

Notice what the system actually destroyed. Not just productivity or morale, but the conditions under which embodied judgment develops. Mentoring: where senior engineers transfer knowledge that cannot be written down. Unstructured conversation: where problems get reframed and assumptions get challenged. Psychological safety: without which no one risks the vulnerability of saying I don't know or I think we're wrong. These are not amenities. They are the organizational infrastructure for integration. TechFlow's monitoring system did not replace human judgment with a better system. It eliminated the environment in which human judgment grows.

The Trading Floor

Rafiq had worked the floor for twenty-five years. While he wasn't the flashiest trader or the one who made huge bets that earned a legendary reputation, he never had a losing quarter. Other traders joked he had a sixth sense for market moves. What they didn't see was that Rafiq read patterns that humans create. He watched how traders reacted to news and sensed when panic was building before it showed in price movements. The line between false bravado and real conviction was easy for Rafiq to see.

The firm had always trained traders on the floor. Junior traders sat next to senior traders for two or three years before they managed their own books. They learned to read the room: the sound of a floor shifting from confident to nervous, the way veteran traders went quiet before a break, the body language of a counterparty who was bluffing versus one who was scared. None of this was in a training manual. It transferred through proximity over years of watching someone like Rafiq work. The slow accumulation of embodied knowledge could not be simulated.

Then a hedge fund acquired the firm. New management brought a proprietary trading algorithm, QuantEdge, and a new philosophy. Backtests showed twenty-three percent better returns than human traders. They restructured training for junior traders to include quantitative modeling, algorithmic strategy, and backtesting methodology. The floor shrank as trading moved to screens. The informal mentorship disappeared. Onboarding programs and simulation software replaced the years of sitting next to Rafiq. More efficient. More scalable. Measurably faster time to productivity.

Management measured what it could see. The new traders were profitable faster than the old ones had been. Time to first solo trade: cut in half. Quantitative test scores: up across the board. What management could not see, because no metric captured it, was what the old pipeline actually produced. Not just profitable traders. Traders who could feel a market before it moved. Experts that could read a counterparty's voice on a phone call and know whether the confidence was real. Lost was the ability of the body to sense the difference between a healthy correction and a systemic break—an instinct cultivated over years of training.

Rafiq raised concerns. He told management the new traders were technically excellent but emotionally blind. Though they could model risk, they couldn't feel it. Management pointed to the numbers proving performance metrics were up and Rafiq was thanked for his perspective.

Over the next several years, QuantEdge absorbed more of the capital allocation. Human traders monitored but did not override. Then a geopolitical event broke. Markets initially stayed calm. Rafiq saw something else. Bond traders' body language had tensed despite stable prices and the energy on the floor was shifting in a way he had learned to recognize over decades. Veteran traders were quietly reducing positions. The newer traders didn't even flinch. They were watching their screens.

> Rafiq went to the head trader. "We need to hedge. Now."
>
> "The algo says stay long."
>
> "The algo doesn't see what I am seeing."
>
> "What are you seeing?"
>
> "Fear. It's spreading. I can feel it on the floor."
>
> The head trader looked at Rafiq, then at his screens. "I can't override a two-billion-dollar position because you feel something."
>
> Forty-five minutes later, the market broke. Flash crash. Eight hundred forty million dollars gone before the algorithm could adjust.
>
> "No," Rafiq said. "You can scale the loss of it."

After the crash, Rafiq and three senior traders left. The firm doubled down on algorithmic trading.

Then, several years later, there was a different crisis: a liquidity event where counterparties stopped honoring electronic orders. Traders needed to pick up phones, read voices, and negotiate in real time with people who were frightened and lying about their positions. The situation required the skills the old floor culture had spent decades building.

No one on the desk could do it. Not because they were unintelligent. Because the institution had eliminated the developmental pathway through which that capacity was built. The training programs never included it and the simulations couldn't model it. The years of sitting next to someone like Rafiq, which was the actual training, no longer existed. The firm took losses it could have managed with three phone calls from someone who knew how to make them.

The emotional intelligence was always invisible to the institutions that depended on it. They measured Rafiq's outputs: consistent returns, no losing quarters. They never measured what produced those outputs: decades of embodied pattern recognition, relational attunement built through thousands of hours of reading human behavior under pressure, a nervous system trained to detect threat before conscious analysis could name it. When they modernized, they optimized for what they could see and eliminated what they could not. They kept the metrics but killed the pipeline. By the time they discovered what they had lost, the capacity to rebuild it had left with the people who carried it.

SYSTEM ADOPTION AS EMOTIONAL BYPASS

There is a deeper pattern at work, and it's not just about efficiency. We adopt systems to avoid emotional complexity. Jordan's analytics platform replaced the effort of sensing what the client felt, easier than the vulnerability of watching a room and not knowing what would be found. TechFlow's monitoring software spared teams the difficulty of having hard conversations about productivity. Easier than a CEO sitting down with an engineer and saying: I need more from you, and here's why. As for the trading algorithm, it replaced the anxiety of human judgment and ultimately bypassed the need to trust a man's gut over a model's math.

System adoption becomes emotional bypass. Emotional bypass, practiced at scale, becomes organizational anesthesia. The company does not feel the injury because it has numbed the nerve endings. It's no longer capable of reading what the numbers cannot contain or holding the full weight of decisions that affect human lives. Reassured by data that looks clean and dashboards that glow green, the capacity to sense what matters most erodes silently—until the moment it is needed but is not there.

This is the mechanism the emotional recession conceals. It is not that people have become less intelligent. It is that systems have been built that make intelligence feel unnecessary. Every tool that removes emotional friction also removes the conditions under which emotional capacity develops. The navigation app that eliminates the need to pay attention to surroundings. Scheduling algorithms that replaces the negotiation of competing needs. AI that drafts the difficult email to avoid sitting with the discomfort of choosing the words. Each substitution is small. The cumulative effect is a population that has fewer and fewer opportunities to practice the skills this book argues are essential.

THE LEADERSHIP VOID

> **PASSIVE ADOPTION** *(noun)*: The delegation of judgment to systems without asking what human capacities atrophy, what wisdom is lost, or what happens when systems fail. A form of slow anesthesia. The loss goes unnoticed until the moment feeling is required and the capacity is no longer there.

Barbara Kellerman at Harvard Kennedy School has documented what she calls "leadership deterioration: not just the emergence of bad leaders, but the decline of leadership as a practice." Leaders are increasingly insulated from consequences, relying on technical competence while delegating judgment and optimizing systems without the wisdom or emotional intelligence to understand what those choices erode. Her warning: "We are producing managers who can run systems but cannot lead humans."

Unfitness for leadership is not malice. It is incapacity. Dissected, it is the inability to tolerate self-scrutiny or to hold discomfort without deflecting. A fit leader would choose integrity over optics and accept accountability without feeling diminished.

Leadership means standing in responsibility for other humans including their livelihoods, professional development, and futures. This is not soft work. It is heavy, emotional work. A leader who cannot hold that weight, who cannot feel the consequences of their decisions for people who depend on them, cannot do the job. They may run systems and hit targets, but they can't lead humans, because leading humans requires the capacity to be affected by them.

Incapacity in a leader is dangerous. Power amplifies everything. A leader's emotional deficits do not stay personal. They become organizational architecture. A leader unable to hold ambiguity drives the organization toward false certainty. One who cannot receive challenge lets feedback loops die. And when discomfort is intolerable, the culture learns avoidance. The leader shapes systems in their own image, then mistakes compliance for alignment and silence for trust.

Low emotional intelligence in leadership presents as composure and certainty, even dismissal, so that the leader appears competent.. They are replicating their incapacity at scale and leveraging public relations (PR) to create illusions of success and competence. The void is more than individual leaders making poor decisions. It is a systemic absence of leaders who see emotional intelligence as their strategic responsibility rather than an HR problem or a soft skill unworthy of attention.

Before deploying any system that replaces human judgment, leaders who retain adaptive capacity ask four questions:

- What human ability does this replace, and what evidence shows that the system performs as well or better?

- How do we maintain that ability?

- What happens when AI and human judgment conflict?

- What is our fallback if the system fails?

These questions are not common. TechFlow's CEO did not ask them. Neither did the trading firm's CEO and Jordan's firm never even considered them. The costs compounded in every case.

Someone must carry the burden of consequences. There needs to be a mechanism to maintain human judgment and the ability to sense what is unmeasurable. Integration across domains goes hand in hand with stewardship of relational capacities. When leaders do not see this as their responsibility, systems fill the void by default. Organizations survive crises through collective judgment, institutional knowledge, trust that enables coordination, and the ability to sense and respond. When these decline, organizations do not stumble. They drift until eventually they hit something.

Rafiq was right: intuition can vanish across an organization. It can be rebuilt just as widely. The emotional recession is not a diagnosis. It is a choice made by default. The next chapter introduces the people who made a different choice, and what became possible when they did.

THIS WEEK: NOTICE ONE DELEGATION

Before you begin skill-building in Part Two, practice awareness. This week, identify one place where you're delegating judgment unnecessarily:

- A decision you defer to an app when your intuition says something different.

- A conversation you avoid by texting when a call resolves it.

- A meeting where you're half-present, attention divided.

- A moment when you reach for your phone to avoid discomfort.

Don't try to change. Just notice. Write down what you observe: What did you delegate? What did you avoid feeling? What was the cost? Awareness precedes change. You're beginning the work of reclaiming what passive adoption erodes.

THE CHOICE

WHAT THEY BUILT

The previous chapter described what passive adoption destroys: the developmental conditions, the mentorship pipelines, the embodied judgment that no metric captures. These are the people who built what passive adoption erodes. Not because they were exceptional. Because someone, at some point, invested in the conditions for their development, or they invested in themselves. To elaborate, meet David, Maya, and Jasmine.

David used to disappear when conversations got hard. Now he stays.

Maya derailed meetings when challenged and was the one other women warned each other about. Now she builds the careers she once would have sabotaged.

Jasmine used to spiral when she failed. Now she fails better than most adults.

What changed was not personality. It was practice.

David

David is forty-five. He spent his twenties and thirties certain he was not an emotional person. His family did not discuss feelings and he had a career that rewarded analysis. Empathy seemed like a personality trait he had missed. When his first serious relationship ended, in his late twenties, his girlfriend said something that stayed with him: "You are not cold. You are just untrained." It stung. He ignored it for another decade.

In his late thirties, he finally started the work. What he thought was set turned out to be undeveloped. He learned to notice his reactions before acting on them. Saying what he felt instead of what seemed acceptable became a daily exercise. Running for the exit in difficult conversations became a thing of the past. He learned these the way he learned to drive: poorly at first, then reliably.

Then came the hardest choice. His first marriage looked successful from the outside: stable, comfortable, financially secure. But there was no love in it anymore, only routine. They had stayed for the children, told themselves it was the responsible thing to do. Only children learn what love looks like by watching their parents and his were learning that marriage means two people performing duty in parallel. Performance was not his goal; growth was, and he knew she wanted it too. Ending it was the kindest thing they could do for each other. The decision cost him money, mutual friends, and two years of uncertainty. He made it anyway.

He has twelve close friendships now. Last month, one of them told him his nonstop work was becoming a problem. Though instinct prepared to argue, he noticed that, waited, and asked instead: "What have you seen?" The conversation lasted three hours. That friendship saved him because it was built through years of honesty, not years of ease.

David can sit with discomfort now without immediately reaching for distraction. Attention holds firm, and he uses meditation not to escape but to practice presence.

When hard things happen, he has a practice for processing them. Write what happened. Name the feeling, specifically: not "bad" but "embarrassed" or "scared" or "guilty." Identify what he can and cannot control. Move his body to discharge the activation. It is just what he does now.

He finds meaning in committing to things that cost him something, bending and recovering along the way.

Maya

Maya is thirty-five. She earned an MBA from a top program, same credentials as thousands of peers. The difference is not talent. It is what her second employer decided to build, and what her first employer revealed about who she had become.

At her first company, she had survived by making herself useful to leadership. That meant performing loyalty, laughing at jokes that were not funny, quietly undermining women who might compete for her access, and tolerating behavior that set a precedent for how all women could be treated. She told herself she was being strategic and complicit even though it came at the expense of respect. The leadership team kept her close because her presence offset their visible homogeneity and their discomfort with women who wanted more. She knew this and played the part anyway.

The reckoning came in a stairwell. A woman she had sabotaged confronted her directly, "I know what you did. I know what you said." Maya had no defense. She had traded this woman's career for her own safety. Two months after that encounter, the colleague left the company.

Her second employer was different. They used AI for everything: code review, demand forecasting, hiring screens, and of course, performance analytics. They had learned the hard way that efficiency without judgment destroys more than it builds. So they invested in judgment.

Maya remembers her first week: new hires had to share a failure that shaped them. She watched a senior VP go first, describing a merger he had botched by ignoring cultural dynamics. His voice caught. The room went quiet. When her turn came, she told the truth about who she had been. She stayed to find out what kind of company this was.

The training started with her body. She learned to read her own signals before meetings: the jaw tension that meant she was about to interrupt, the flush that meant she was taking something personally. Then she learned to shift her own state before difficult conversations. The first dozen times felt ridiculous. By year two, it was automatic. Part Two of this book teaches the method. What matters here is that it worked, and that it cost her something: months of feeling incompetent at skills she thought adults were supposed to have already.

Now leading a division, she can read a room and name what others are avoiding. Her feedback lands well, and she can sit with competing priorities until the right path clarifies.

The path was not smooth. Promotions have passed her by, and she has damaged relationships by being too direct, rebuilt them, and damaged them again. Last month she snapped at a team member during a crisis. She apologized in front of the same people who witnessed it, asked what she had missed that made her reactive, and scheduled a follow-up to make sure the relationship was repaired. She also does something she never did before: she sponsors junior women. Not mentors. Sponsors. She puts her credibility behind their advancement and ensures they are in rooms she once would have kept them out of. It does not erase what she did. It is what she does now.

Jasmine

Jasmine is fifteen. Her school uses AI for personalized learning but defines education as more than knowledge transfer.

The transition was not easy. When the school added emotional intelligence to the curriculum, parents complained that test scores dipped. Teachers struggled with new autonomy after years of scripted lessons. Enrollment dropped in year two. By year four, students outperformed district averages on both traditional metrics and measures of wellbeing. Now there is an admissions waiting list.

Jasmine's teachers are not content deliverers. AI handles the routine from administrative tasks to progress tracking and resource suggestions. Teachers do what screens cannot: noticing when a student is struggling but will not ask for help, guiding someone through confusion without just giving the answer, modeling how adults handle uncertainty honestly.

Jasmine is learning to think critically about information. Staying focused without algorithmic prompts and tolerating frustration have become integral to her learning. She works with people who approach problems differently and discovers what interests her through exploration rather than recommendation.

She still struggles. Last semester she nearly quit the robotics team after weeks of failures. Her teacher did not rescue her. Instead they worked on something specific: noticing when frustration was building (her voice getting clipped, her movements getting sharp), naming what kind of frustration it was ("I am not good enough" versus "I hate this"), and then reframing it ("This is hard, but I can handle it"). She stayed anyway. The robot never worked perfectly but she learned more from that project than from any success.

The development is not confined to special classes. In math, she notices when difficulty tempts her to quit and practices perseverance. History teaches her to hold perspectives that are not her own. Science asks ethical questions with no clean answers.

Her generation shows measurably stronger critical thinking, collaboration, and emotional range than cohorts educated purely for test performance. They are not invulnerable. Attention is still a struggle in a world designed for distraction. They fall apart under extreme pressure. Jasmine still cries after some failures, still has days when she wants to quit everything. The difference is she has learned those feelings pass, and she does not make permanent decisions while they are loud.

Remember Jordan from the previous chapter: brilliant, optimized, unable to read a room. Jordan and Jasmine are the same age cohort with different developmental conditions. Jordan was built by a system that treated emotional capacity as inefficiency. Jasmine is being built by a system that treats it as infrastructure. The difference is not talent. It is what someone decided to invest in.

THE PATH FORWARD

David, Maya, Jasmine. Different domains, same foundation. They built what most people leave to chance.

The divergence was not luck. David decided his ex-girlfriend was right and did the work she named. Maya's company offered training and she took it; 40% of her peers did not. Jasmine's parents chose a harder school.

Notice what each of them paid. David lost a marriage, mutual friends, money, and two years of certainty. Maya lost her reputation, absorbed being passed over, and had to stand in front of colleagues and account for her own failures. Jasmine's school lost enrollment for two years before results justified the investment. Emotional intelligence is not free. The literature is full of what it gives: better leadership, stronger relationships, improved outcomes. Almost no one talks about what it costs. Discomfort. Humiliation. The slow, unglamorous work of sitting with what would rather be avoided. The willingness to be bad at something important before becoming competent at it.

The choice this chapter describes is not whether to develop. It is whether to pay.

None of them are finished. All of them still fail, still struggle, still lose their way. The difference is they know how to find it again.

The method is not mysterious. It begins with the body, with learning to read what the nervous system already knows. It develops into the capacity to choose responses when pressure wants to make the choice. It matures into the ability to stay present with other people's pain, complexity, and difference without collapsing or retreating. Each stage is learnable. Each requires practice. Part Two is the work.

PART 2
FROM INSIGHT TO ACTION

THE LANDSCAPE

"You do not rise to the level of your goals.
You fall to the level of your training."
Archilochus

Part One made the case. Part Two is the work. What follows is structured, sequential, and demanding. The framework rests on three pillars of emotional intelligence, composed of eleven skills. These practices build capacity the way miles build endurance: not by reading about running, but by running.

Some of this will feel obvious, but do it anyway. At times, the work will feel uncomfortable, and that is the point. The gap between knowing and embodying is where most people stop; this work closes the gap.

Begin where everything begins: **the body.**

Earlier we met David, Maya, and Jasmine and followed them as they began building new capacities. Now consider what that required of each of them. David stayed in a conversation that every instinct told him to leave. Maya learned to read the tension in her own jaw before it became the word she could not take back. Jasmine sat with weeks of failure until the failure taught her something success never could. What they built is not mysterious. It is the result of capacities developed through deliberate practice. What follows is the method.

A note on language. This book calls these skills. A skill is a capacity that can be taught, practiced, measured, and improved. It develops the way all competencies develop: poorly at first, then reliably, then automatically. Everything in Part Two follows this pattern.

The eleven skills form an integrated system in which each capacity enables the next. Interoception—the ability to sense internal bodily states—supports emotional literacy, laying the foundation for meta-awareness. Modern science traces this concept to 1906, when Charles Scott Sherrington introduced the term and delineated three sensory domains, establishing the foundation for the study of internal awareness.

With interoception as the foundation, self-awareness develops into self-mastery, which in turn shapes relational mastery. A person with empathy but no self-awareness absorbs others' pain without knowing why, demonstrating that these skills depend on one another. Likewise, having an emotional vocabulary but no interoception means they can label feelings they cannot actually feel, revealing how the capacities build on each other. That interdependence is what makes this an intelligence rather than a list.

These skills are foundational because personal agency, growth, and connection all depend on some combination of these capacities. Leadership is not trained directly. Instead, the skills that make leadership possible are developed.

THE THREE PILLARS

Each pillar builds on the previous. Self-awareness enables self-mastery. Both enable relational mastery. Progress in any area strengthens the others. Weakness in any pillar limits everything above it.

TABLE 3: The Three Pillars of Emotional Intelligence

PILLAR	SKILLS	CHAPTER
Self-Awareness	Interoception Emotional Literacy Meta-Awareness Values Alignment	Chapter 7
Self-Mastery	Emotional Self-Command Discomfort Tolerance Resilience	Chapter 8
Relational Mastery	Empathy Communication Conflict Navigation Persuasiveness	Chapter 9

Self-Awareness

Self-awareness is the first pillar because it is impossible to regulate what cannot be detected. The nervous system reacts moments before conscious awareness of anger appears. Physiological shifts begin: heart rate climbing, hands becoming clammy, muscles tensing. For most people, these signals pass by unnoticed until after a reaction has taken place. The work here is learning to decode in real time.

Introspection is operational intelligence. Feeling activation rising before it peaks creates a window for choice that reactive people never have. Naming emotions with precision, not just "bad" or "stressed" but the specific texture of disappointment, frustration, or fear, engages the capacity for regulation. Vague feeling remain unnamed. Named feeling becomes workable.

Chapter Seven builds four skills that move from body to meaning.

- Interoception: sensing what the body knows.

- Emotional literacy: translating sensation into language.

- Meta-awareness: observing personal patterns as they unfold.

- Values alignment: clarifying what actually matters to the self when pressure strips away pretense.

Self-Mastery

Self-mastery is where awareness becomes reliable action under pressure. And the emotion that shows up most often under pressure is fear. Failure, rejection, exposure, and loss are all different expressions of the same underlying response. Most of what derails people in high-stakes moments is fear in disguise.

This work is not about eliminating fear. Fear is the foundation of courage. Courage is acting in alignment with personal values when there is a perceived cost, which is why it requires the values clarity developed in the first pillar. It is impossible to hold the line on something that has not been identified. No price can be paid for a principle not yet named.

The work here is learning to feel fear fully and act anyway. This allows the nervous system to complete the stress cycle and return to baseline rather than accumulating damage. It also trains the ability to stay remain present in discomfort without collapsing or fleeing.

> **Suppression is not mastery.** Suppression stores activation in the body; it does not resolve it. What looks like control is often delayed explosion or a slow leak. True regulation means the emotion moves through completely: accessed, expressed appropriately, and released.

Chapter Eight builds three skills.

- Emotional self-command: choosing a response when the nervous system wants to react.

- Discomfort tolerance: staying present with what is painful without collapsing or fleeing.

- Resilience: recovering so that today does not still carry the residue of last month.

Relational Mastery

Relational mastery is where these capacities meet other people. Presence with others depends on first being present with oneself, and full listening is impossible when personal activation drowns out the signal. Conflict cannot be navigated without collapsing or escalating unless the capacity to hold discomfort has been trained. The first two pillars are prerequisites.

Relational skill is not just individual capacity applied socially. Something additional happens between people. When a person is genuinely attuned to another, physiological systems begin to coordinate. This is measurable. It is also what is felt in the presence of someone who somehow steadies without saying a word, or the colleague whose anxiety registers even over video.

Chapter Nine builds four skills.

- Empathy: feeling what another person experiences without losing perspective.

- Communication: conveying ideas clearly, not just being heard.

- Conflict navigation: holding disagreement without rupturing the relationship.

- Persuasiveness: influencing others without manipulation.

HOW TO USE THIS SECTION

Each skill chapter explains what the capacity is, what it produces, and how to build it. The practices are specific and progressive. The performance indicators let you track whether you are actually developing.

Work sequentially if you want comprehensive development. Master body sensing before you try to regulate what you cannot yet detect. Master regulation before you try to stay present with someone else's pain. Work selectively if you have a specific gap. If you collapse under conflict, that is discomfort tolerance and conflict navigation. If you miss signals until it is too late, that is interoception and meta-awareness.

Developing and ultimately mastering these capacities is a personal responsibility that cannot be outsourced, even in a world increasingly shaped by AI. Cultivating awareness, regulation, and relational skill ensures that each response remains intentional and human.

CHAPTER 7

SELF AWARENESS

THE FOUNDATIONS OF SELF-AWARENESS

"The limits of my language mean the limits of my world."
Ludwig Wittgenstein

The Body Speaks First

Kevin's fingers fidgeted as he walked into the room. Twenty-two years old, eight months into his first professional role, he had arrived at coaching after a performance review that blindsided him. His manager's feedback: hard to read, disengaged, shuts down under pressure. He hadn't seen it coming. On his wrist, a small device quietly tracked his heart rate, breath patterns, the subtle physiological signatures of a nervous system on high alert.

This was 2025. The device could predict his emotional state with remarkable accuracy. It knew he was anxious before he did. What it couldn't do was teach him the emotional language of his own inner world.

Over the next three months, through weekly sessions and daily practice, he would learn to identify something that no algorithm could provide: the foundational skills of self-awareness, **interoception** (sensing what the body knows), **emotional literacy** (naming what the body feels), **meta-awareness** (observing his own patterns), and **values alignment** (acting from what matters most even under pressure).

In a world where AI can recognize emotional patterns in speech, predict behavioral responses, and simulate empathy, the question becomes urgent: have we outsourced our inner lives to algorithms, gradually losing fluency in our own emotional language?

A person cannot regulate what they have not recognized. Truly connecting with others is difficult to impossible without knowing what is happening within oneself first. This is why self-awareness anchors everything that follows. Without it, the skills in the next two chapters have no foundation.

From Sensation to Fluency

Mastering any complex domain begins by learning its language. Like any skill, fluency develops through consistent effort. For this domain: can we feel it, name it, reflect on it, and discern what aligns?

What follows are four skills that build this capacity. We begin with the body's wisdom, learning to hear its signals. Then we learn the vocabulary that gives those signals meaning. From there, we begin to notice the patterns in our own thoughts and responses, like discovering the grammar of the language. Finally, we learn to align our actions with what matters most, putting the language into practice and learning to speak it in our daily lives. Each skill concludes with a specific, low-friction practice you can begin today.

SKILL 1: INTEROCEPTION

Train the Observer

> What am I feeling right now,
> and where do I feel it?

This is the first skill in the self-awareness sequence. Here the focus is simply on noticing signals, without yet interpreting or naming them. Before we can work with emotions, we must learn to detect them in the body.

Kevin chose the chair farthest from her desk, knees pulled up tight. The room smelled faintly of coffee and printer paper. His fingers gripped the edge of the seat, grounding grounding him against its cool surface.

His coach waited, watching his shallow breathing. She had learned that silence was often the first teacher.

"Do you ever feel something in your stomach? Like it flips or sinks?"

He nodded once. He didn't like that feeling. It meant something bad was coming.

"That could be nervous. Or maybe unsure. Or maybe scared. What do you think it is for you?"

"It's when I think I'm in trouble. Even when I haven't done anything wrong." He paused, "It happens before team meetings. Before I've even said a word. My manager walks in and it's already there."

"Your body always speaks first," she said. "That's called interoception. It means you're noticing what's happening inside your body. That comes first. Then comes the emotion, like fear or anger. Then your mind makes meaning of it. And once you name it, once you say it out loud, that's when language helps you understand."

> ## FROM THE KEVIN'S JOURNAL, WEEK 1
>
> *Stomach drops before team meetings. Before I've said a word. She says my body knows things before my brain does.*

Language is not always made of words. It can take the form of images, rhythms, gestures, or somatic impressions. The body speaks in its own vocabulary, and listening to it is the first step toward clarity.

Understanding Interoception

When the psychologist asked about his stomach, she was introducing him to something science has only recently begun to fully understand.

Interoception is the brain's ability to sense, interpret, and integrate signals from inside the body: dizziness, bracing, hunger, temperature, muscle tension. It forms the raw data of emotional experience. The key is perception. Not fixing. Not controlling. Just noticing, recognizing, becoming fluent in the signals from the body. This work leads to somatic awareness, nervous system tracking, and eventually, presence.

Interoception gives rise to our earliest sense of self. It informs us whether we are safe or threatened, energized or depleted, and whether we are aligned or off-course.

Research links higher interoceptive awareness to more effective emotion regulation including lower anxiety and faster recovery from stress. People who can sense subtle shifts earlier have more time to choose their response instead of being swept away by it.

IMPORTANT NOTE

For some, the work is learning to hear signals that have been numbed or ignored. For others, especially those with a history of trauma or anxiety, the signals are already too loud. For them, the work is not "turning up the volume," but learning to relate to the signals with curiosity rather than reflex, transforming the body's message from a constant alarm into usable information.

A Timeless Intelligence

Kevin's journey connects to something much older than coaching. The ability to sense internal bodily states is one of the oldest skills humans have cultivated. Long before neuroscience named it, spiritual traditions wove it into practices that centered the body as a source of wisdom and divine insight. For thousands of years, interoceptive awareness has been a gateway to transformation that brings healing and alignment.

Modern science now validates what ancient traditions always knew. **Bud Craig,** a prominent neuroscientist who reframed Sherrington's work on interoception, traced how interoceptive signals travel from the body to the brain, converging in the anterior insula, the part of the brain involved in self-awareness and emotional experience. His work reframed interoception as a neural basis of subjective feeling itself.

"Gut feelings" are not metaphors; they are biological status updates sent to the brain to ensure survival. To ignore them is to cut off your own data feed.

Building on this, **Lisa Feldman Barrett** advanced the theory that the brain constantly predicts internal states based on experience as informed by context and probability. After the sensations are processed, the brain forms an emotion. Barrett calls this "the theory of constructed emotion."

We feel first, then label.

> *"Interoception is the brain's representation of the body's internal world."*
> **Lisa Feldman Barrett**

The Integration Practice

Like Kevin learning to recognize that "dropping" feeling in his stomach, we all can develop this awareness. Machines can reveal the signal and enable a micro- and macro-level view. In a world that tracks everything, we can deepen our edge with more information, but it's the synthesis of that information that gives us power.

There are no shortcuts. Emotional intelligence cannot be downloaded. It must be lived. Felt. Practiced. Chosen.

TRY THIS: 2-Minute Body Scan

Close your eyes. Starting at the top of your head, slowly move your attention down through your body. Notice any areas of tension or discomfort. Are there signals of warmth or cold? Don't try to change anything. Just notice. When you reach your feet, ask yourself: *What is my body telling me right now?* There's no right answer. The practice is the noticing.

TABLE 4: Interoception

CATEGORY	DETAILS
Subskills	• Body scanning: Systematic attention to physical sensations • Heartbeat awareness: Detecting cardiac signals without external measurement • Somatic tracking: Following sensation patterns through the body
Skillsets	• Somatic Awareness: Reading the body's native language of sensation
Tools	• Body scan meditation; Sensation journals; Breathwork practices; Biofeedback devices
Performance Indicators	• You can pause and locate physical sensations during emotional activation, distinguish between different types of internal signals, and use body awareness to inform decisions before cognitive processing.

KEY TAKEAWAY

Your body speaks before your mind does. Interoception is the skill of listening. You do not need to interpret or fix what you feel. Just notice. That noticing is the foundation everything else builds on.

SKILL 2: EMOTIONAL LITERACY

Build Your Vocabulary

> Can you name five emotions you felt today and
> identify where they showed up in your body?

This is the second skill in the sequence. Having learned to notice body signals, we now give names to those signals. Naming transforms raw sensation into usable information. Without this step, we feel but cannot work with what we feel.

We think of language as expression. In emotional intelligence, language is the architecture of awareness. It is how we build our internal world. That world shapes how we learn and lead, and forms how we love.

Four weeks into their work together, Kevin was ready for the next step. He could feel the signals in his body, but he didn't yet have language precise enough to work with them. This is where emotional literacy begins: the bridge between raw sensation and conscious understanding.

She pulled out a small emotion wheel from the side table. At the same time, she tapped her tablet. A gentle interface appeared, showing words that orbited a simple outline of a human figure: *Guarded. Protective. Cautious.*

"This will help you figure out what your body might be saying."

He leaned forward slightly. She noticed the shift, a sign of curiosity engaging his parasympathetic nervous system.

"That feeling in your chest, the rock. What would you call it?"

"Maybe... anger? I don't know. Maybe..." He looked at the wheel. "Protective anger."

"So the anger keeps something safe."

"Yeah. I don't want them to know it hurt."

> ### FROM KEVIN'S JOURNAL, WEEK 4
>
> *Found out there are different kinds of angry. Mine is the protecting kind. It's like armor, but on the inside.*

Kevin was learning that emotions are not just feelings; they're internal information systems. That rock in his chest wasn't his enemy. It was his protector, built from years of experiences where showing vulnerability felt unsafe.

The Power of Naming

The moment when Kevin named his "protective anger" represents a fundamental shift in how humans process emotion. From a tight chest to the words "I feel anxious," this act of naming transforms raw sensation into usable emotional data.

Naming what we feel, a process known as **affect labeling** in neuroscience, activates the prefrontal cortex, which supports executive functioning and regulation, and quiets the amygdala, the part of the brain responsible for the fight-or-flight response. **Matthew Lieberman's** brain imaging studies demonstrated this mechanism directly: brain scans showed reduced amygdala activation within seconds of participants naming their emotions.

We do not have to "solve" the feeling to reduce its power. Simply naming it accurately flips the switch from reaction to regulation.

Without this step, we might default to suppression or projection. When we name it, *"I am scared," "I am disappointed," "I am hopeful,"* we gain the power to respond rather than react.

Over time, this precision does more than calm the nervous system; it refines judgment. When we can distinguish *fear* from *dislike*, or *shame* from *sadness*, we are less likely to misread others, project our own stories onto them, or let unexamined emotions quietly drive decisions.

Kevin's growing vocabulary connects to decades of research on how humans create meaning from feeling.

This precision has deep scientific roots. Marc Brackett built the RULER framework at the Yale Center for Emotional Intelligence around this principle, demonstrating that emotional labeling is a teachable skill, not an innate gift. Antonio Damasio's somatic marker hypothesis goes further: the body encodes past emotional experiences as physiological markers that guide future choices, often before conscious reasoning engages. Patients with damage to emotion-processing regions of the brain retain full cognitive ability yet cannot decide what to eat for lunch because every option carries identical weight. Emotion is not the enemy of rationality. It is its prerequisite. Dan Siegel captured the mechanism simply: "name it to tame it." Labeling integrates different brain regions, turning overwhelming sensation into workable information.

Research shows that **emotional granularity**, the ability to find the precise word for a feeling, is associated with lower rates of depression and better coping under stress. It is not just a language game; it is a resilience skill.

The Machine Mirror: A Crucial Distinction

This human process, naming to understand, has an instructive parallel in how we taught machines to process language.

Geoffrey Hinton pioneered neural network architecture by modeling how the brain encodes associations. **Tomas Mikolov** introduced Word2Vec, transforming words into numerical vectors: each word becoming a point in mathematical space, defined by its relationships to other words. **Jacob Devlin's** BERT processes context bidirectionally, enabling machines to interpret nuance based on surrounding text.

The parallel runs deep. When Kevin names his "protective anger," he creates an internal reference point, a location in his emotional landscape he can return to, recognize, and work with. When a language model processes the word "anger," it creates a vector embedding, a location in mathematical space defined by statistical relationships to other words.

Both systems depend on naming. Both build increasingly sophisticated maps. Both improve with more data.

Here is where the parallel breaks: Kevin feels what the name points to. The machine does not. This distinction explains something puzzling from Part One: why AI systems can score highly on emotional intelligence assessments while possessing no emotional intelligence at all. Those tests measure the map—pattern recognition, correct labeling, knowledge about emotional dynamics. Kevin is building something the tests cannot see: the territory itself. His nervous system changes when he names the feeling. His body responds differently to "protective anger" than to undifferentiated distress. The label reorganizes his physiology, not just his cognition.

A machine can label anger in text with impressive accuracy. It cannot feel the rock in the chest soften when the right word arrives. It cannot experience the relief of being understood by itself.

Emotional literacy is not just vocabulary acquisition. It is the integration of language with living tissue, the moment when naming becomes a bodily event. No amount of training data replicates this. No embedding captures it. Kevin's four-word journal entry, "Mine is the protecting kind," represents something no language model can achieve: felt meaning.

TRY THIS: Emotion Vocabulary Expansion

The next time you feel "bad" or "stressed," pause and ask: *What specifically is this? Frustrated? Disappointed? Overwhelmed? Anxious? Resentful? Lonely?* Try to find at least three words that come closer to the actual feeling. Notice how precision changes your relationship to the emotion.

TABLE 5: Emotional Literacy

CATEGORY	DETAILS
Subskills	• Affect labeling: Naming emotions with precision • Emotional vocabulary: Expanding the range of emotional terms • Emotion differentiation: Distinguishing between similar emotional states
Skillsets	• Linguistic Precision: Using language to transform overwhelming sensation into manageable experience
Tools	• Emotion wheels; Vocabulary expansion exercises; Journaling with emotional specificity; RULER framework
Performance Indicators	• You can name three to five specific emotions when activated rather than generic terms, distinguish between similar emotions, and notice how naming shifts your experience.

KEY TAKEAWAY

Naming what you feel is not a language exercise. It is a neurological event that shifts your brain from reaction to regulation. The more precise the word, the greater the shift. Move beyond "stressed" and "fine." Precision is power.

The Bridge to Action

As Kevin discovered, naming isn't just for self-regulation. It's the beginning of ethical foresight. When we know what we feel, we are less likely to act from fear, insecurity, or unconscious bias. This matters for leadership. It matters for justice. It matters for love.

FROM KEVIN'S JOURNAL, WEEK 6

Realized I have scared-angry and sad-angry and even protective-angry. They all feel different in my body. Scared-angry is hot and fast. Sad-angry is heavy and slow. Protective-angry is like a wall.

The next skill asks a harder question: once it can be felt and named, is it possible to step back and watch the pattern?

SKILL #3: META-AWARENESS

The Witness Within

> What story are you telling yourself right now, and is it true?

Interoception and emotional literacy grant access to an inner world. But awareness doesn't stop at sensing and naming. The deeper work begins with developing the ability to observe what's being noticed: witnessing patterns, questioning stories, and aligning actions with what matters most.

Kevin was ready for something more: the ability to step outside his experience and examine it.

Building on the foundation of body awareness and emotional literacy, these skills explore the higher-order capacities of self-awareness: **meta-awareness** is the ability to observe one's thoughts and patterns, and **values alignment** is the practice of living in accordance with what matters most.

The Evolution of Awareness

Seven weeks ago, Kevin couldn't name what he felt. Now he was ready for something deeper.

"I noticed something," Kevin said as he settled into his chair. Several sessions of practice had shifted his posture. His movements were more thoughtful than reactive.

"In yesterday's meeting, when Amanda kept cutting off Harry, I felt that rock again. But this time I knew what it was."

He paused, organizing his thoughts. "It wasn't about me. It was about Harry. I felt bad for him, but I also felt scared to say anything. Like two feelings at the same time."

"What did you do with that information?"

"I thought about it. Why was I scared? What was I protecting? I think I was protecting myself from becoming a target, too. But that meant leaving Harry alone."

"How do you feel about that choice now?"

"Guilty. Like when you know you should have done something but didn't."

> ## FROM KEVIN'S JOURNAL, WEEK 7
>
> *Starting to see my patterns. When I'm scared, I protect. When I protect too much, I feel bad later. There's probably another way.*

What was emerging was the third foundational skill: the ability to step outside experience and observe it, to ask not just *"What am I feeling?"* but *"What am I thinking about what I'm feeling? And is that thought serving me?"*

Develop the Witness

Kevin was discovering something profound: he wasn't just his thoughts and feelings. There was a part of him that could watch them, understand them, even question them. This is meta-awareness, and it changes everything.

The Architecture of Observation

Dr. Aaron Beck, founder of Cognitive Behavioral Therapy, demonstrated through decades of clinical research that **metacognition,** our ability to think about our own thinking, is key to identifying and reworking cognitive distortions. Complementing this, **Dr. Jon Kabat-Zinn's** work cultivates nonjudgmental awareness that reduces emotional reactivity. Together, these capacities create the pause needed to observe our own mental processes.

This pause allows us to catch the brain's fast, automatic reactions—what **Daniel Kahneman's** calls "System 1"—as they happen. Without meta-awareness, we are captives of our conditioning. With it, we gain the gap between stimulus and response.

Reflection and meta-awareness give rise to deeper internal capacities: pattern recognition across time and situations, narrative reframing of life experiences, emotion-thought differentiation, compassionate self-observation (witness, not judge), and the foundation for intuition.

Over time, this observer self also becomes the **editor-in-chief**. A person can ask, *"Is this the story I want to keep living?"* and begin to write a different one. This is how we move from inherited narratives ("people like me never succeed") toward chosen ones.

The Power Tool: Journaling

If you don't journal, start. It is one of the most underrated tools for this work.

Kevin had discovered it on his own. Like emotional labeling, journaling is deceptively simple and incredibly powerful. Polymaths, philosophers, and world leaders have all used journaling to organize thoughts and reflect on experiences. The practice has deep roots. The Stoic emperor Marcus Aurelius used it to govern himself. The Renaissance inventor Leonardo da Vinci used notebooks to refine ideas. Scientists such as Marie Curie, Albert Einstein, and Nikola Tesla also kept journals as part of their thinking process.

> ### FROM KEVIN'S JOURNAL, WEEK 8
>
> *Tried something new today. When I felt the scared-angry feeling, I asked myself: 'What would I do if I wasn't afraid?' The answer surprised me.*

Journaling activates multiple neural mechanisms at once. When we write what we feel and reflect on our actions, we organize scattered fragments into coherent stories. This supports cognitive coherence between the brain's emotional and rational regions. The practice strengthens memory consolidation, aids emotional regulation, and promotes clarity by slowing reactivity. Writing engages the prefrontal cortex in a sustained dialogue with the limbic system, producing the very integration this chapter describes. It is, in a real sense, self-awareness made tangible.

As Kevin's self-observation deepened, two unexpected capacities emerged: **intuition** and **courage**.

Nobel laureate **Herbert Simon** defined intuition as "nothing more and nothing less than recognition": rapid identification of familiar patterns developed through experience. Alongside intuition, another quality cultivated through this work is courage. Not impulsive boldness, but a steady willingness to see clearly and act in alignment, even in the face of discomfort.

Brené Brown defines courage not as heroic action, but as the willingness to show up when the outcome cannot be controlled. Her research links emotional courage to self-awareness, showing how reflection and pattern recognition build the resilience required to act with integrity. Brown's two decades of qualitative research on vulnerability demonstrate that the people who exhibit the most consistent courage are not those who feel less fear. They are those who have practiced naming it, sitting with it, and acting on it despite the fear. This is not personality. It is training.

> ## FROM KEVIN'S JOURNAL, WEEK 9
>
> *Saw Amanda cut off Harry again in the meeting. Felt the rock (protection) and something else; like a pull to help. Didn't do anything, but I stayed aware of both feelings. That's new.*

One of the most critical shifts in meta-awareness is seeing our own filters. **Daniel Kahneman** showed that unconscious biases stem from fast, automatic thinking, while conscious reflection (slow thinking) is required to override these distortions. Thoughts like "People like me never succeed," can be seen as cognitive patterns rather than facts.

Meta-awareness leads to **meta-intelligence**. This is the capacity to observe the mind's operating system, notice when old programs no longer serve, and write new code.

TRY THIS: The Witness Pause

When you notice a strong reaction (anger, defensiveness, anxiety), pause and silently narrate what's happening: *"I notice I'm feeling defensive. My shoulders are tense. I'm thinking that this person doesn't respect me."* Simply observing the reaction, without trying to change it, creates space. Notice what happens to the intensity of the feeling when you watch it instead of becoming it.

TABLE 6: Meta-Awareness

CATEGORY	DETAILS
Subskills	• Observe self: Watching thoughts and emotions without fusion • Pattern recognition: Identifying recurring emotional sequences • Intuition development: Synthesizing unconscious pattern recognition into actionable insight
Skillsets	• Witness Consciousness: Maintaining observational distance while remaining engaged
Tools	• Mindfulness meditation; Trigger mapping; Reflective journaling; Pattern tracking sheets; Intuition logs
Performance Indicators	• You can notice your automatic reactions before acting on them, identify patterns in your emotional responses, and distinguish between intuition and impulse.

KEY TAKEAWAY

You are not your thoughts. You are the one who watches them. Meta-awareness is the skill that turns patterns from invisible forces into visible choices. The question is not "What am I feeling?" but "What story am I telling myself about what I am feeling, and is that story true?"

SKILL #4: VALUES ALIGNMENT

Align with Your Compass

> Are your daily choices aligned with your deepest
> values, or are you living someone else's priorities?

This is the fourth and final skill, and it draws on all three that came before. Having learned to feel, name, and observe, we now learn to act from what matters most. Values alignment means making choices that reflect one's deepest principles, especially when the environment encourages ignoring them.

Week Ten marked a turning point. Kevin had developed something new: the ability to notice and then trust.

By their tenth session, he began to sense when his choices were aligned versus merely reactions to pressure, expectation, or fear, and to distinguish between the tight, protective feeling of fear and the warm, expansive feeling of acting in alignment with his values.

"Amanda cut off Harry again in yesterday's meeting," he said. "But this time was different."

"How so?"

"I felt the rock, but I also felt something else. Like a pull toward helping him."

"What did that pull feel like?"

"Warm. Right here." He touched his heart. "Different from the rock. The rock is cold and hard. This was warm and... right."

"What did you do?"

"I spoke up. Asked Harry to finish his point."

"How did that feel?"

"Scary. But also good. Like I was being myself."

> ## FROM KEVIN'S JOURNAL, WEEK 10
>
> *Did something that scared me today. Spoke up for Harry. The scared feeling was still there, but something stronger was there too. It felt like me.*

Kevin had discovered the fourth skill: values alignment. The ability to recognize what matters most and act from that place, even when it is uncomfortable.

Behavior, Not Doctrine

Values are lived out in behavior, not doctrine.

Belief systems offer structure, but alignment comes from real-time choices. A person may be a devoted religious family person at home, yet display bias, dishonesty, and manipulation in the workplace. This is a reflection of the absence of value alignment as a skill. Kevin experienced this gap in miniature. He valued fairness, and in turn wanted to speak up for Harry. Yet for weeks, his behavior chose safety over that value. The gap was not a moral failing; it was a skill deficit. He had not yet learned to act from what mattered most when the cost was real.

Misalignment inherently limits growth because it begins with self-deception. Values alignment trains individuals to integrate their principles across all domains of life, leading to integrity.

The Biology of Conscience

What Kevin described, that "warm pull," is often dismissed as sentimentality. We casually refer to it as our "Jiminy Cricket," the conscience or inner voice in *Pinocchio*. Neuroscience suggests this compass is not a cartoon fantasy; it is a living, trainable biological system.

Conscience is a form of **moral intuition**. It creates quick, emotionally charged judgments about right and wrong that appear in awareness without step-by-step reasoning (*"this feels wrong," "this is the decent thing to do"*). These intuitions arise from neural networks linking bodily and emotional systems (the insula, cingulate, and amygdala) with frontal regions that appraise situations and goals. It is a biological blend of gut feeling and high-speed interpretation.

Jonathan Haidt's social intuitionist model captures this: most moral judgments start as fast intuitions, with reasoning often arriving afterward to explain what we already feel.

This system is not fixed; it grows. Developmental research shows that young children start by internalizing rules based on fear (*"I don't want to be punished"*). As we mature, repeated experiences of empathy and modeling shift the compass inward. We move from fear of authority to internal resonance (*"I feel bad if I hurt someone or betray what I believe is right"*).

The compass is biologically prepared, but it is culturally educated. Every time it is honored, the signal sharpens. Every time it is overridden, it dulls.

The Neuroscience of Living Aligned

Most of us don't stop to consider whether our daily choices align with our deeper values. Life moves fast, and this kind of uncomfortable inner work often gets pushed to the margins. But here's the shift: the cost of misalignment is quiet, cumulative, and real.

Kevin's discovery connects to something fundamental about human nature. Research across psychology, anthropology, and neuroscience confirms that we share deep-rooted ethical instincts.

Social scientists have studied the values that guide human behavior. **Shalom Schwartz**, a psychologist, found ten fundamental values recurring across more than eighty cultural groups. **Jonathan Haidt**, a moral psychologist, identified six universal moral foundations. **Martha Nussbaum**, a philosopher, outlined essential human capabilities as the ground of dignity. The cross-cultural persistence of these patterns suggests they are more than preferences. They are structures that support human flourishing.

Neuroscience confirms this at the biological level. **Joshua Greene's** brain imaging studies demonstrated that moral decision-making originates in emotional centers and is only later rationalized by the cognitive mind.

The Cost of Fragmentation

When there's a disconnect between values and behavior, it generates **cognitive dissonance.** There's a name for what happens when we repeatedly betray our values: **moral injury.** Originally from military psychology, the concept describes what happens when we encounter experiences that violate our deepest beliefs about right and wrong, creating a profound sense of inner turmoil. Neuroimaging research shows moral injury activates different neural pathways than trauma, involving regions associated with self-concept, empathy, and moral reasoning.

While initially studied in soldiers, moral injury is now recognized in additional professions with heavy moral responsibilities such as healthcare and law enforcement. Even in corporate settings people can feel compelled to enact policies they perceive as wrong, a pattern that can lead to shame, withdrawal, and loss of meaning.

In short: a lack of values alignment slowly convinces a person that they have to choose between success and self-respect.

Research reveals that this misalignment erodes well-being at three levels:

The Physical Cost: Misalignment is a chronic stressor. Studies across healthcare and mental health practitioners show that value incongruence is strongly associated with higher burnout, emotional exhaustion, and physical complaints such as headaches and sleep disturbance. When values are suppressed, the body keeps score.

Identity Fragmentation: Many workers feel forced to adopt a "work self" that enables practices they privately oppose. Researchers call the antidote **identity integration,** a sense that the self expressed at work and the self expressed at home are reflections of the same underlying identity. The more fragmented those selves become, the harder it is to feel authentic or act with consistent integrity.

Relational Withdrawal: Unresolved value violations often lead to social isolation and cynicism. When we feel compromised, we withdraw from others to protect ourselves from further conflict.

The choice to align is not just about feeling good; it is a structural necessity for sustainable performance.

- It protects well-being: when personal and organizational values are congruent, people show lower burnout and better mental health.

- It preserves integrity: value congruence predicts not only wellbeing but also ethical behavior under pressure.

- It stabilizes relationships: value-congruent environments have higher trust and lower turnover; misalignment breeds cynicism, quiet quitting, and ethical drift.

- It clarifies the exit: when alignment is systematically blocked, the most emotionally intelligent choice is often to change the system or leave it, because no amount of personal resilience can offset a structure that requires ongoing self-betrayal.

> ## FROM KEVIN'S JOURNAL, WEEK 11
>
> *Realized I've been protecting myself so much that I forgot what I was protecting. Maybe being safe isn't the same as being okay.*

Values as a Trainable Skill

Kevin was learning what most people never discover: values alignment is not a personality trait. It is a defensive skill, the one that protects a person not from others, but from becoming someone unrecognizable.

Psychologist **Carl Rogers** called it "congruence." Researcher and author **Brené Brown** describes authenticity as a daily practice rooted in courage. Leadership expert **Stephen Covey** framed values as guiding principles.

While these perspectives name the importance, few present values alignment as a trainable skill of self-awareness.

Psychologists call this **psychological flexibility**: the ability to feel fear, shame, or pressure and still take a step toward personal values. Research in Acceptance and Commitment Therapy links this capacity to higher well-being. When difficult emotions are interpreted as the cost of living according to one's values rather than as signs to avoid, the brain's threat response changes. Distress becomes information to work with, not a command to retreat.

Crucially, this is not about weaponizing "authenticity" to excuse reactivity. It is about **emotionally intelligent authenticity**: telling the truth in a way that honors both our values and the humanity of others.

TRY THIS: The "System versus Human" Audit

Modern workplaces often incentivize us to shut down our humanity to survive. We confuse "professionalism" with emotional suppression. Ask yourself these three questions to see where the system might be overriding your values:

The Exit Test: When a colleague is "let go," do you reach out to them as a person? Or do you distance yourself because they are no longer "inside" the tribe? Notice the fear that keeps you from sending that text. That fear is the system speaking, not your values.

The Jargon Trap: Do you refer to humans as resources, headcount, or capital? Do you discuss "restructuring" without acknowledging the grief it causes? Notice if your language is designed to numb you to the reality of others.

The Authenticity Gap: In your last difficult meeting, did you say what was true, or what was safe? Did you nod along with a decision you felt was wrong?

Pick one of these areas this week. Send the text to the former colleague. Change the term "resources" to "people" in your next email.

Say the true thing in the meeting. **Notice not just how the system reacts, but how your body reacts—the jaw unclenching, the breath returning. That somatic shift is your nervous system register-ing alignment.**

TABLE 7: **Values Alignment**

CATEGORY	DETAILS
Subskills	• Values clarification: Identifying core principles that guide action • Integrity audits: Checking alignment between stated values and actual behavior • Moral reasoning: Navigating ethical complexity with wisdom
Skillsets	• Ethical Integration: Living in alignment with deeply held principles
Tools	• Values hierarchies; Decision frameworks; Integrity journals; Ethical dilemma practice; Values-based goal setting
Performance Indicators	• You can name your top three to five core values, identify when behavior conflicts with values, and make decisions that honor your principles under pressure.

KEY TAKEAWAY

Values alignment is not a personality trait. It is a trainable skill. The cost of misalignment is quiet and cumulative: burnout, iden-tity fragmentation, relational withdrawal. The practice is simple and difficult: notice when your actions split from your principles, and be willing to change direction.

THE ERROR-CORRECTION SYSTEM
Self-Awareness Loop

Together, these four skills function like an internal error-correction system: a loop that runs continuously, each skill feeding the next. The loop is fast. With practice, it becomes automatic. It is not reactive: it is responsive. The difference is everything.

Watch how Kevin used it in week eleven, in a moment that would have undone him just a few earlier:

His manager called an impromptu review of the quarter's project outcomes. Kevin had made a visible error in a client-facing report. The room was small. The silence was pointed.

- **Interoception:** He felt the rock in his chest (cold, hard) and something tightening across his shoulders. His breathing went shallow. He recognized it before it became a flood.

- **Emotional Literacy:** He named it precisely: not shame, not anger. Exposed. The word landed differently than "stressed" would have. It told him something true about what was actually at stake.

- **Meta-Awareness:** He noticed the familiar pattern rising: go quiet, make yourself small, wait for it to pass. He saw it as a habit, not a requirement. He had a choice.

- **Values Alignment:** He felt the pull toward self-protection and something else. The pull toward being the kind of person who owns his work. He chose the second one.

"I made the error," he said. "Here is what I missed and here is how I will correct it."

The fear did not disappear. He acted anyway, because he knew what kind of person he wanted to be.

The whole loop took seconds. Without any single skill, it breaks down. Without **interoception,** he would not have noticed the two distinct signals, just a general sense of a "bad feeling" that he would avoid or suppress. Without **emotional literacy**, he could not have separated protective fear from care. Both would have blurred into anxiety, and anxiety usually chooses safety. Without **meta-awareness**, he would not have seen his own pattern. He would have assumed his hesitation was rational ("it's not my problem") rather than habitual ("this is what I always do"). Without **values alignment**, he might have seen the choice clearly but still defaulted to self-protection. Seeing is not choosing. He needed to feel the pull of who he wanted to become.

This is the architecture of self-awareness: a system that detects, names, observes, and aligns—fast enough to operate in real time, accurate enough to catch the stories we tell ourselves, and connected enough to our values that we can act from them even when afraid.

Kevin did not learn four separate skills. He built one integrated capacity. The skills are how we teach it. The loop is how it works.

> **Interoception:** detects the early signal—*something is happening in the body.*
>
> **Emotional Literacy:** assigns a label—*this sensation has a name*
>
> **Meta-Awareness:** checks the story—*is what I am telling myself true, or just familiar?*
>
> **Values Alignment:** determines the response—*given what I now understand, what action reflects who I want to be?*

Week Twelve: The Integration

Twelve weeks after their first session, Kevin walked into the room differently.

Still choosing the same chair, still keeping some protective distance, but now moving with a quiet confidence that hadn't been there before. The device on his wrist, which had tracked his journey from chronic stress to increasing coherence, now showed the steady rhythms of a nervous system beginning to trust itself. The numbers could measure the change.

They could not explain what the change meant; that would require Kevin's own words.

"I want to show you something," he said, pulling out a small notebook. "I've been writing down what I notice."

FROM KEVIN'S JOURNAL, WEEK 12

Tuesday: *Felt tight in my shoulders before the client presentation. Named it as worried about failing. Asked myself: Is this thought true? Maybe, but worrying isn't helping me focus. Took a walk and did a breathing exercise.*

Wednesday: *New hire started today. Watched Amanda work the room before lunch. I've seen this before. She gets threatened, especially by other women, and she moves fast. By afternoon she was already in leadership's ear. I went to my manager. Laid it out clearly. He listened, nodded, said he'd keep an eye on it. I know what that means. Three good people have left this team in eighteen months. Each one said the same thing on their way out, quietly, to the people they trusted. Nobody upstairs connected the dots. Or if they did, they decided the dots weren't worth the discomfort. That is not a culture problem. That is a leadership problem. And leadership problems compound. I've been watching Amanda longer than anyone here knows. She doesn't need to be respected. She needs to be seen by the people with power. As long as leadership treats her like she's capable, she can survive the rest. I recognize that. I used to need the same thing. The difference is I had someone who taught me there was another way. She never got that. I don't excuse what she does. I just understand it now. Felt the rock the whole time. Named it. Not just frustrated. Grieving, maybe. For the new hire. For the ones before her. For Amanda too, if I'm honest. The loop didn't fix the system. It just kept me from going numb inside it.*

> **Friday:** *Harry thanked me for having his back. Felt warm and proud, but also something else. Looked it up. Grateful. I'm grateful that I learned to be myself instead of just being safe. That I don't need to add to the harm.*

The transformation was profound but not complete. Kevin still faced difficult situations, still felt fear and uncertainty, still sometimes chose protection over connection. He now had tools.

"What's different now?" she asked during their final session.

"I know what I feel and why I feel it. I know what I think and when my thoughts are helping or hurting. And I know what I care about, really care about, not just what I'm supposed to care about."

"And how does that change things?"

"When I started here, my manager said I was hard to read. I thought that was their problem. Then I realized I was hard to read because I couldn't read myself. I had no access. Not to what I was feeling, not to why I was reacting, not to what I actually valued underneath all the noise. I was just responding to everything, all the time, with no ground under me."

He was quiet for a moment.

"When you're inside a place that performs culture instead of building it, that confusion gets louder. You start to think the problem is your competence, your politics, your ability to play the game. It took me a long time to understand that I wasn't confused because I was failing. I was confused because I was paying attention. The gap between what they said and what I felt every day was real. I was reading it accurately. I just had nothing solid enough to stand on."

"And now?"

"Now I have the ground. I know when something is wrong before I can name it. I know the difference between my instinct and my fear. I know what I will and won't do, and why. That clarity cost me something. I put in my notice last week."

She waited.

"They don't want it fixed. I understand that now. Toxicity is easier to manage than people who think for themselves. Leadership that lacks emotional intelligence doesn't just tolerate a culture like that. It depends on it. The confusion, the politics, the performance. It keeps people off balance. People who are off balance don't ask hard questions."

"I'm asking hard questions now. I can't unknow what I know. And I won't pretend the ground isn't there just because it makes them uncomfortable."

She said nothing. Some endings don't need commentary.

He walked out, shoulders straight, breathing deep.

Six months later, she received a message from Kevin: "Wanted you to know I landed somewhere that actually means what it says. First week, my manager asked me what I needed to do my best work. I had to sit with that for a minute. Nobody had ever asked me that before. I knew the answer. That's the whole point, isn't it."

He picked up his notebook. "Thank you for teaching me that my feelings are not the boss of me, but they're not my enemy either. They're just...information I can use."

The skills he built were his. They lived in his body now, not on a page. Self-awareness is only the ground. Knowing what is felt, naming it accurately, observing the patterns, choosing from personal values: this is the base. What rises from it is the next question.

The young man who walked out of that room, shoulders straight and breathing deep, learned what it means to be present to himself. What you learn to move through in yourself, you become capable of leading others through.

Values alignment is where the sequence becomes ethical action. Power carries responsibility. To lead is to hold others in your care. Decency is not a quality that enhances leadership. It is a requirement of it. Self-awareness without conscience is not wisdom. It is sophistication in service of the self.

What is remarkable is how universal values are across cultures, traditions, and time. It is not a coincidence. It is what it means to be human.

A young man speaking up for a colleague in a meeting room because he knows who he wants to be is not a small thing. It is how humanity moves toward its better self.

The leaders whose influence outlasted their authority carried this in their body. As choices made in alignment with what mattered compounded over time, that alignment became who they were and what they offered the world.

AI can accelerate the development of these skills by making what was previously invisible observable: the body's signals, the patterns in our language, the gap between our stated values and our actual behavior. What it cannot do is close that gap. That remains the work of a human being willing to be changed by what they see. The capacity to be changed by your own experience, to integrate what you feel into who you become, to lead others from a self that has been tested and held, remains irreducibly human.

Self-awareness shows the territory. Self-mastery teaches how to move through it.

KEY TAKEAWAYS

The Four-Skill Loop

Self-awareness is not four separate skills but one integrated capacity:

- **Feel it** (Interoception): Notice the physical sensation before the story starts.

- **Name it** (Emotional Literacy): Give precise language to what you notice.

- **Observe it** (Meta-Awareness): Step back and watch your patterns.
- **Align it** (Values Alignment): Choose action based on what matters most.

The loop runs continuously. With practice, it runs fast. The goal is not to eliminate difficult emotions but to stop being ambushed by them.

What Makes This Human

AI can track heart rates, predict emotional states, and label sentiment in speech. It cannot feel the rock in the chest soften when the right word arrives. It cannot experience the relief of being understood by itself. The skills in this chapter build something no algorithm replicates: **felt meaning**.

The Cost of Skipping This

Without interoception, one reacts before knowing why. Without emotional literacy, everything feels like "stress" or "fine." Without meta-awareness, our patterns run us. Without values alignment, we optimize for safety instead of meaning. The cumulative cost is a life spent performing rather than living.

One Practice to Start

Pause for ten seconds and ask: *What is my body telling me right now?* No judgment. No fixing. Just notice. This is how fluency begins.

> *"Between stimulus and response, there is a space. In that space, we have the power to choose our response. In our response lies our growth and our freedom."*
> **Viktor Frankl, Man's Search for Meaning**

CHAPTER 8

SELF MASTERY

THE ALCHEMIST

> *Without fear, there is nothing to overcome.*
> *Fear is the foundation of courage, not its opposite."*
> **Joseph LeDoux, neuroscientist and**
> **author of *The Emotional Brain***

Where Self-Awareness asks, *"What is happening in me?"* self-mastery asks, *"What will I do with this?"*

Self-mastery is built on three trainable skills:

- **Self-Command:** the ability to generate and direct useful emotional states.

- **Discomfort Tolerance:** the capacity to stay engaged when things are hard.

- **Resilience through Recovery:** the discipline of completing intense experiences in order to begin again.

Kevin from the previous chapter learned to feel, name, observe, and align. Knowing feelings is not the same as commanding them. What happens when the fear is too strong to name? When the pattern seen is one that cannot be broken? When values are clear but the pressure to betray them is overwhelming?

Self-mastery answers these questions.

It separates insight from leadership. A person can be emotionally intelligent in perception yet still lack the tools to regulate, motivate, and recover. They know what they feel, but cannot change their response. The patterns are recognizable, but repeated regardless.

Self-mastery is where perception becomes discipline. In the face of challenges and unpredictability, it is the ability to stay grounded, direct energy with purpose, and recover without losing momentum. It is not about suppression. It is about emotional precision: the ability to remain aligned even when conditions are hard. Intelligence only matters when tested in real conditions. When challenged, collapse is not the path forward. Expansion follows hardships. Rising becomes inevitable.

From Awareness to Agency

In the previous chapter, Kevin built four skills which gave him a map of his inner world. Self-mastery asks a harder question: Can he read that map while the ground is shaking?

The leap from awareness to mastery is the leap from perception to purposeful action, called agency. Agency is not a new skill. It happens when the awareness skills operate fast enough, reliably enough, and under enough pressure to produce intentional action rather than mere insight. Kevin saw his pattern; the act of speaking up was agency. The difference was not knowledge. It was speed, reliability, and willingness under load.

Self-mastery trains that speed. It takes the four-skill loop from Chapter Seven and runs it at professional velocity: an actress reads her body, names the fear, observes her options, and chooses to recruit the fear into vulnerability, all seconds before the curtain rises. A soldier runs the same loop under combat load: interoception detects the spike, literacy names it as productive adrenaline, meta-awareness checks whether he is still thinking clearly, and values alignment keeps him oriented toward the team. The loop is identical. The conditions are extreme. That is the difference between awareness and mastery.

Emotions Are Superpowers

Many people view their emotions as intruders: disruptive forces that hijack the nervous system. Biologically, they are neural instructions designed for survival. They are not noise; they are data.

Consider the spectrum of human feeling not as a list of problems to solve, but as a catalog of potential energy.

- **Fear,** often vilified, is the architect of focus; it heightens perception and prepares the body for speed. Without fear, there is no courage, only recklessness.

- **Anger,** when stripped of its volatility, is simply mobilized energy designed to defend boundaries and correct injustice.

- **Sadness** slows the metabolic rate to process loss, creating the biological conditions for depth and connection.

- **Disgust,** the most primal rejection, is the root of moral discernment: the ability to know instantly what violates personal standards.

- **Surprise** triggers the cognitive reset needed for adaptability.

- **Contempt** signals social misalignment.

- **Happiness** cements the social bonds that allow us to build trust.

The alchemist is a master of transformation. She does not repress emotional signals. She transmutes them. She takes the raw lead of terror and turns it into the gold of situational awareness. She takes the heat of rage and forges it into a boundary.

The Emotional Redirection Map

These raw signals can be redirected through skills into constructive action. The emotion can be felt without obeying it.

Mastery is about being aligned with core values in moments when most people lose themselves. It is clarity when others shut down, connection when others disconnect, and courage when others retreat. This is not just emotional freedom; it is a strategic advantage. This capacity is what makes leadership credible, trust possible, and performance sustainable.

The Performer and The Soldier

We turn to two high-performance domains that seem opposites but share a secret language: the theater stage and the special operations unit.

The theater performer and a soldier's work is not equivalent in stakes. The soldier risks death; the actress risks a bad review.

Yet both demand something rare: precise emotional control under conditions that would destabilize most people. Both have developed systematic training over decades. They represent opposite applications of the same foundational skills.

The actress in this chapter trained in the Konstantin Stanislavski method. What made this approach revolutionary was its insistence that actors could not simply *pretend* to feel. To be believed, they had to access genuine emotion through *emotional memory*: the deliberate recall of personal experiences that produce the required physiological state. This was not performance of feeling; it was trained generation of feeling. The nervous system does not distinguish between remembered grief and present grief. The body responds the same way.

The military tradition arrived at the same insight from the opposite direction. NATO's human performance laboratories and the U.S. Army's Performance Enhancement and Resilience (PEAR) program have produced detailed research on how trained operators maintain cognitive function when fear, exhaustion, and chaos would overwhelm untrained individuals. What researchers found contradicted the stereotype: elite warriors do not suppress emotion. They regulate it with surgical precision.

The actress trains to access emotional depth. Her craft requires her to genuinely feel grief, rage, or tenderness because audiences detect inauthenticity instantly. She must open fully to the emotion and let it flow into visible expression.

The soldier trains to maintain emotional agency. His effectiveness requires him to experience fear and aggression without being hijacked by them. He must function clearly *despite* the feeling, not because of it.

Same fire. She fans it into a flame the audience can feel. He banks it into heat he can use.

SKILL #1: EMOTIONAL SELF-COMMAND

Become the Driver

> Can you generate the emotional state that serves
> your purpose, or does your state choose for you?

This is the first skill of mastery: the trained ability to access, generate, and direct emotional states with intention. It is the move from being a passenger in one's own body to being the driver.

NINETY SECONDS TO CURTAIN

The murmur of the audience hums behind the heavy red velvet curtain. Even after more than thirty performances, the scene still unnerves her.

Tonight is the scene where Elena buries her son. To play it, the actress will reach for a memory carried from age nineteen: the morning her mother called to say her brother had died in a motorcycle accident. Standing in a rehearsal hall in New York, 3,000 miles from home, the floor tilted. The exact quality of the silence after the phone went dead stays with her, a silence she has drawn on hundreds of times on stage. It always comes at a cost.

With short, sharp breaths, a tension builds in the chest and the buzz in her limbs is not forced away. She takes note of the charge. The energy. Before it shapes into anything else.

Fear coils low in her abdomen, rising to protect. She notices it, expands her stance, and grounds through her feet. *You're safe.*

Her eyes slide shut to begin the ritual. Only in her mind, she walks on stage, feels the warmth of the lights, hears the silence of the house. This isn't daydreaming; it's embodied rehearsal with the nervous system responding as if it's happening now.

Breathing begins in a square rhythm: inhaling for four counts, holding for four, exhaling for four, holding for four. The long exhale mechanically activates the parasympathetic nervous system, quieting the fight-or-flight response just enough to restore access to clear thought. She gets herself to baseline to access *receptivity*.

A body scan registers the warmth in her palms and the rhythm of the pulse, each sensation an adjustable data point. Anxiety crackles in her throat, demanding certainty. She lengthens her exhale, narrowing focus to the first line of the script. Anxiety wants control, so she gives it structure.

Excitement tingles in her limbs. She lets it rise, drawing it into movement, shaking arms and rolling shoulders. Fear isn't suppressed; she recruits it. Each emotion is a current of energy with a purpose. The body speaks. The mind listens. Together, they decide what gets expressed.

This is the moment most people miss. She has options: let the fear freeze her, grief and memory flooding in, or let excitement scatter her. Awareness gave her all of the signals simultaneously. Agency is the act of choosing which current to ride. Tonight, she chooses grief because Elena needs it. With fear sharpening her focus and excitement fueling energy, the channel to her brother is opened. The choice isn't cognitive. It's felt: a turning of attention, like adjusting a lens until the image resolves.

She is ready to feel.

0400 HOURS: PRE-MISSION

The operator folds his daughter's drawing, a purple house with a lopsided sun, and tucks it inside the left breast pocket of his tactical vest. He has carried something of hers on every operation since she was born. It's not superstition. It's a compass point: a physical reminder of who he is when the mission strips away everything but reflex. Later, if the fear becomes enormous, he'll feel the paper crinkle against his chest and know what needs protecting.

The operator's preparation follows an exact sequence.

"The cave you fear to enter holds the treasure you seek."
Joseph Campbell

The visualization is tactical. Eyes closed, he runs through the breach. He feels the weight of his gear, the sting of the desert heat, the specific resistance of the trigger. The mission is encoded into muscle memory so that when chaos hits, his body knows the answer before his mind asks the question.

His interoception is operational. He scans for the optimal level of activation: enough adrenaline for speed, but not so much that it compromises fine motor control. He knows his personal markers; if his heart rate spikes too early, his vision will tunnel.

Adjustments are made in the quiet of preparation, breathing in a four-count rhythm. Breathing does not eliminate fear because that's what keeps him alive. He breathes to sharpen it into hyper-vigilance, channeling it into tactical awareness. The drawing crinkles against his chest. He registers it, lets the warmth settle for half a second, and returns to the scan.

He is ready to act.

The Shared Secret

This is the same process available to everybody before a board meeting, a difficult conversation, or a presentation. It is not about "faking it." It is about recruiting real emotional states in alignment with values, rather than defenses. The difference between someone who is overwhelmed before a high-stakes moment and someone who performs through it is not courage or talent. It is whether they have trained the awareness-to-agency loop: feel what is happening, name it, observe the options, and choose which energy to recruit. Preparation is only half the story. Watch what happens when the curtain rises.

CURTAIN UP

As she walks onstage, Elena emerges. Grief narrows her throat and vulnerability trembles through her fingers. She notices these sensations and names each one. When the lights brighten, the audience sees confidence. What they are witnessing is emotional fluency in motion: self-awareness and self-regulation synchronized through disciplined, trained, physical expression.

Then something shifts. A laugh lands early. A hush deepens in the back row. She feels it. Adjusts her rhythm. Holds a beat longer. The room merges with her breath. She is in sync with the other actors on stage and the pulse of the audience between them.

This is not just a performance; it is a relationship. The theater becomes a dojo for emotional agility. In the grief scene, she reaches for her brother. The memory arrives not as a thought but as temperature: a sudden cold in her hands, a weight behind her eyes. Twenty years and it still floods her nervous system. She lets it come, trained for exactly this: not to perform grief, but to open the channel and let it pass through her into the room. The audience does not know what they are seeing. They only know it is real.

CONTACT

Execution unfolds at 0437.

The operator's body has done this in training a thousand times. When the door breaches, conscious deliberation steps back and trained response takes over. Heart rate spikes. He expected this, does not fight it. Fear floods his system and he lets it convert to hypervigilance. Every sense amplifies. Time seems to slow as processing speed increases.

He clears his sector, registers threats, makes split-second decisions that would paralyze untrained individuals. The emotional state he generated before the mission (controlled intensity, contained aggression) is now operational. Fear isn't suppressed; it's information: this is dangerous, stay maximally alert. It sharpens rather than scatters attention.

Contact. The plan adapts in real-time. A teammate takes fire; he is exposed, covering the extraction. Fear surges, and he has trained for exactly this. The feeling is enormous, but it doesn't flood. Access to judgment is maintained as he moves, shoots, and communicates: the triad drilled into reflex.

Here is where awareness becomes agency. Two signals are competing: the survival instinct screaming move to cover, and the trained response that says hold position, the team needs you here. An untrained person would obey the louder signal. The operator does something different. He observes both, recognizes the survival instinct as fear doing its job, and chooses the trained response because it aligns with what matters more than his own safety. The choice takes less than a second. It isn't suppression. It's selection: the values alignment is operating at lethal speed.

The drawing crinkles. For a fraction of a second, the purple house flashes behind his eyes. It doesn't distract him. It steadies him.

He knows what he is fighting for, and the knowing isn't cognitive. It lives in the warmth against his chest.

Forty-three minutes of sustained intensity. Decisions with life-or-death consequences made in fractions of seconds. Emotional states that would incapacitate most people channeled into precise, effective action.

Mission complete. The team extracts. His heart rate begins the long descent from combat activation.

The work is not finished.

THE PRE-PERFORMANCE RESET

Before your next high-stakes moment (presentation, difficult conversation, performance review), try this sequence:

Three box breaths (four counts in, four hold, four out, four hold).

Interoceptive scan: Locate tension, temperature, activation level.

Visualize the first thirty seconds going well, with physical detail. Use all four senses.

Name the emotion present without trying to change it.

Ask: *"What state serves me here?"*

The sequence takes ninety seconds. Practice until it becomes automatic

TABLE 8: Emotional Self-Command in Practice

CATEGORY	DETAILS
Subskills	• State induction: Creating or amplifying desired emotional states as needed • Emotional redirection: Channeling intense emotions into constructive action • Regulation under load: Maintaining executive function during activation
Skillsets	• Emotional Engineering: Systematically constructing and rehearsing emotional states in advance for key moments
Tools	• State rehearsal/visualization; Recovery protocols (movement, breathwork, expressive writing); State anchoring techniques; Adaptive exposure exercises; Biofeedback devices for heart rate tracking; After-action debriefing
Performance Indicators	• You can articulate which strategies work for you to rapidly shift into a focused or calm state under pressure, sustain composure in rising emotional intensity, channel intensity into constructive action, and move smoothly between emotional states without becoming stuck or overwhelmed.

KEY TAKEAWAY

You are not at the mercy of your emotional states. Self-command is the trained ability to generate the state that serves your purpose, not suppress what you feel, but recruit it. The actress and the soldier use the same tools: breath, visualization, interoceptive scanning. The difference is direction, not capacity.

SKILL #2: DISCOMFORT TOLERANCE

Transform the Burn

> When difficulty arrives, do you collapse, numb,
> or find the meaning that lets you stay?

Without the tolerance of discomfort, values collapse the moment conditions become hard.

If self-command is the spark, discomfort tolerance is the fuel. It is the ability to sustain action when the state becomes painful, transforming the relationship with difficulty itself.

> *"Enthusiasm is common. Endurance is rare.*
> *The capacity to tolerate discomfort in service of a greater purpose*
> *transforms potential into performance."*
> **Jim Loehr, performance psychologist**

THE THIRD ACT

By the final act, the actress's body rebels. Her feet ache. The lights are oppressive. She has cried real tears fifty times, and tonight it must be done again.

She draws from something deeper than comfort: the commitment to truth. The discomfort isn't an obstacle; it's information. Her tired feet ground her in the character's exhaustion. She doesn't transcend the discomfort; she includes it and stays in the scene because the story matters more than her fatigue.

There is a moment in the third act where Elena sits alone on an empty stage and says nothing for twelve seconds. Twelve seconds of silence in a theater is an eternity. The temptation, every night, is to fill it: a gesture, a shift, something to prove she is still acting. Tonight she resists, sitting in the silence as the audience feel the weight of what has been lost. Her exhaustion becomes the character's exhaustion. The ache in her feet becomes the ache of a woman who has carried too much for too long. She doesn't act the pain. She is in the pain, and she stays.

This is the skill: not enduring discomfort by going numb, but staying present inside it long enough for it to become something useful.

She could leave. Not the stage, but the feeling. She knows how to perform grief on autopilot: the gestures, the timing, the catch in the voice. The audience would never know the difference. The temptation to go mechanical is the discomfort her body is trying to escape. Agency, here, is the choice to stay embodied: to keep feeling the ache rather than performing it. The cost is real. The result is the difference between a good performance and the kind that changes someone in the audience.

HOUR 48

Two days without sleep. The operator's body is consuming its own reserves.

He knows that discomfort is data, not a verdict. The cold means his circulation is prioritizing core organs. The hunger means he is running on ketones. He is still operational.

At hour thirty-six, a voice in his head started negotiating. Just close your eyes for two minutes. Nobody will know. He recognized the voice: it was the same one that whispered "quit" during Hell Week, the same one that promised rest if he just stopped swimming. He has learned not to argue with it. Arguing gives it weight. Instead, he returns to the protocol: next task, next breath, next step. The voice doesn't stop, but it's no longer trying to steer. This is agency under sustained load: not the absence of the impulse to quit, but the trained capacity to hear it without obeying it.

At hour forty-two, something shifts. The misery is still there, but it becomes backdrop rather than foreground. He finds himself noticing things with unusual clarity: the exact pattern of stars through the cloud break, the rhythm of his teammate's breathing. Researchers call this the "second wind" of sustained effort, the moment when the nervous system stops fighting the discomfort and begins integrating it.

His motivation isn't comfort; it's completion. He stays in the mission because the team matters more than his pain.

The Architecture of Grit

Research confirms that how we view stress determines its impact. **Alia Crum**, a Stanford University psychologist and mindset researcher, shows that viewing stress as energy mobilization alters our actual physiology. At the University of Rochester, **Jeremy Jamieson** researches stress reappraisal, revealing that reframing anxiety as excitement boosts high-stakes performance.

The Yerkes-Dodson law shows that peak performance occurs at moderate stress levels: too little leads to complacency, too much causes overwhelm. The challenge is learning to surf this middle zone.

This requires **dual consciousness**: the capacity to experience intense pain or emotion while simultaneously observing it. The soldier feels the panic chemicals but observes them as "information." The actress feels the exhaustion but observes it as "depth." This separate "observer self" prevents the sensation from becoming a command. It is the difference between drowning and learning to breathe underwater.

Crucially, this skill applies to meaningful difficulty: the discomfort of growth, not the harm of abuse. Staying in a toxic system is not discomfort tolerance; it is self-betrayal. The skill is learning to distinguish between the burn of exercise and the burn of injury.

TRY THIS: The Discomfort Reframe

The next time you feel stress rising before a challenging situation, try this internal script:

"This sensation is my body preparing to perform. The activation I feel is energy being mobilized. This difficulty means I am doing something that matters."

Notice what shifts when you interpret the same physical sensations as preparation rather than threat. The reframe may feel forced at first; that is expected. The goal is not to believe it immediately but to interrupt the automatic "stress is bad" narrative.

TABLE 9: Discomfort Tolerance in Practice

CATEGORY	DETAILS
Subskills	• Stress reappraisal: Viewing stress as energy mobilization rather than system breakdown • Purpose connection: Linking difficulty to meaningful goals • Dual consciousness: Experiencing intensity while maintaining observer awareness
Skillsets	• Adaptive Persistence: Sustaining effort through discomfort by connecting to purpose
Tools	• Stress reappraisal exercises; Purpose journaling; Deliberate discomfort practice; Performance under pressure simulations; Motivational interviewing techniques
Performance Indicators	• You can maintain performance during extended challenge, reframe stress as enhancing rather than debilitating, connect difficult moments to meaningful goals, and distinguish between productive discomfort and harmful strain.

KEY TAKEAWAY

Discomfort is not the enemy of performance. It is the price of meaning. The skill is not endurance through numbness but presence inside difficulty. When you can reframe the burn as information rather than verdict, you stop collapsing at the threshold where growth begins.

SKILL #3: RESILIENCE THROUGH RECOVERY

Complete the Cycle

> After intensity, do you recover fully, or do you
> carry the residue into the next moment?

Without recovery, every success leaves a residue that eventually turns into burnout. Self-command generates the state. Discomfort tolerance sustains it. Resilience is what allows it to be done again tomorrow. Recovery is not what happens after the work; it is part of the work.

THE RETURN

As the final bow ends, the actress faces her hardest task: returning to herself. She's lived in another's skin, and her nervous system is flooded with emotions that don't belong to her. If she goes home now, she'll carry the character's grief into her kitchen.

So she has a ritual. She shakes out her limbs to physically discharge the tension. She wipes off the makeup, creating a boundary between roles. She journals three things she learned, closing the cognitive loop.

She speaks her own name aloud, grounding herself in her own reality.

Tonight the grief lingers longer than usual. She reached deeper for the brother memory, and it doesn't want to let go. She sits at her dressing room mirror and writes: "The silence in Act Three was real tonight. I let it be real. That cost me something. I am putting it down now." She reads the words back to herself, and something in her chest loosens. This isn't weakness. This is the discipline of completion: naming what the performance took from her so she doesn't carry it home to the people she loves.

By the time she leaves the theater, she is whole.

THE DEBRIEF

The operator's recovery is rigorous. He creates a physical discharge through controlled exercise to burn off the circulating stress hormones. He engages in a structured debrief (facts first, feelings later) to process the chaos into coherence.

He reconnects with his team, using shared experience to metabolize the trauma.

In the debrief room, the team lead asks the same question he asks after every operation: "What did you feel that you didn't expect to feel?" The question is not therapeutic softness. It is operational intelligence. An unexpected emotion, rage at a target who turned out to be a teenager, guilt over a call that saved the team but cost a civilian structure, these are the residues that, unprocessed, become the stress injuries that end careers. The operator answers honestly: "When the drawing crinkled during the extraction, I felt homesick. Not afraid. Homesick. That surprised me."

The team lead nods. "That is the one to sit with tonight."

Research from the Army's PEAR program documents that operators who master these recovery techniques have fewer stress injuries and longer careers. They do not just "bounce back"; they integrate the stress and grow stronger.

Unscripted

Unlike the actress or the soldier, life rarely grants a clear curtain call or mission end. The stress of a difficult marriage or a high-pressure job clings to us. This **incomplete intensity** accumulates as a residue that leads to burnout.

This is why we must invent our own rituals of release when we push ourselves. We must learn to complete the cycle.

Physiology resets through breath, sleep, and movement. Consumer wearables now make this visible: Oura Ring or WHOOP band tracks Heart Rate Variability (HRV), showing whether the nervous system is recovering or depleting. When HRV crashes on Sunday nights anticipating Monday's demands, it can be adjusted through experiment. Does a body scan help? Does preparing tomorrow's logistics reduce the anticipatory stress? The measurement becomes a development tool: not just data but feedback that accelerates learning.

Emotion releases through expression. Reflection turns chaos into coherence. Community assures us we are not alone.

Resilience is the difference between finishing the day depleted and finishing the day emptied-and-refilled, available again for your own life.

TRY THIS: The Completion Ritual

After any intense experience (difficult meeting, emotional conversation, high-stakes performance), practice completion:

Physical discharge: Shake, move, walk, or exercise for two to five minutes.

Name three things: What you learned, what you release, what you carry forward.

Grounding: Feel your feet, name where you are, recall your own name.

Connection: Brief contact with someone who knows the real you.

TABLE 10: Resilience in Practice

CATEGORY	DETAILS
Subskills	• Recovery awareness: Recognizing when you need restoration before burnout • Stress cycle completion: Processing activation fully rather than suppressing • Integration practice: Transforming difficulty into growth

CATEGORY	DETAILS
Skillsets	• Recovery Architecture: Designing personalized systems for restoration
Tools	• Sleep optimization protocols; HRV-guided recovery; Social support mapping; Post-failure analysis frameworks; Energy management systems; Strategic rest practices
Performance Indicators	• You can identify your personal signs of depletion before burnout, implement effective recovery strategies, extract learning from setbacks without excessive rumination, and maintain sustainable performance over extended periods.

KEY TAKEAWAY

Recovery is not weakness. It is the discipline that makes sustained performance possible. Without completion, intensity accumulates as residue that eventually becomes burnout. The actress journals. The soldier debriefs. Both understand that what you do after the performance determines whether you can perform again tomorrow.

The Same Foundation, Different Mastery

The actress and the soldier never meet. Their worlds share no obvious common ground. One bows to applause in a room designed for beauty. The other debriefs in a facility that officially does not exist.

They have trained in the same foundational capacity through different applications.

What makes their parallel instructive is not the symmetry of their techniques. It is the asymmetry of their relationship to the same emotions. The actress trains to open. The soldier trains to contain. She succeeds when feeling becomes visible. He succeeds when feeling becomes fuel. Yet both require the same underlying capacity: a disciplined, conscious relationship with their own nervous system.

This is why self-mastery is not a personality type or a temperament. It is an infrastructure. The actress did not arrive at Stanislavski's method because she was naturally emotional. She arrived because raw emotion without training produced performances that were chaotic, not moving. The soldier did not arrive at tactical breathing because he was naturally stoic. He arrived because unregulated fear in combat produces not bravery but paralysis.

Both discovered the same truth: unmanaged emotion is noise and trained emotion is power. The question is not whether we feel intensely. The question is whether the infrastructure has been built to use what is felt.

The mechanism is the same one Kevin discovered, operating at higher speed. Feel the signal (interoception). Name it precisely (emotional literacy). Observe the choice point (meta-awareness). Select the response that aligns with what matters (values alignment). Then direct the energy with trained intention (self-command), sustain it through difficulty (discomfort tolerance), and complete the cycle so it can be done again (resilience). Seven skills, one continuous loop. Self-awareness provides the map. Self-mastery is the ability to read it while the earth quakes underfoot.

It is not faked. It is formed.

The Mastery Integration

The actress and the soldier teach the same truth. Self-mastery is not about control or release; it is about conscious choice. The three skills form a continuous loop that handles pressure without breaking.

It begins with **self-command**. Fear rises before the pitch; instead of suppressing it, breathe, name it, and channel it into focus. As the challenge lengthens and fatigue sets in, **discomfort tolerance** takes over; reconnect to purpose (*why this matters*) and use the exhaustion as fuel to listen deeper rather than checking out. Finally, when the day ends, **resilience** completes the cycle. Instead of carrying the tension home, take ten minutes to walk, debrief, and reset. Return to life whole, ready to begin again tomorrow.

These skills show up in every domain where stakes are real and performance matters: the ICU nurse managing her sixteenth hour, the teacher holding space for troubled students, the leader navigating layoffs with dignity. Every context requires the same fundamental capacities: to direct emotional energy consciously, to find meaning in difficulty, and to recover completely from intensity.

The Bridge to Relational Mastery

Self-mastery gives command over internal world. Emotional intelligence ultimately lives between people. The steadiest nervous system in the room means nothing if it cannot attune to others, repair ruptures, or build the trust that makes teams function.

The final pillar asks: **What do you do with your mastery when you turn it outward?**

Before you continue, ask yourself:

- Can you access courage when you feel fear?

- Can you find meaning in discomfort that makes it bearable?

- Can you recover fully without numbing or carrying residue?

KEY TAKEAWAYS

The Three Skills in Action
- **Command it (Self-Command):** Generate the state that serves your purpose.

- **Channel it (Discomfort Tolerance):** Transform pressure into performance through meaning.

- **Complete it (Resilience):** Process fully and integrate cleanly.

The loop runs continuously. With practice, it becomes the difference between performing under pressure and being crushed by it.

> *"Knowing others is intelligence; knowing yourself is true wisdom.*
> *Mastering others is strength; mastering yourself is true power."*
> **Lao Tzu,** *Tao Te Ching*

RELATIONAL MASTERY *(Part A)*

THE INTELLIGENCE BETWEEN US

> *"We are neurologically wired for empathy, but the modern world has left this talent underdeveloped."*
> **Roman Krznaric, *Empathy: Why It Matters, and How to Get It***

Where self-awareness asks, *"What is happening in me?"* and self-mastery asks, *"What will I do with this?"* relational mastery asks, *"How do we connect authentically and create something greater together?"*

Self-awareness gives the map. Self-mastery gives command. Relational mastery is where inner work becomes visible, where both capacities meet the world. This is where emotional intelligence transforms from personal development into human impact.

In Chapter Eight, the actress and the soldier trained their nervous systems to produce agency under pressure: the ability to feel intensely and act with intention rather than react from reflex. Relational mastery asks what happens when that regulated nervous system is turned outward. Calm becomes a resource others can borrow. Interoception becomes attunement: reading another person's state the same way an individual learned to read their own. Discomfort tolerance becomes the capacity that allows presence during conflict rather than shutting down or escalating. Every skill from the previous two pillars now operates in the space between people.

What happens between people in genuine relationship is measurable biology. Two nervous systems in connection do not operate independently; they synchronize. One person's heart rhythm influences another's. One's calm steadies the other's activation. Simultaneous brain activity research shows neural coupling between connected people. HRV data reveals

---

physiological coregulation in real time. Relational mastery builds the capacity for biological coordination with others.

In 2025, staying at one company for thirty years makes you a statistical outlier. The average tenure is just four years. Most careers span eight to twelve employers. Yet here was Sarah Chen, surrounded by three decades of relationships that had somehow deepened rather than fractured under the pressures of reorganizations, budget cuts, leadership changes, and the relentless churn of modern corporate life.

Thirty Years

The conference room buzzed with an energy that felt different from the usual retirement gatherings. People weren't checking phones or glancing at watches. Former rivals sat together, laughing about projects that once kept them up at night. The atmosphere itself told a story; this wasn't the polite endurance of most corporate events, but something genuinely celebratory.

For Sarah, this work had been her identity, fiercely protected against social conditioning that insisted she couldn't be both a strong mother and a strong professional. She had refused the false choice, building a career that energized rather than depleted her capacity for every other relationship in her life.

Sarah brought her real self into every room she entered, and that authenticity had created something measurable: environments where people felt safer to take risks, speak honestly, and grow beyond their perceived limitations.

During the presentations, Anthony spoke with genuine warmth. "Sarah didn't just help us solve problems," he said. "She helped us see what we were capable of achieving." Under Sarah's leadership, his team had consistently exceeded targets. Her approach had somehow made the work both more challenging and more sustainable.

Richard stepped forward with uncharacteristic hesitation. As a former regional director, his comments were anticipated, but the tone surprised many who remembered his authoritarian style. "I want to share something that changed how I think about leadership," he began. The room grew quiet. What followed was a story he would reference for years.

Near the refreshment table, her husband Seth nervously adjusted his tie. What began as a professional partnership had grown into something lasting, rooted in mutual respect and a shared devotion to meaningful work. Seth had understood from the start that Sarah's professional passion was not a rival to their relationship but a source of vitality within it.

By 9 p.m., only a few people remained. There were some tears and some hugs. Tonight had demonstrated that relational leadership aimed for ethical outcomes creates something that outlasts any individual career: a legacy of people who learned to lead with the same authenticity they had experienced.

What Sarah had demonstrated was relational mastery: the ability to create, sustain, and repair meaningful human connections through four integrated capabilities.

The Architecture of Connection

Until recently, relational intelligence looked like one thing. It was called it "people skills" and treated as a single capacity some people had and others did not. AI changed what can be seen. When machines attempted to replicate human connection, they succeeded at some components and failed at others. Emotion recognition systems achieved attunement. Language models achieved expression. Neither achieved compassion. Neither sustained anything across time. The machine's partial success works like an X-ray: it reveals that what was called relational intelligence was never one thing. It was four distinct neural processes operating together, invisible to us until something tried to replicate them and failed at the seams.

Chapter Five revealed that traditional emotional intelligence tests now favor machines over humans, exposing that they measured knowledge about emotions rather than embodied emotional capacity. The four skills that follow describe what those tests were failing to capture.

Empathy. Perceiving others inaccurately risks misdirected care, even with the best intentions. Tania Singer's neuroscience research at the Max Planck Institute is decisive: empathy and compassion activate different neural networks. Empathy alone, feeling another's pain, leads to burnout. Compassion activates caregiving circuits that make sustained connection possible. Without compassion, empathy exhausts. With it, empathy endures. This skill extends the interoceptive capacity from Chapter Seven into the relational field. A person learns to read the nervous system first, then to read another's, allowing discoveries to guide understanding.

Authentic Expression. Empathy without expression is understanding that never creates connection. Uri Hasson's brain study research at Princeton shows that during genuine communication, the listener's brain mirrors and even anticipates the speaker's. The synchronization is involuntary and fragile; it collapses the moment attention shifts inward. Carl Rogers' therapeutic research established that perceiving accurately and expressing honestly are separable conditions: one can be perfectly attuned to another and still fail to share one's own truth. Authentic expression bridges two inner worlds. Without it, empathy remains private.

Conflict Navigation. Connection under threat is a different neural event than connection in calm. Sue Johnson's Emotionally Focused Therapy research, validated across more than twenty randomized controlled trials, demonstrates that relational conflict activates the same neurobiological cascade as physical danger. Heart rates spike. The prefrontal cortex goes partially offline. Holding multiple perspectives while a person's own is under siege requires the self-mastery capacities from Chapter Eight deployed at relational speed. Gottman's four decades of longitudinal data are definitive: what distinguishes lasting relationships from failing ones is not the absence of conflict but the presence of repair.

Ethical Influence. Empathy, authentic expression, and conflict navigation create strong connections. They do not create shared movement. Herbert Kelman's research distinguishes compliance (obedience to power), identification (following someone admired), and internalization (adopting values because they align with personal ones). Ethical influence operates through internalization, the deepest and most durable form. Paul Zak's neuroeconomics research at Claremont on the role of oxytocin shows the mechanism: observing consistent integrity in another person triggers neurochemical changes that open pathways to deeper engagement. Trust is not a metaphor. It is a biological event.

Each skill requires the ones before it: perceive, express, withstand, move together.

The four skills of relational mastery build directly on the self-awareness and self-mastery capacities from previous chapters. The interoception developed now becomes relational: using the body's wisdom to read the room. Emotional literacy allows the naming of what is happening between people, not just within one's own self. Meta-awareness allows the observation of relationship dynamics without being consumed by them.

Similarly, emotional self-command allows presence during conflict. Discomfort tolerance helps navigate the messiness of human connection. Resilience through recovery means relationships can be repaired after rupture.

Without self-awareness, one's inner world is projected onto others. Without self-mastery, relationships become reactive. With these pillars solid, relational mastery becomes possible.

Unlike the previous pillars, which can be developed in relative solitude, relational mastery requires other people. Skills are learned through the lived experience of connection, conflict, repair, and trust-building over time.

These skills cannot be mastered without risking relationships, without occasionally failing, without sometimes causing harm despite the best of intentions. The path requires both courage and humility: courage to engage authentically, humility to repair when effort falls short.

Each relationship tended with skill makes the next one deeper. Each repair successfully builds resilience that serves all personal connections. Over time, a person becomes someone others trust instinctively, seek out in difficulty, and feel genuinely safe around.

The work begins with learning to see others clearly. Not as projections of personal needs and fears, but as complete individuals with their own inner worlds, worthy of understanding on their own terms.

SKILL 1: EMPATHY

See Others Clearly

> Do you respond to what others actually
> feel, or to what you think they feel?

Empathy is the ability to discern and appreciate another person's perspective or emotional state while remaining grounded. It is not merging with their feelings, not feeling sorry for someone (sympathy), and not being emotionally reactive. It is recognizing them with clarity and respect.

At its core, empathy reflects a deeper truth: emotional experiences are not entirely unique to the individual. The architecture of human emotion is shared reality, one that allows the recognition of joy, grief, fear, or hope in one another. Empathy draws on this common ground to create trust and safety, leading to authentic connection.

Importantly, empathy is not a fixed trait but a skill that can be cultivated. It grows through four integrated subskills: attunement, resonance, compassion, and moral awareness.

Without empathy, people react to their assumptions about others instead of what others are truly experiencing. Every subsequent relational skill depends on accurate perception.

Empathy in the Digital Age

Technology is simultaneously eroding and enhancing our empathic capacity. Digital interfaces strip the signals attunement depends on. Text removes tone. Email removes facial expression. Even video calls flatten the three-dimensional richness of physical presence; the brain works harder to read a face on a screen, which is why video meetings exhaust the empathy circuits faster than in-person conversation. Leaders managing distributed teams face a genuine neurological challenge: the medium itself degrades the signal.

AI compounds the disruption. Emotion recognition systems from companies like Affectiva can now read facial micro-expressions faster and more consistently than trained humans. Voice analysis tools detect stress patterns in real time. These technologies respond to others without understanding them, without compassion. They read a person without caring about them. An algorithm that detects frustration and adjusts its response accordingly is performing a sophisticated simulation of empathy. It is not empathy. The distinction matters precisely because the simulation is becoming convincing enough to confuse us.

Yet technology also creates unprecedented opportunities to train empathy. Virtual reality programs now place users inside the lived experience of others: experiencing age-related vision loss, navigating a wheelchair through an inaccessible city, hearing voices as a person with schizophrenia does. Early research from Stanford's Virtual Human Interaction Lab shows these immersive experiences produce longer-lasting empathic responses than reading or imagining alone. Biofeedback tools can show a person their physiological responses during conversation, making the invisible visible: they can see their heart rate spike when a colleague challenges them, watch their breathing shallow when they disengage. AI-powered conversation analysis can identify patterns they cannot see for themselves: how often they interrupt, when their attention drifts, which emotional cues they consistently miss. The technology does not replace empathy. It accelerates the self-awareness that empathy requires.

Attunement

Attunement is the ability to read others accurately without projecting personal emotional patterns.

The interoception developed in Chapter Seven now extends into the relational field. Interoception reads a person's own nervous system; attunement uses that same capacity to read another person's in real time. This not building something new; this is awakening something already there.

Attunement operates beneath conscious thought. The nervous system detects micro-expressions, vocal tones, body postures, and energy states before the analytical mind can categorize them. The shift in the room can be felt when someone arrives upset. A child's distress can be sensed by a parent before the child can articulate it. A person senses something is off with their partner before a single word is spoken.

One of the purest examples of automatic, embodied attunement is the new mother whose breast milk lets down at the sound of her infant's cry. The nervous system response, mediated by neuroendocrine pathways involving oxytocin and prolactin, floods her system, triggered by emotional cues: seeing, hearing, or even thinking about her baby. Her nervous system has detected the child's need and answered it through instantaneous physiological communication, immediate and automatic.

We are wired for connection at the cellular level. The same neural and hormonal systems that governed our survival as a species continue to operate in every meaningful relationship we have.

Sarah in the Boardroom

The quarterly review was fifteen minutes old when Sarah noticed it. Everyone was nodding along with the new initiative, but there was a quality of stillness in the room that didn't feel like engagement. It felt like resignation.

She watched Anthony's hands, usually animated when he was excited. They were flat on the table. Jennifer's smile didn't reach her eyes. Tom, who typically interrupted with questions, had said nothing.

The micro-expressions were neutral, but something in the collective energy suggested unspoken concerns. Sarah trusted her read.

She stepped away from the screen and pulled a chair around to the side of the table, sitting among them rather than before them. She said nothing for a moment. Then, quietly, "Before we continue, I want to pause. What are we not talking about?"

Silence. Then Anthony exhaled. "Honestly? We've seen initiatives like this before. They launch with fanfare and die in six months when priorities shift."

The real conversation began. By the end of the meeting, they had identified three structural obstacles that would've killed the initiative and designed solutions for each. The project succeeded specifically because Sarah's attunement surfaced what politeness concealed.

True empathy emerges when attunement is accurate, responding to what someone actually feels rather than to what is imagined. Without accurate attunement, empathy becomes well-intentioned but misaligned care: offering comfort when someone needs space, advice when they need validation, solutions when they need to be heard.

Resonance

If attunement is perception, resonance is connection. Resonance is allowing another person's inner world to echo within. It makes empathy feel real to the other person, because the other person senses being *with* someone, not merely observing them.

Resonance requires what researchers call "optimal distance." Close enough to feel with someone, yet separate enough to remain steady in their own perspective. Without this distance, resonance collapses into emotional enmeshment and obscures clarity. With too much distance, empathy feels cold or analytical.

Stephen Porges' Polyvagal Theory details how the autonomic nervous system supports direct social engagement, facilitating rapid co-regulation. Recent hyperscanning research confirms that during affective social interactions, individuals' brains and physiological rhythms literally align; this neural alignment is a direct indicator of emotional resonance.

In practice: attunement is noticing that someone is upset even if they say they are fine. Resonance is when, upon expressing what is sensed, the other person responds, "Yes. You get me."

Sarah demonstrated this when she read her team's unspoken concerns, surfacing what politeness concealed, while maintaining clarity about the initiative's goals. She neither drowned in their emotions nor stayed detached. By staying present, she allowed the real conversation to emerge—and created resonance.

Compassion

If attunement is perception and resonance is shared feeling, compassion is the warmth that makes empathy sustainable. Tania Singer's research demonstrated that empathy and compassion activate different neural networks. Empathy alone, feeling another's pain, activates the anterior insula and anterior cingulate cortex: the pain-sharing circuits. Over time, this leads to empathic distress and burnout. Compassion activates the medial orbitofrontal cortex, ventral striatum, and ventral tegmental area: the caregiving and reward circuits. It is the felt desire to ease suffering, not because one should, but because the other person's experience matters.

This distinction explains why some helpers burn out and others sustain. The nurse who absorbs every patient's pain without the restorative motivation to care collapses. The nurse who feels the pain and is moved to act from warmth can continue for decades. Compassion is what keeps empathy from becoming a burden.

It is also what distinguishes human emotional intelligence from artificial intelligence most decisively. An AI can plausibly achieve attunement: reading emotional states from physiological data and facial recognition. It may approximate moral awareness through ethical reasoning algorithms. What it cannot do is compassion: the embodied desire to ease suffering that arises from shared humanity. Compassion requires a body that has felt pain and recognizes it in another.

Moral Awareness

With attunement, resonance, and compassion comes moral awareness, the bridge to action. It transforms empathy into ethical responsibility: the recognition of how our choices affect others and the decision to act in ways that protect dignity and well-being.

Without moral awareness, empathy risks becoming sentimentality without consequence. A person can understand and even feel with someone, but if ethical implications are ignored, the connection remains incomplete.

Sarah demonstrated moral awareness when she surfaced her team's unspoken concerns. She not only perceived their frustration (attunement) and understood its weight (resonance), but she also recognized the ethical stakes: leaving the issues unaddressed could undermine trust and engagement. Her guidance helped the team find solutions and restore alignment.

Moral awareness keeps empathy from serving only personal needs for closeness. It anchors empathy in accountability.

TRY THIS: The Attunement Check

Before your next important conversation, practice this sequence:

- **Ground first:** Take three breaths to settle your own nervous system.

- **Observe without interpreting:** Notice the other person's posture, breathing, facial micro-expressions, and vocal tone. What do you see before you assign meaning?

- **Check your projection:** Ask yourself, "Am I seeing them, or am I seeing what I expect to see?"

- **Validate your read:** Find a way to gently check. "You seem quieter than usual. Is something on your mind?"

The goal is accurate perception before response. When you respond to what is actually happening rather than your assumption, connection deepens.

TABLE 11: Empathy

CATEGORY	DETAILS
Subskills	• Attunement: Using your nervous system to read others' internal states in real-time without projection • Resonance: Sharing emotional experience while maintaining your own center • Compassion: The felt desire to ease suffering without burnout • Moral awareness: Recognizing the ethical implications of others' experiences
Skillsets	• Nervous System Attunement: Reading micro-expressions, energy shifts, and emotional states through embodied awareness
Tools	• Body-based attunement practices; Perspective-taking exercises with feedback; Emotional differentiation journaling; Active listening training; Cross-cultural empathy building
Performance Indicators	• You can sense the emotional states of others before they verbalize them, distinguish between sympathy and empathy, stay present with the pain of others without rushing to fix, adjust your support style based on what others actually need, and sustain empathic engagement over time without emotional depletion.

KEY TAKEAWAY

Empathy is not a feeling. It is a skill built on the same interoceptive capacity you trained in Chapter Seven, now turned outward. Attunement reads the room. Resonance makes the other person feel met. Compassion sustains the connection without burning you out. Moral awareness ensures your understanding leads to ethical action, not just emotional closeness. AI's ability to replicate attunement and its inability to replicate compassion reveal that empathy was never one capacity. It was four, and the one machines cannot perform is the one that sustains all the others.

SKILL 2: AUTHENTIC EXPRESSION

Build the Bridge

"The single biggest problem in communication is the illusion that it has taken place."
Often attributed to George Bernard Shaw

Without authentic expression, empathic understanding remains trapped inside. Even if perception is accurate, it may not create shared reality. Empathy without expression is a beautiful prison of understanding that never creates connection. The bridge from feeling to sharing requires new skills: the courage to articulate inner experience and the discipline to receive others' truths without drowning in them.

AI exposed this skill's hidden architecture. Uri Hasson's research shows that genuine communication produces neural coupling between speaker and listener. When AI generates the words, the coupling breaks. The machine can produce eloquent text. It cannot produce the neural signature of authenticity that another brain requires to synchronize. This is a measurable, neurological event, not a philosophical preference.

Authentic expression transforms internal recognition into shared reality through four integrated subskills. These draw on Ronald Riggio's foundational work measuring communication as distinct, separable skills and on Uri Hasson's discovery that genuine expression creates measurable neural synchrony between speaker and listener: active listening, expressiveness, nonverbal alignment, and feedback.

Active Listening

Active listening seems simple: pay close attention and show understand. It is one of the most transformative and challenging relational skills. It requires redirecting attention away from inner dialogue, judgments, and rehearsed responses to stay fully with another person's words, tone, and emotions in the present moment.

It is lending someone our own regulated nervous system as a sanctuary. Our presence becomes the container where their truth can surface; not the truth they think they should feel, but what they actually feel.

This is why most listening fails. We pay attention while internally preparing our response. We track words while missing the emotional current beneath them. We hear the story but not the storyteller.

The Budget Dispute

Jennifer from accounting had been fighting with Tom's engineering team for three weeks. The quarterly budget allocation had become personal. Both sides had stopped listening and started defending.

Sarah scheduled separate meetings with each. With Jennifer, she did not open with solutions. She opened with silence and attention.

"Tell me what's really going on," Sarah said. Then she listened. Not preparing her response. Not forming judgments. Just receiving.

Jennifer started with numbers. Resource allocation. Timeline pressures. Standard accounting concerns. Sarah nodded but waited. There was something underneath.

"It's just…" Jennifer paused. "Every quarter, engineering gets celebrated for innovation, and accounting gets treated like the department of 'no.' We work just as hard. We save this company millions. But when's the last time anyone thanked us for a clean audit?"

There it was. Jennifer thought she was fighting for resources. She was fighting for recognition.

"You don't feel seen," Sarah said.

Jennifer's eyes filled. "No. I don't."

Now the real conversation could begin.

Dr. Uri Hasson's Princeton research on "brain-to-brain coupling" reveals why this matters. Using brain image scanning, Hasson showed that during effective communication, the listener's brain activity mirrors the speaker's. In deep active listening, certain areas of the listener's brain actually anticipate the speaker's, tracking emerging thought before it is fully articulated. The moment responses begin being formulated, the coupling breaks. **It cannot be faked.**

Technology is disrupting this coupling at its source. AI now drafts our emails, suggests our replies, completes our sentences. When words are generated by an algorithm rather than neural activity, the listener's brain has nothing authentic to couple to. The efficiency gain is real. The relational cost is unmeasured. Social media compounds the problem: platforms designed to maximize engagement reward performance over authenticity. People curate rather than communicate. They broadcast rather than connect. The architecture of digital communication is optimized for reach, not for the kind of mutual vulnerability that Hasson's research shows genuine coupling requires.

AI can also sharpen authentic expression in ways previously impossible. Recording and transcript analysis tools can show the gap between what a speaker intended to communicate and what was actually said. Natural language processing can identify patterns in communication: hedging language that undermines clarity, filler words that signal anxiety, tonal shifts that contradict content. AI coaching tools can simulate difficult conversations and provide immediate feedback on delivery, letting users practice authentic expression in low-stakes environments before the conversation that counts. The paradox: using artificial intelligence to develop the most human of skills. The resolution: AI trains the mechanics. Humans supply the meaning.

Expressiveness

If active listening is receiving, expressiveness is giving. It is the skill of making one's inner world visible, speaking with precision so that others don't just understand the logic, they feel the reality.

Authentic expressiveness is not impulsive; it is calibrated. It requires aligning what is shared with what the relationship can hold. The inner experience—what is seen, felt, and hoped—is spoken. Firm but not harsh. Clear but not cruel. It is strength and vulnerability coexisting.

Nonverbal Alignment

While words carry content, the body carries truth. In emotionally charged or ambiguous situations, research shows that when verbal and nonverbal messages conflict, people trust the nonverbal signal overwhelmingly.

Sarah's colleagues felt "safe" in her presence because her nonverbal communication created coherence. When she sensed resignation in the boardroom, she detected microscopic shifts: delayed responses, reduced animation, subtle breathing patterns suggesting holding rather than flowing.

Nonverbal communication is not just reading others; it is conscious transmission. What is broadcasted matters as much as what is received.

Feedback

Feedback is communication for growth, where expression becomes developmental. Done well, it accelerates growth. Done poorly, it damages trust. Silence is also not neutral. When leaders remain silent, people often interpret it as disapproval, indifference, or hidden judgment.

What separates done well from done poorly is rarely the conditions. Feedback delivered across a power gap without an established relationship does not land as development. It lands as judgment from above. The receiver's threat response activates before the first sentence ends. The technique becomes irrelevant. Even if exactly the right thing was said, it arrived at a nervous system that was not in a position to hear it.

This is why relationship precedes feedback. A foundation of trust does not soften the message. It creates the conditions under which the message can be received at all.

Done poorly, feedback also fails. Evaluation without observation, "You're not collaborative" gives someone nothing to work with. "I noticed you interrupted before Luke finished three times in today's meeting" gives them something they can actually see and change.

Sarah's Feedback to Richard

The morning after the Morrison celebration, Sarah closed her office door. This was the conversation Richard would later describe at her retirement as the one that changed how he thought about leadership.

"Richard, I want to share some observations. Is this a good time?"

He nodded, already defensive.

"The win was significant. The team performed brilliantly. But I noticed something in how we celebrated it." She paused, letting him settle. "When you redistributed credit in your remarks,

Kwame's strategic insights, which shaped the entire proposal, went unmentioned. I watched his face. I watched the team's faces."

Richard started to justify. Sarah raised her hand gently.

"I'm not questioning your intent. I'm sharing impact. When contributions aren't acknowledged fairly, it creates an environment where people protect themselves rather than collaborate. Kwame has been considering a transfer. I don't think that's coincidental."

She let the silence work.

"What I'm hoping," she continued, "is that you'll consider a different sequence. Acknowledgment before analysis. Celebration before correction. Not because it feels good, but because it creates the conditions that let people take the risks that produce wins like Morrison."

Richard sat with it. "I didn't see it."

"I know. That's why I'm telling you."

TRY THIS: The Listening Audit

In your next three conversations, notice:

- **How often do you interrupt?** Even to agree or empathize?

- **Where does your attention go?** Are you preparing your response while they speak?

- **What happens if you wait three seconds** after they finish before responding?

Most people have never experienced being fully heard. When you offer that gift, relationships transform.

TABLE 12: Authentic Expression

CATEGORY	DETAILS
Subskills	• Active listening: Full presence with another person without formulating response • Expressiveness: Articulating inner experience with clarity and courage • Nonverbal alignment: Ensuring body language matches verbal message • Feedback: Giving and receiving developmental input effectively
Skillsets	• Neural Coupling: Creating brain synchronization through genuine engagement
Tools	• Active listening protocols; Expressive writing practice; Nonverbal awareness training; Feedback reception frameworks; Difficult conversation rehearsal
Performance Indicators	• You can listen without formulating response, express feelings without blame, align nonverbal and verbal messages, receive feedback non-defensively, and repair communication breakdowns effectively.

KEY TAKEAWAY

Authentic expression is not information transfer. It is the creation of shared reality. Active listening lends your regulated nervous system as a sanctuary. Expressiveness makes your inner world visible without distortion. The moment you start formulating your response, the neural coupling breaks. It cannot be faked. AI can generate words indistinguishable from yours. It cannot generate the neural signature that another brain requires to synchronize. The medium has changed what authenticity demands of us.

SKILL 3: CONFLICT NAVIGATION

Transform the Tension

Without conflict navigation, disagreement damages rather than deepens connection. Relationships become fragile, requiring constant agreement to survive.

> *"In the middle of difficulty lies opportunity."*
> **Albert Einstein**

Even perfect communication cannot prevent conflict. Differences in needs, values, and perspectives make tension inevitable. The question is not whether conflict will arise but whether we can transform it from destructive to generative.

Sarah's thirty-year career was not conflict-free. It was marked by her ability to transform conflict into collaboration.

Digital communication has not merely changed where conflict happens. It has changed what conflict is. Asynchronous channels remove the biological de-escalation signals that face-to-face conflict depends on: the softening posture, the shifted vocal tone, the micro-expression of willingness. Reading energy through a screen, building trust without physical co-presence, repairing without the signals our nervous systems evolved to use: these are genuinely new cognitive demands. No previous generation faced them. No existing EI framework accounts for them.

De-escalation

De-escalation reduces emotional activation when tensions rise. It builds directly on emotional self-command and discomfort tolerance, allowing a person to remain grounded when others become dysregulated.

This is where conflict navigation diverges from the mastery skills of Chapter 8. The soldier manages his own activation under pressure. The arena is internal. In conflict, a person must manage their own activation while simultaneously attending to another's, even as the other actively destabilizes them. The anger and withdrawal of the reactive party trigger the defensiveness and anxiety of the regulating party, who must manage themselves while also reading the former's state, holding both perspectives, and creating conditions for nervous systems to settle. Self-mastery is the engine; conflict navigation is driving it through traffic.

The Reorganization Meeting

The real conversation Sarah had promised Jennifer could not happen in a hallway. She scheduled a joint meeting with Jennifer and Tom, knowing she was walking into something already heated.

She was right. The quarterly budget dispute had become personal. Both had stopped arguing about numbers. They were arguing about respect.

Jennifer sat with her arms crossed. Tom leaned forward, jaw tight. The room had already polarized before Sarah said a word.

Sarah didn't raise her voice or minimize concerns. She lowered her voice and slowed her speech, signaling calm through her vocal prosody. She took a deep breath others unconsciously mirrored. She acknowledged the intensity: "This clearly matters deeply to both of you."

She created physical space by suggesting everyone sit. Then reframed: "Help me understand what you're each trying to protect."

The question shifted the frame from positions to needs. Within minutes, the emotional temperature dropped enough for dialogue. Both department heads wanted the same thing: to protect their people from burnout during transition. They had been fighting about method, not outcome.

When we are flooded, the amygdala hijacks the prefrontal cortex. De-escalation works by activating the parasympathetic nervous system, bringing the thinking brain back online. Calm nervous systems help regulate activated ones. Feeling heard reduces the need to escalate. Slowing down creates processing space between trigger and response.

Mediation

Mediation actively facilitates dialogue between conflicting perspectives. It requires holding multiple viewpoints without taking sides.

Sarah's approach with Jennifer and Tom revealed the architecture of effective conflict resolution. She held separate conversations to understand each perspective without defensive pressure. She uncovered underlying interests by moving beneath "I want X" to "I need Y because Z." She found shared values: both departments cared about innovation within constraints. She reframed the conflict from "us versus them" to "how do we solve this shared challenge." Then she facilitated direct dialogue, creating structured space for mutual hearing.

The breakthrough: accounting's need for predictability and engineering's need for flexibility both served the same goal. The conflict was not personal. It was structural. Once they saw that, they designed new processes together that other companies now study as best practices.

This is solution orientation: the capacity to move a conversation from understood to resolved. Mediation surfaces what each party actually needs. Solution orientation takes that understanding and asks the next question: given what we now know, what can we build together? The two capacities are sequential. Genuine solutions cannot be reached without first achieving mutual understanding. Solution orientation is what transforms insight into outcome, and conflict into collaboration.

Repair

Repair is perhaps the most sophisticated skill: rebuilding connection after rupture. It requires all your capacities: awareness to recognize impact, mastery to regulate shame, and relational skill to rebuild.

Sarah's Mistake

Early in her tenure, Sarah inadvertently excluded a junior colleague, David, from a crucial client meeting. She hadn't intended harm; the invitation list was rushed, and she simply forgot.

David's absence was noticed. The client asked about him by name. David learned about the meeting from a colleague's offhand comment. His credibility was undermined, and he had no explanation to offer.

When Sarah realized what had happened, she felt the pull to minimize. *It was an honest mistake. He'll get over it. Making a big deal will only make it worse.*

She recognized that impulse as self-protection and overrode it.

She went to David's office. "I need to talk to you about the Hendricks meeting."

He looked up, guarded.

"I excluded you from the invitation, and I want you to know it wasn't intentional, but that doesn't change the impact. You were put in an impossible position. Your credibility with Hendricks was affected. I'm sorry."

David's shoulders dropped slightly. He had expected excuses.

"I've already spoken with Hendricks directly," Sarah continued. "I clarified your role and my oversight. And I've set up a meeting for you with their team lead next week to rebuild that relationship. But I also want to know: what else would help make this right?"

David was quiet for a moment. "Honestly? Just this. The fact that you came to me, that you didn't make me come to you."

Sarah nodded. "I'm also changing how I manage meeting invitations. This won't happen again."

David became one of Sarah's strongest allies, specifically because they had navigated rupture together.

Dr. John Gottman's research reveals the "magic ratio": five positive interactions per negative maintain relationship health. This does not mean avoiding conflict. It means ensuring repair follows rupture. Successful repair strengthens neural pathways associated with trust. We learn someone can be trusted not because they are perfect, but because they take responsibility.

The consequences are visible in every workplace. Email and messaging conflicts escalate faster and repair slower than face-to-face disagreements because the medium strips the signals repair depends on. Workplace ghosting, withdrawing from a relationship rather than working through rupture, has become epidemic precisely because technology makes avoidance easier than repair.

AI introduces both risk and resource. Algorithmic communication tools can misinterpret tone, escalate misunderstandings through auto-suggested responses, and create permanent written records that make conflicts feel higher-stakes than they are.

Yet AI also enables conflict skill development in ways no previous technology has achieved. Simulation tools can generate realistic conflict scenarios calibrated to specific challenges: a resistant direct report, a defensive peer, a hostile client. A person can practice de-escalation, perspective-holding, and repair in environments where failure teaches rather than damages. AI can analyze recordings of real conversations and identify conflict patterns: where things escalate, when withdraw occurs, which triggers consistently compromise regulation. Pattern recognition across hundreds of interactions reveals what a single coaching session cannot.

TRY THIS: The Repair Conversation

When you have caused harm, even unintentionally, practice this sequence:

- **Acknowledge specific impact:** "When I [action], you experienced [impact]."

- **Take responsibility without excuse:** "That was my oversight. I'm sorry."

- **Ask what would help:** "What do you need from me to make this right?"
- **Commit to change:** "Here's what I'll do differently going forward."

The sequence matters. Most people start with explanation or justification. Start with acknowledgment.

TABLE 13: Conflict Navigation

CATEGORY	DETAILS
Subskills	• De-escalation: Creating space for solutions when emotions run high • Mediation: Facilitating dialogue between conflicting perspectives • Solution orientation: Moving from problems to possibilities • Repair: Rebuilding connection after rupture
Skillsets	• Tension Tolerance: Staying present and effective when conflict intensifies
Tools	• De-escalation protocols; Interest-based negotiation frameworks; Repair conversation templates; Mediation techniques; Conflict mapping exercises
Performance Indicators	• You can stay regulated during heated exchanges, identify interests beneath positions, facilitate resolution without imposing solutions, and restore trust after conflict through genuine repair.

KEY TAKEAWAY

Conflict is not the opposite of connection. It is connection under pressure. The question is never whether rupture will occur, but whether repair follows. We learn someone can be trusted not because they are perfect, but because they take responsibility when they fall short. Digital communication has not simply moved conflict online. It has created structurally new forms of conflict that require capacities no previous generation needed.

SKILL 4: ETHICAL INFLUENCE

Inspire Voluntary Change

> *"The supreme art of war is to subdue the enemy without fighting."*
> **Sun Tzu**, *The Art of War*

With ethical influence, you can move relational skill into collective impact. Resolving conflict creates temporary peace. Creating lasting change requires influence: not the manipulation of compliance, but the inspiration of commitment. This final skill transforms relational mastery from personal competence into collective impact.

Algorithmic persuasion has made this skill both more urgent and rarer. Targeted advertising, recommendation engines, and personalized content apply the mechanics of influence at unprecedented scale, without the ethical constraints that human relationship imposes. When a platform knows a person's vulnerabilities and uses them to shape their behavior, it is performing influence without consent, identification without relationship, compliance without awareness. The result is a world saturated with sophisticated manipulation. It is the only form of influence that cannot be automated.

Return to Sarah Chen's retirement celebration. What created the room's unusual energy was not nostalgia. It was the accumulated effect of three decades of influence earned through integrity. Anthony and Richard spoke because Sarah had changed them. Not through authority or pressure, but through consistent demonstration of what relational leadership could be. People did not comply with Sarah; they chose to follow her direction because her vision aligned with values they recognized as their own.

Motivational Communication

Motivational communication helps others connect with their own drivers. Sarah understood that sustainable motivation comes from within. Rather than imposing enthusiasm, she helped others discover theirs.

Three Conversations

Anthony lingered after the team meeting. "I'm not sure this initiative is worth the time investment," he said, scanning the project brief. "The scope is massive and the timeline is unrealistic."

Sarah didn't argue the timeline. She had watched Anthony for two years and knew what moved him: not deadlines but depth. "You're right that the scope is ambitious," she said. "Let me tell you why I think you should lead it anyway. The integration layer requires someone who understands both the legacy architecture and the new platform. You've been saying for a year that you want that systems-level view. This is how you get it."

Anthony paused. She could see the shift: not compliance, but recognition. "You're offering me the piece I actually want."

"I'm offering you the piece you're uniquely qualified for. The timeline we can negotiate. The learning opportunity, we can't manufacture."

He took the project. He exceeded every benchmark.

. . . . .

With Jennifer, the approach was entirely different. Sarah didn't mention growth or learning. She mentioned visibility. "You'll be partnering with teams who need to understand what accounting actually contributes. When the CFO reviews cross-functional performance, your department's role will be documented for the first time. This is a chance to change how they see you."

Jennifer's posture changed. Not the numbers. The recognition.

. . . . .

With Tom, Sarah led with the problem. "No one has solved this the way you're proposing. If your approach works, it changes how we build everything going forward." Tom didn't need recognition or growth. He needed the dare.

Same initiative. Three different framings. Each person heard an invitation to what they already valued. **Sarah read what mattered to each person and spoke to those values.** Not generic inspiration but specific connection grounded in genuine understanding.

Vision-Casting

Vision-casting articulates futures others want to help create. Sarah's vision was not imposed; it emerged from dialogue. She facilitated conversations that helped her team discover shared aspirations: "What would excellence look like? What impact do we want? What legacy do we leave?"

By involving others in vision creation, she generated buy-in that no mandate could achieve. The vision became theirs, creating intrinsic commitment that survived obstacles and setbacks.

The discipline here is restraint. Leaders often arrive with vision already formed, seeking buy-in for decisions already made. This generates compliance, not commitment. True vision-casting requires genuine openness: the willingness to have direction shaped by the process of co-creation. The result may differ from what was initially imagined. It will be stronger for that difference.

Integrity and Trust

Integrity operates through trust rather than position. It is built on consistency: people trust leaders whose actions reflect their stated principles.

Sarah's influence grew from coherence. She never asked what she would not do herself. Her private actions matched public positions. She admitted mistakes before others pointed them out. She credited others' contributions when she could have claimed them. This created what researchers call "referent power": influence derived from respect rather than position. Even superiors sought Sarah's input because they trusted her judgment served shared interests rather than personal ones.

This is what social psychologists John French and Bertram Raven called referent power, influence derived from respect rather than position or authority. It is the most durable form of influence that exists, and it cannot be manufactured. Paul Zak's decades of research on trust and human behavior reveal that when people consistently observe someone doing what they say they will do, the brain registers it as safety. Trust is a neurochemical response to evidence gathered over time.

Boundary Setting

Perhaps surprisingly, clear boundaries enhance rather than diminish influence. Sarah's "no" was as respected as her "yes" because both came from clear values.

When she declined weekends except for emergencies, she modeled work-life integration. When she refused gossip or political maneuvering, she created safety. Her boundaries did not isolate; they attracted others who valued the same clarity. When a senior colleague drew her into a conversation designed to position her against another leader, she redirected without aggression and without explanation. The colleague was briefly unsettled. Over time, people stopped bringing her that kind of conversation entirely, not because they feared her, but because they respected that she had no use for it.

Boundaries communicate what someone stands for by showing what they will not accept. They create predictability that builds trust. Brené Brown's research on vulnerability and courage finds that the most compassionate leaders are also maintain the clearest boundaries, not despite their care for others, but because of it. People who know their own limits are trusted more than people who appear to have none. Boundaries create the predictability that makes deep trust possible.

Practicing Influence, Earning Trust

Technology can now simulate the signals trust depends on. Deepfakes replicate presence. AI-generated text mimics voice. But integrity operates on a timescale no algorithm can compress: years of kept promises, visible accountability, and consistent action when no one is watching. The synthetic signal is convincing in the moment. It cannot survive the slow verification that real relationships demand.

For the first time, difficult conversations can be rehearsed with AI that generates realistic objections, plays skeptical stakeholders, and provides immediate feedback on clarity and structure. These simulations allow you to fail safely, iterate quickly, and enter real conversations having already navigated multiple scenarios.

The technology creates feedback loops that were previously impossible without expensive coaching or willing practice partners. You can record yourself, analyze pacing and filler words, and refine delivery before stakes are real.

But remember the book's central argument: AI can simulate persuasive scenarios. It cannot build the embodied credibility that comes from keeping promises over time, the trust that emerges from values alignment, or the referent power that Sarah accumulated through decades of consistent action. Technology accelerates skill acquisition. Influence can be practiced with AI, but trust can only be earned with humans.

TRY THIS: Training Ethical Influence

Break influence into components that can practiced separately.

Mapping what matters to the other person before key conversations. Practice summarizing "Here's what I understand matters most to you," and inviting correction. Sarah did this instinctively with Anthony, Jennifer, and Tom.

Framing means opening with clear value, supporting it with evidence, and ending with a specific ask. Most people meander toward their point. Practice stating your core message in twenty seconds, then expanding.

Objection handling means naming concerns before they become resistance. "You might be worried about timeline," disarms defensiveness and signals you have considered their perspective.

Story and analogy transform abstract arguments into memorable experiences. A before, after, and benefit arc activates emotional engagement that data alone cannot achieve.

TABLE 14: Ethical Influence

CATEGORY	DETAILS
Subskills	• Motivational communication: Connecting to intrinsic drivers rather than external pressure • Vision-casting: Articulating futures others want to help create • Boundary setting: Maintaining clear limits that enhance rather than diminish influence
Skillsets	• Referent Power Development: Earning influence through character and competence over time
Tools	• Audience insight mapping; Framing practice; Objection handling; Story and analogy development; AI-assisted rehearsal; Progressive practice from friendly to skeptical audiences
Performance Indicators	• You can influence without manipulation, set boundaries without aggression, cast vision that inspires voluntary commitment, and build referent power through consistent values-aligned action over time.

KEY TAKEAWAY

Ethical influence is not charisma. It is the accumulated credibility of consistent values-aligned action over time. It persuades not through argument but through demonstration. People do not comply with this kind of leadership—they choose it. In a world saturated with algorithmic persuasion, influence earned through integrity is the only form that cannot be automated.

The Shadow Side

Relational skill is morally neutral. The same capacities that enable deep connection can be weaponized for manipulation. The difference lies in intent and impact.

Recognizing Manipulation

Manipulation uses relational skills for unilateral benefit. Attunement becomes surveillance for exploitation. Resonance becomes mirroring for false trust. Expression becomes persuasion without consent. Influence becomes coercion disguised as choice.

The signs are often felt before they are understood: feeling drained after interactions, confusion about what was agreed upon, guilt without clear cause, boundaries repeatedly "misunderstood," one person's concerns minimized while the other person's escalate.

The Contrast

Consider two leaders facing the same situation: a team member resistant to a new initiative.

The manipulator uses attunement to identify the person's insecurities, then leverages them. "I noticed you've been struggling with the new systems. This initiative could really help you catch up." The message beneath the message: the team member is behind, and compliance is their path to safety. The person agrees, but feels vaguely ashamed without knowing why.

The relationally masterful leader uses attunement to understand the resistance. "You seem hesitant. Help me understand what concerns you." The conversation surfaces a legitimate worry about implementation timeline. They problem-solve together. The person commits because their concern was heard and addressed.

Same skill. Opposite intent. Different outcome.

Bias as Relational Failure

Bias is fear moving through the body before it becomes ideology. The body reacts first: posture straightens when someone unfamiliar enters, heat rises when status feels threatened, the body tightens before judgment or exclusion occurs.

Neuroscience supports this sequence. David Amodio's brain activity research shows the amygdala firing within milliseconds of exposure to difference, long before conscious thought or deliberate judgment. People do not think their way into bias. They feel their way into it.

His work also shows something hopeful: the brain is capable of regulating these responses when they are detected early. Awareness changes the trajectory.

Then comes ego. Fear initiates the reaction by saying, "I might be harmed." Ego rationalizes the reaction by saying, "I am superior." Together they construct stories that justify what the body has already decided.

This is why bias is not a knowledge problem. Fear cannot be educated out of someone. Susan Fiske's research documents the neural signatures of dehumanization, showing how quickly the mind strips others of full human status under perceived threat.

Artificial intelligence has reinforced this truth. When algorithms trained on human data reproduce racial, gender, and socioeconomic disparities, they are not inventing prejudice. They are reflecting accumulated fear and ego at machine scale.

This is precisely why self-awareness is the first skill emotional intelligence trains. Detection is the intervention. Bias is a relational failure that begins with a failure of self-awareness: not noticing what is happening in the body before it shapes behavior toward others.

ETHICAL USE OF RELATIONAL SKILL

Relational mastery carries responsibility.

- **Consent:** Is influence transparent and voluntary?

- **Mutual benefit:** Does the outcome serve all parties?

- **Dignity:** Are you protecting others' agency and autonomy?

- **Sustainability:** Will this strengthen or strain the relationship long-term?

- **Accountability:** Can you own the full impact of your actions?

When relational skill serves only your interests, it becomes manipulation regardless of how sophisticated the technique. When it serves mutual flourishing, it becomes the foundation of trust.

Relationships as Development

The strongest predictor of health and happiness is not wealth, achievement, or even physical fitness. It is the quality of our relationships.

The Harvard Study of Adult Development, tracking lives for over eighty years, confirms what poets and philosophers have long known: we are wired for connection, and our well-being depends on the depth, consistency, and authenticity of our bonds with others.

The contemplatives of Chapter Three arrived at these same capacities through different vocabularies. Buddhist metta practice trains compassion as a daily discipline, not a spontaneous feeling. Stoic self-examination under relational pressure, what Marcus Aurelius practiced in the chaos of imperial politics, trains conflict navigation. The Yoruba concept of iwa-pele, gentle character, describes the ethical influence that emerges from sustained integrity. Ubuntu, "I am because we are," is a philosophical framework for the biological reality this chapter describes: that human nervous systems are not designed to operate alone. Relationship is the medium through which emotional intelligence exists.

Human beings require different types of relationships to thrive. We need:

- **Intimate bonds** where we learn vulnerability and co-regulation.

- **Friendships** where we practice authenticity without hierarchy.

- **Professional relationships** where we translate personal skills into structured contexts.

- **Community connections** that teach us to hold differences and contribute to something larger.

- **Mentoring relationships** where we practice developmental care across experience levels.

There is skill transfer between contexts. The parent who learns patience with teenagers discovers it transforms their leadership style. The manager who masters difficult conversations at work finds they can finally have honest discussions with their spouse. The friend who becomes skilled at repair applies those principles to customer relationships.

Life becomes the laboratory. Every relationship reflects a person's capacity for empathy, skill in authentic expression, and ability to create trust and repair when it breaks. Everything we build depends on the quality of connection between the people who comprise it.

From Skill to Transcendence

Chapter Four described the mechanism of collective transcendence: one person's integration creating the conditions for another's. Baldwin at Cambridge demonstrated it at societal scale. Sarah demonstrates it at relational scale.

This is what relational mastery produces when all four skills operate together. Empathy perceives accurately. Authentic expression makes that perception available. Conflict navigation sustains the connection under pressure. Ethical influence creates shared direction. The integration of all four, practiced over time, produces something greater than skill. It produces the conditions under which other people transform.

RELATIONAL MASTERY *(Part B)*

THE DEEPEST APPLICATION: LOVE

> *"The greatest thing you'll ever learn is just to love and*
> *be loved in return."*
> **Eden Ahbez**

The four skills of relational mastery find their fullest expression in one context: love. Not sentiment or infatuation. Love as sustained practice, the arena where every relational capacity is tested and deepened over time.

Love's Crucible

Love is not a category. It is a crucible.

Every relational skill you have built faces its hardest examination in sustained intimacy. Empathy is easy when you are fresh. Try it at year twenty, when you think you already know what your partner feels. Authentic expression is manageable in a boardroom with professional distance. Try it when the person across from you knows exactly which words will land hardest. Conflict navigation works with colleagues you see forty hours a week. Try it with someone you see every morning for the rest of your life. Love does not require different skills. It requires the same skills at closer range, higher stakes, and longer duration.

If relational mastery means applying emotional intelligence in real time, love is where those skills meet their edge. You are asked to be independent and connected, open and guarded, safe and changed. These tensions are not obstacles. They are the mechanism.

Sarah and Seth

It was a Tuesday evening, two years before the retirement party, when Seth said the thing Sarah had been avoiding.

"You're disappearing again."

Sarah felt the familiar tightening.

She wasn't disappearing. She was preparing for the biggest product launch of her career.

That was her first impulse. Her second was softer and harder: he was right.

She'd been home for dinner every night that week. Physically present. Emotionally elsewhere. Seth could feel the difference because thirty-two years of attunement had taught him to read her the way she read a boardroom. Her laugh was half a beat late. Her questions about his day were careful rather than curious. She was performing presence, not living it.

"I know," she said. Two words that cost more than any boardroom admission.

What followed wasn't a fight. It was repair in its most intimate form. Seth didn't need Sarah to cancel the launch. He needed her to acknowledge that the gap existed, that she saw it, and that she would close it. Not perfectly. Not immediately. Consistently enough for him to trust.

"I won't be fully available until March," she said. "That's the truth. What I can do is stop pretending I am. I would rather be honestly absent for two hours than dishonestly present for five."

Seth nodded. "That's all I'm asking for."

This was the marriage: not the absence of strain, but the willingness to name it before it calcified. Every skill Sarah used at work—attunement, honest expression, repair—operated here at deeper stakes and closer range. The boardroom tolerated her imperfections. Seth had to live with them.

The Paradox of Freedom

Previous generations often did not have this choice. Structured paths dictated whom they married and which community held them accountable. Staying was not always virtue; sometimes it was necessity.

In many societies, there is now unprecedented freedom. People can exit relationships responsibly, relocate for opportunity, build networks reflecting their values. For the first time in history, love is almost entirely voluntary.

Freedom creates a paradox. It is easy to mistake options for growth, to confuse the ability to leave with wisdom about when to stay. Some exits are essential; love does not require enduring harm or coercion. The question is whether departure reflects discernment or reflexive avoidance.

For traditions that understand marriage as sacrament, this framing sharpens rather than weakens commitment, naming it as shared discipline of growth and repair rather than mere endurance.

Yet many use freedom to avoid transformation entirely. Technology amplifies this escape: AI companions calibrated to soothe, algorithms promising compatibility without friction, apps shielding people from vulnerability. The relationship that never challenges a person also never changes them. This pattern crosses generations. The sixty-year-old filling evenings with busyness to avoid intimacy makes the same choice as the twenty-five-year-old swiping left at the first sign of friction.

The label does not make it sacred. Duty does not make it love. Marriage should not be a hiding place from real intimacy, a way to preserve control while escaping truth.

The Cost of Comfort

What happens when we choose comfort over transformation?

The cost is measurable. Individually, emotional range narrow and relationships turn transactional. Vulnerability begins to feel like exposure rather than connection, because what it produces when it is met with care has been forgotten.

The consequences scale. When enough people choose protection over authenticity, trust erodes. Institutions depending on good faith (marriages, teams, communities, democracies) hollow out. People remain proximate but not bonded.

The U.S. Surgeon General declared loneliness a public health crisis in 2023: more connected technologically, more isolated relationally than ever before. The obstacle is not circumstance. It is choosing comfort when growth is available.

The antidote is values alignment: acting from personal values toward another person's well-being, consistently, over time. Clear boundaries, honest feedback, rapid repair make love tangible. They make it a source of safety, belonging, trust.

Love Beyond the Personal

This alignment is physiological, not only ethical. Love is real in the body. Oxytocin, vasopressin, and dopamine fire in feedback loops of warmth. Love also appears in physiological alignment: holding hands, breath slowing together, attention synchronizing. The body responds. Regulation improves.

In high-attunement relationships, consciousness shifts. A person is no longer only a self. They become part of a shared field. Whether it is called spiritual or simply meaningful, it is understood that love asks more of people than most things ever will. And somehow, they still choose it.

AI has inadvertently clarified why. The individual components of emotional intelligence are separable: pattern recognition, response calibration, even empathy simulation. Machines can isolate and perform each one. What cannot be separated is the integration of all of them, sustained over time, in a body that ages, fails, repairs, and persists. Love is where that integration becomes visible, because love is the only context that lasts long enough to reveal it. The meaning that accumulates between two people across decades of imperfect practice is not a skill. It is what skills produce when they are held together by commitment rather than optimization. Machines optimize for prediction. Humans optimize for meaning. Love is where the difference is no longer theoretical.

This is why love is not only personal. The safety created between two people radiates outward. Children raised in secure attachment develop greater capacity for connection. Teams led with genuine care outperform those managed through fear. Communities bound by mutual regard prove more resilient than those organized around self-interest.

Emotional intelligence is not a solo performance. It is revealed, refined, and realized in the space between us.

KEY TAKEAWAYS

Core Insights

Connection is built, not found. Deep relationships require deliberate practice. The myth of effortless compatibility keeps people searching for what can only be constructed.

Conflict is the mechanism, not the obstacle. Navigating disagreement skillfully deepens relationships. Couples who never fight often never grow.

Influence flows from trust, not position. Lasting persuasion comes from consistent integrity over time.

Love creates fields of development. Authentic care establishes conditions where everyone involved can grow.

The Bridge Forward

Unlike previous pillars, relational mastery requires other people. Every interaction becomes practice. Every relationship becomes curriculum.

The skills you have built are yours. They live in your body, not on a page.

A person with profound self-awareness can be destroyed by a workplace that punishes honesty. A master of repair can be broken by an institution that treats conflict as betrayal.

Part Three of this book asks the harder question: How do we build systems that make emotional intelligence possible at scale?

> *"We are not just social beings; we are beings whose very neurobiological architecture is built for connection."*
> **Louis Cozolino**

PART 3
SCALING HUMAN WISDOM

FROM INDIVIDUAL MASTERY TO COLLECTIVE INTELLIGENCE

THE SYSTEM

A man reports ageism.

At fifty-seven, he has twenty-three years with the company and exceptional reviews. His last rating called him "indispensable." Then a new VP arrived. Within weeks, the man was excluded from the AI team he had been promised. His project went to someone hired eighteen months ago. The VP, in a meeting: "We need people who didn't grow up with fax machines making these decisions." Others laughed. The man did not.

Now he sits across from someone trained to help, who nods with concern and says the right words.

Behind that concern, a calculation runs: legal exposure, the VP's relationship with the CEO, investigation cost versus settlement cost, how close this man is to retirement anyway.

The room feels different than he expected. The questions narrow rather than understand. He walked in with evidence but leaves knowing he has been processed.

This is not one bad HR department. This is structure.

How We Got Here

Before it was a system, it was a decision. Someone looked at a human being and saw a unit of production.

Industrial management controlled labor at scale. Judgment mattered less than compliance. Then workers organized, and for a few decades, accountability returned.

The institutional response was absorption. Worker protections were diffused, not dismantled. Responsibilities accumulated inside HR. When hiring, training, discipline, culture PR, and legal defense share one function, accountability collapses. The same office supports employees and shields the firm. This conflict is design, not accident.

Many who enter HR do so to help. They believe proximity to power lets them advocate from within. The system metabolizes good intentions. The caring professional learns which concerns can be raised. They learn to call this discernment, not defeat.

Then AI arrived, doing to cognitive work what mechanization did to physical: centralizing power, displacing accountability into systems that appear neutral. Workers face this moment with weaker protections and systems built to contain risk, not honor claims.

What Can Be Redesigned

What was designed can be redesigned.

Parts One and Two built internal capacity: how to read nervous system, regulate under pressure, connect authentically, repair when connection breaks. Part Two revealed when machines attempted to replicate these capacities, they succeeded at some components and failed at others. That partial success exposed what could not previously be seen: emotional intelligence was not one capacity but many, each with distinct neural architecture and each vulnerable to different systemic failures. Systems either support these capacities or erode them.

Collective emotional intelligence is not the sum of individual skills. It is emergent: how systems are designed, how power is distributed, how conflict is navigated, how values are enacted under pressure.

The Foundation: Justice

If individual capacity is not sufficient, what determines whether systems develop it or destroy it?

> *"The opposite of poverty is not wealth. The opposite of poverty is justice."*
> **Bryan Stevenson,** *Just Mercy*

Justice determines whether humans can coordinate at scale and trust the institutions that govern them.

At the root of most institutional injustice is a failure of emotional intelligence. Low emotional intelligence in a person without power is a personal limitation. In a person with authority over careers, compensation, and termination, protected by systems that treat complaints as threats, low emotional intelligence is a structural danger.

The harm is well established: leaders ill-equipped to manage other humans replicate their incapacity at scale. The harm is specific, measurable, and compounding. Justice is the only structural protection the people below that leader have.

Justice requires emotional intelligence. An emotionally intelligent society requires justice.

Justice is the mechanism through which individuals participate in their own governance. When that mechanism fails, it does not just harm the person in front of it. It revokes agency. A progressive society promises its citizens the structural capacity to speak, to seek redress, to act on their own behalf. When the systems meant to honor that promise instead absorb complaints, silence witnesses, and protect power, the society has not merely failed one person. Everything this book trains, the awareness, the regulation, the relational skill, becomes trapped inside people who have no structural path to use it. This is not a workplace problem: it is a civilizational one.

A leader with low emotional intelligence and a pen could harm dozens, while one with an algorithm can harm thousands, faster, with less visibility, and with systems that make the harm appear neutral. Every measurement capability described in Chapter Ten, behavioral analytics, physiological tracking, pattern reconstruction, can serve development or surveillance. Justice is what determines which.

The guardrails that governed prior generations of justice were designed for physical workplaces with observable behavior. They do not account for algorithmic hiring decisions no applicant can audit, biometric monitoring no employee consented to, or behavioral analytics that reconstruct patterns across data an individual never knew was collected. Participating in the next generation of justice requires guardrails built for the technology that now mediates power.

The cautionary lesson from IQ testing still stands: measurement without justice principles can reinforce exclusion and surveillance.

What Fails

The most seductive failure: trying to purchase emotional intelligence as a service.

A company notices burnout. Leadership responds with the Emotional Intelligence Starter Pack: wellness app, offsite retreat, mindfulness room, executive coach.

Six months later: 23% app adoption. The offsite made good photos. The mindfulness room is a nap zone. The coach helps leaders manage their feelings about how nothing is changing.

This is not emotional intelligence. It is theater.

The app suggests breathing exercises while meetings silence dissent. The retreat invites vulnerability while the workplace punishes it. Coaching soothes executives without confronting power.

These tools are not bad. Meditation helps. Retreats spark. Coaching works. Without systemic change, they become pressure release valves: helping people cope with what should be challenged.

The deeper barrier is that people already know their inner lives are being read. Every email carries emotional signatures. Every Slack message has a timestamp that reveals what was engaged with and what was avoided. Every video call captures micro-expressions that weren't intended to be shared. The digital fingerprint of a person's emotional life already exists. When organizations claim they want access to "emotional intelligence," employees hear surveillance dressed as development and shut down. Inner experience is sacred terrain. The systems asking for access have not yet earned trust with it.

There is a path forward: reframing emotional intelligence as observable, learnable skills rather than access to someone's inner world. Real organizational EI requires changing the system, not helping people survive it.

The Chapters Ahead

Chapter Ten: Measuring What Matters. When machines score well on those assessments, they confirm it: what the tests captured was knowledge about emotions, not embodied capacity. New technologies can now measure what the tests miss. This chapter provides frameworks for measurement that serves growth without creating control.

Chapter Eleven: The Tribunal. What happens when emotional intelligence fails at scale. Every failure maps to capacities this book has trained.

Chapter Twelve: The Work Ahead. Back to you. The capacities you have developed are not skills bolted onto a fixed self.

The man who reported ageism deserved a system that would weigh it. Welcome to scaling wisdom.

MEASUREMENT

> *Tell me how you measure me, and I will tell you how I will behave.*
> **Eliyahu Goldratt,** *The Haystack Syndrome*

THE PATTERN WE KEEP REPEATING

The dashboard looked impressive. Green indicators across every metric: 87% engagement score (up 4% from last quarter), 94% training completion, 78% psychological safety rating, zero formal complaints.

Leadership presented these numbers to the board with confidence. The emotional intelligence initiative was working.

This is what the dashboard didn't show:

The engagement survey went live the same week as performance reviews, and everyone knew their managers could see who submitted responses. The 87% didn't measure engagement. It measured fear of being seen as disengaged.

The training completion rate measured who clicked through modules, not who learned anything. People discovered you could play videos at double the speed while answering emails. Complete the quiz by elimination. Certificate generated. Box checked.

The psychological safety question was answered by people who had watched colleagues get managed out after "not being a culture fit." They understood what answers kept them employed.

And that zero formal complaints? The whistleblowing form went directly to the HR director, who reported to the CEO, who was the problem. Everyone knew reporting meant career suicide.

Everyone knew even though everyone pretended not to know. And the metrics said everything was fine.

This is measurement dysfunction at scale. Not because the tools are flawed, but because the system measures what protects power, not what reveals truth.

How do we know our capacity is growing? How do we track progress? And how do we protect ourselves from systems that could use these same measurement capabilities against you?

The thesis is simple: Emotional intelligence should be measured to support growth and justice, not to extract performance or justify control.

Before We Measure: The Definitional Question

Before we can measure emotional intelligence, we must confront an uncomfortable question: What exactly are we measuring?

The field has never fully resolved this. Mayer and Salovey defined EI as ability: perceiving, using, understanding, and managing emotions. Goleman expanded it to include personality traits and social competencies. Bar-On framed it as emotional-social intelligence spanning intrapersonal ability, stress management, and general mood. Each definition produces different assessments that correlate only modestly with each other.

This book has taken a position: emotional intelligence is the embodied capacity to integrate emotional data with cognition under real conditions. This definition emphasizes biology over trait, process over personality, and performance under pressure over abstract knowledge. The measurement approaches that follow differ substantially from traditional psychometric tests.

They also differ from something older. This book has documented civilizations across five thousand years independently cultivating the same capacities, each through its own practices and vocabulary. What matters for measurement is that those traditions also had their own methods for recognizing when integration was present and when it was absent.

They assessed character through sustained observation over years, not snapshot tests. They evaluated capacity through how a person behaved under communal pressure, not controlled conditions. They understood emotional intelligence as collective and relational, not individual and cognitive.

Western psychometrics arrived with instruments calibrated to one culture's narrowest definition of the phenomenon, then treated the results as universal. The measurement revolution described in this chapter is using technology to affirm and expand our understanding.

Why Traditional Tests Fail

The Shadow of IQ

Emotional intelligence measurement did not emerge in a vacuum. It grew in the shadow of IQ testing—and inherited its methodology, its assumptions, and its blind spots.

When Alfred Binet developed intelligence tests in 1905, he had a developmental purpose: identifying children who needed educational support. He explicitly warned against treating scores as fixed or innate. When American psychologists imported his tests, they stripped away the caveats. Scores became reified as measuring "innate intelligence." Within decades, the same tools justified racial hierarchies, immigration restrictions, and forced sterilization.

The flaw was structural: snapshot tests measuring performance on specific cognitive tasks were treated as measuring fixed, essential capacity. They captured what could be learned and practiced, then called it something immutable.

EQ testing, the emotional intelligence parallel to IQ testing, repeated this pattern. When the formal measurement of emotional intelligence emerged in the 1990s, it borrowed IQ's methodology wholesale: standardized tests with "correct" answers, controlled conditions, snapshot assessments, and the assumption that test performance equals real-world capacity. The instruments were different. The fundamental approach was the same.

The Evolution of EQ Measurement

The formalization emerged through three instruments:

Bar-On's EQ-i (1997) made EI accessible through self-report but relies on self-awareness to assess self-awareness. If a person lacks insight into their emotional patterns, they will be rated inaccurately.

MSCEIT (2002) represented the gold standard: performance-based, objective, resistant to self-deception. It requires controlled conditions, expert scoring, and captures a snapshot rather than patterns over time.

EQ-360 provides behavioral evidence from real relationships, the most ecologically valid measure. It depends on rater honesty and captures perception rather than capacity.

These tools proved emotional intelligence was real, measurable, and developable. But meta-analytic work finds only modest convergence between self-report, ability-based, and 360 measures—supporting the point that definitional fragmentation produces measurement fragmentation. And they shared a limitation not fully understood until recently.

The AI Revelation

In research settings, advanced language models can perform competitively with humans on components of widely used EI assessments, including tasks modeled on MSCEIT branches. Systems with no body, no relationships, no lived experience perform well on tests used for decades to identify emotionally intelligent humans.

This finding forces a reset. It reveals that what tests capture is emotional problem-solving knowledge and pattern recognition, not the biological integration this book argues is central.

Traditional tests measure pattern recognition in facial expressions, knowledge about how emotions work, and ability to identify "correct" responses in emotional scenarios. These are cognitive skills about emotions, not embodied emotional capacity.

Part One established that emotional intelligence requires embodiment including felt sense, nervous system response, and biological coordination with others. Traditional tests assess what can be learned from books and examples. They do not assess what can only be built through lived experience.

What the tests miss is what requires biological existence: the neural integration built practicing regulation under pressure, the physiological flexibility developed through stress cycle completion, the interpersonal synchrony created through genuine attunement.

Now we can measure these.

What We Can Now Measure

Each skill practiced in Part Two maps to neural and physiological substrates that new technologies can track. Interoception strengthens insula function. Emotional literacy activates prefrontal regions. Resilience improves heart rate variability. Empathy builds capacity for physiological synchrony with others.

TABLE 15: Three Pillars/Skills → Measurement Validation

Pillar/Skill	What Was Practiced	Neural/Physiological Substrate	What Can Be Measured
SELF-AWARENESS			
Interoception	Body scans, sensation tracking, heartbeat awareness	Insula activation, interoceptive networks	Improved heartbeat detection accuracy
Emotional Literacy	Naming emotions precisely, expanding vocabulary	Prefrontal activation during labeling	Emotion word diversity in communication
Meta-Awareness	Observing thought patterns, noticing triggers	DMN connectivity, self-referential processing	DMN functional connectivity strength
Values Alignment	Checking actions against values	vmPFC integration	Consistency between stated values and behavior
SELF-MASTERY			
Emotional Self-Command	Generating states, performing under pressure	Prefrontal-limbic integration	EEG coherence during regulation
Discomfort Tolerance	Staying present in difficulty	Sustained prefrontal activation	HRV stability during challenge
Resilience	Recovery, stress cycle completion	Autonomic flexibility	HRV recovery time, sleep quality
RELATIONAL MASTERY			
Empathy	Attunement, perspective-taking	Shared neural representations, simulation networks	Physiological coupling during interaction
Authentic Expression	Active listening, clear expression	Language-emotion integration	Turn-taking patterns, repair attempts
Conflict Navigation	Staying regulated in disagreement	Maintained prefrontal function	De-escalation patterns
Ethical Influence	Inspiring voluntary change	Social cognition integration	Influence without coercion markers

The Three Domains

Three domains of measurement now exist that did not when MSCEIT was designed.

Natural language processing can now analyze sentiment, linguistic patterns, and emotional markers across millions of communications. Wearable sensors track physiological states continuously, not just during lab visits. Machine learning detects patterns across time scales and data volumes no human observer could process. Hyperscanning technology measures brain-to-brain coupling in real time.

These represent a categorical shift: from asking people about their emotional intelligence to observing it in action, continuously, at scale.

Domain One: Digital Behavior Patterns

A person's digital footprint is vast, and it reveals more than any questionnaire ever could.

Consider what a single workday generates:

- Dozens of emails show measurable response latency, word choice, and tone.

- Slack messages with timestamps indicate engagement and avoidance.

- Calendar patterns highlight who is prioritized and who is neglected.

- Video calls capture facial expressions, vocal patterns, speaking time, and interruption frequency.

- Document edits reveal collaboration markers.

- Mouse movements and typing cadence carry emotional signatures.

Multiply this across months and years. The average knowledge worker generates thousands of data points weekly. Across an organization of 10,000 people over five years, the behavioral dataset numbers in the billions. Traditional EI tests sample a few dozen responses in controlled conditions. Digital behavior captures patterns across real stakes, real relationships, and real pressure—continuously.

What emerges is not noise. It is signal.

Chapter Nine argued that digital communication has not merely changed where these interactions happen. It has changed what they are. Managing conflict over text, sustaining empathy through a screen, reading emotional tone without vocal cues or body language are structurally new cognitive demands. The behavioral patterns below do not simply measure familiar skills through a new medium. Some measure capacities that did not exist as discrete demands until the medium created them.

Consider six months of manager-employee digital interactions:

Manager A

- Response times are consistent regardless of message emotional tone.

- Turn-taking in written exchanges is balanced.

- Linguistic markers indicate acknowledgment of others' perspectives.

- Uses repair language after disagreements.

- Maintains consistent patterns regardless of organizational pressure.

Manager B

- Response time increases dramatically to emotionally difficult messages.

- Dominates meeting talk time.

- Uses "I" pronouns far more than "we."

- Never acknowledges others' emotional states in writing.

- Patterns intensify during high-pressure periods.

Self-report asks both managers, "How well do you listen?" Both rate themselves seven or eight out of ten. Behavioral analytics across 10,000 interactions tells a different story—one that traditional assessment cannot see.

Scale this across an organization and different patterns emerge. Communication analytics can show that one department receives acknowledgment responses from leadership at half the rate of another. Repair language after disagreements predicts promotion more reliably than performance ratings. Teams led by managers with consistent response patterns exhibit clustering of linguistic markers of psychological safety, while those led by managers whose engagement drops under pressure show none. None of this is visible in quarterly surveys, but all of it is becomes apparent in six months of digital behavior. While individual measurement provides insight into a manager, systemic measurement illuminates the culture as a whole.

TABLE 16: Digital Behavior Patterns → Three Pillars/Skills

Digital Behavior	Maps to Skill	High EI Pattern	Low EI Pattern
SELF-AWARENESS			
Emotion word diversity	Emotional Literacy	50+ distinct terms	5-10 basic terms repeated
Self-correction frequency	Meta-Awareness	Edits before sending	Sends impulsively
Calendar-values alignment	Values Alignment	Time matches priorities	Says X, spends time on Y
SELF-MASTERY			
Typing speed in conflict	Emotional Self-Command	Steady patterns	Spikes 80%+
Response time to difficult messages	Discomfort Tolerance	Consistent 2-4 hour	24 hour or more to conflict
Communication after setbacks	Resilience	Returns to baseline	Prolonged withdrawal
RELATIONAL MASTERY			
Empathic language	Empathy	Increases with validation	Absent when signaled
Consistency of voice in exchanges	Authentic Expression	Balanced turn-taking, repair language	Dominates or withdraws under pressure
Repair attempts	Conflict Navigation	Acknowledges, reconnects	Avoids or doubles down
First-person pronouns (I/we/us)	Ethical Influence	Integrity markers, values consistency	Compliance pressure, authority references

Domain Two: Physiological Truth

HRV measures the variation between heartbeats—a well-validated proxy for autonomic flexibility and stress recovery. High HRV means the nervous system can shift fluidly between activation and recovery. Low HRV indicates a system stuck in chronic stress, unable to downregulate even when the threat has passed.

Chapter Eight taught this with practice completing stress cycles. HRV measurement validates whether those practices built actual capacity. Traditional assessment asked, "Do you manage stress well?" The answer was usually, "Mostly, yes." HRV shows the nervous system's actual flexibility, independent of what a person claims or believes.

A high school teacher's HRV drops predictably every September. In the first year, it stayed suppressed through June and never recovered. By the third year, after she developed regulation practices, her HRV still dips in September but returns to baseline by October. The stressor is the same, but the capacity is different. The body tells the truth.

She had not planned to look at the data. Her school offered HRV tracking through a voluntary wellness program offering a personal device for privacy of results. For months the app sat unused. Then a Sunday evening panic attack sent her to the emergency room. Her heart was fine, but her nervous system was not. She opened the app the next morning. What she saw changed how she understood her own body: HRV had been declining since August. It was not a sudden collapse but rather a slow erosion she could not feel because she had normalized the exhaustion. The graph showed her what her self-report could not. She started regulation practices and by October she could see the line climbing. That visibility was the intervention.

Burnout is not just feeling tired. It is when the nervous system stops recovering and the baseline changes.

Domain Three: Relational Synchrony

Chapter Nine's empathy and attunement practices built measurable biological coordination capacity. When people interact, their physiological systems do not operate independently. They synchronize.

Studies using dual-brain scanning and cardio-respiratory measures show that romantic couples exhibit significantly greater brain-to-brain coupling and heart rhythm synchronization than strangers, especially under stress or during touch. Controlled experiments demonstrate that when one partner achieves heart coherence, the other partner's heart rhythms shift toward coherence too, even without verbal communication.

You have felt this. Maybe it is the friend whose presence steadies your breathing without a word spoken. Perhaps the colleague whose anxiety is contagious even over video call. Or the leader who walks into a room and somehow makes everyone calmer—or more tense.

Chapter Nine established that AI-generated communication breaks this coupling. Machines can produce words indistinguishable from a human's, but they cannot synchronize. Hyperscanning can now detect the difference: authentic communication produces measurable interpersonal coherence. Attunement is not cognitive recognition of others' states. It is physiological resonance. The biological infrastructure for synchrony is what Part Two's empathy practices built, and although measurement is still cutting-edge, it is now possible.

The Integration

The most powerful insight comes from combining physiological sensing with behavioral pattern analysis.

Consider this example employee, whose data reveal both strengths and hidden challenges

Physiology and behavior:

- High HRV (good physiological regulation)

- Communication patterns reveal systematic conflict avoidance

- Response latency increases 400% for difficult messages

- Never initiates hard conversations

- Agreeable in all written communication

Interpretation:

- Physiological regulation achieved through behavioral avoidance, not engagement

- Employee maintains calm by not entering difficulty

Development need:

- Additional regulation techniques are unnecessary; employee maintains sufficient calm

- Develop willingness to experience fear and act despite it

Chapter Eight established that courage is not the absence of fear. It is action in the presence of fear. Growth requires discomfort. This person's nervous system has learned to avoid discomfort so efficiently that it registers as health, though the measurement reveals it is not.

Single modality can mislead. Triangulation reveals truth.

What triangulation converges on is integration itself: cognitive, emotional, physiological, and relational systems coordinating in a living body in real time. That is what this book's definition of emotional intelligence describes and what every contemplative tradition was cultivating. This is exactly what the three domains are each trying to capture from a different angle: digital behavior reveals the cognitive and relational patterns, physiology reveals the autonomic architecture, and synchrony reveals the interpersonal field.

None of these capture integration directly. Together, they approximate it. The phenomenon they are circling is the felt experience of being a whole person under pressure, choosing rather than reacting, connecting rather than performing. We sought to understand it because we recognized it was happening inside us long before we had instruments.

The Measurement Paradox

How Measurement Corrupts What It Measures

Not everything meaningful is measurable. Not everything measurable is meaningful. And the act of measurement itself changes what is being measured.

The measurement paradox works like this:

1. Engagement is measured through surveys. Initially useful. People who feel safe express concerns. Problems surface. Decisions improve.

2. Survey scores become a key performance indicator (KPI). Managers get evaluated on engagement numbers. The survey becomes political. People learn that expressing dissatisfaction leads to awkward HR "check-ins."

3. Gaming emerges. Teams have pre-survey "alignment conversations." Managers coach on "balanced feedback." Response rates from dissatisfied groups drop.

The metric that once revealed truth now conceals it. Same tool, opposite function.

What economists call Goodhart's Law captures this structurally: when a measure becomes a target, it ceases to be a good measure.

The sophistication of biometric measurement does not solve this—it intensifies it. A person can learn to slow their breathing to improve HRV scores without building genuine regulation. Physiological metrics can be gamed just as easily as surveys.

The paradox does not invalidate measurement. It makes humility essential. Measurement is more advanced than ever before, but it is not perfect. Systems must be designed to account for human incentives to perform rather than to be.

The Unmeasurable Core

Some aspects of emotional intelligence may resist quantification not because instruments are inadequate, but because measurement and the phenomenon are structurally incompatible.

Wisdom involves knowing when rules apply and when they don't, when to follow data and when to override it. Any metric for wisdom would immediately become a pattern to recognize, missing the point.

Moral weight describes the felt significance of ethical stakes. Physiological arousal can be measured during moral decisions, but it does not indicate whether the person grasps why the decision matters. A sociopath may show identical activation patterns to a person of deep conscience; the difference is meaning, not measurement.

Presence involves being fully there with another person. Neural synchrony, HRV coherence, and behavioral mirroring can be measured and are correlates of presence, not presence itself. Someone could manipulate every physiological marker while remaining internally disconnected.

Integration under novel pressure is the capacity this book argues matters most. Integration can be measured in controlled conditions. The whole point of emotional intelligence is that it operates when conditions are not controlled. The moment observation is structured, the phenomenon is changed.

The Surveillance Risk

Imagine this scenario, technically feasible today:

Every interaction generates assessment data. Wearable HRV devices track data continuously. Laptops analyze typing patterns in real time. Video calls are processed for facial microexpressions, voice tone, and linguistic markers. All this feeds into an aggregate "EI score" that affects performance reviews, promotion decisions, and career trajectory.

What happens to an employee's behavior?

Performance replaces genuine expression. Behavior is optimized for what is measured, not what is meaningful. Authenticity becomes impossible because the context eliminates the conditions it requires.

The measured emotional intelligence becomes the performance of emotional intelligence.

Measurement can also protect when governed well: identifying burnout before collapse, surfacing bullying patterns, ensuring fairness in who gets developed. The difference between surveillance and support lies entirely in how the system is designed along with the rules for consent and control of the data.

The Justice Dimension

The measurement revolution does not affect everyone equally. Those with power get privacy, while those without it are subjected to surveillance.

Executive communications are not analyzed at a granular level; that would be intrusive. On the other hand, call center workers have every interaction monitored, scored, and reviewed.

Some people were systematically denied environments developing EI: trauma, poverty, and discrimination create developmental barriers. Emotional suppression was survival strategy. Now measurement reveals the cost of that survival and may penalize it.

"Professional" emotional expression reproduces power dynamics. Whose emotions are valued versus policed varies by power. Anger at injustice from subordinates is "unprofessional." The same anger from executives is "passionate leadership."

The IQ precedent—detailed earlier in this chapter—provides the warning. What began as developmental assessment became weaponized within decades. EQ measurement faces the same risk.

Who gets labeled "low EI"? Disproportionately, it is those expressing legitimate anger at injustice, those whose cultural norms differ from Western instruments, and those without developmental opportunities others take for granted. The traditions documented earlier in this book assessed emotional capacity through sustained communal observation, not standardized testing. Instruments calibrated to Western norms do not measure universal human capacity. They measure conformity to one culture's expression of it.

Technologies That Protect

There is no need to choose between measurement capability and privacy protection. Technology exists to do both.

- **Edge Computing:** Personal devices do the analysis. Raw data never leaves. Only aggregated insights sync anywhere, and only with explicit consent.

- **Federated Learning:** Devices learn from each other's patterns without sharing actual data. The system improves while individual information stays private.

- **Differential Privacy:** Mathematical noise protects individuals while patterns stay clear. Organizations can identify systemic patterns ("stress concentrates in this department") without identifying individuals.

- **Secure Aggregation:** Cryptographic protection means even if the server is hacked, only meaningless noise would be exposed. Multiple individuals' contributions combine in ways that mathematically prevent disaggregation.

- **User Control:** The user chooses what is measured, when it is measured, and who sees it. Data can be deleted at anytime and permissions are granular. Tracking can be paused without explanation.

Major consumer ecosystems already use on-device processing, strict consent, and cryptographic protections for data. In well-designed implementations, privacy-preserving approaches achieve accuracy comparable to centralized models.

Why the Gap Exists

If privacy-preserving technology exists, why is it not standard? Several factors explain why:

- Data monetization incentives
- Engineering convenience
- Competitive advantage from centralized databases
- Regulatory lag
- User awareness gaps

When organizations deploy surveillance architectures despite privacy-preserving alternatives, they are choosing that data value matters more than user protection.

The technology exists. The question is political: will users demand it?

Why Measure at All?

Measurement is not neutral. It directs attention, creates incentives, and shapes what organizations value. Before asking how to measure well, we must ask why we measure at all.

The case for measurement:

- **Visibility enables development.** Many people cannot improve what they cannot see. The teacher who sees her HRV data discovers she never recovers, even on weekends. That visibility enables change.

- **Patterns reveal structure.** Individual data points mean little; patterns across time and context reveal the architecture of capacity. Measurement surfaces distinctions that matter.

- **Accountability requires evidence.** The tribunal in Chapter Eleven works because behavioral analytics document patterns that witnesses might miss or deny. Measurement makes the invisible visible.

The case against measurement:

- **Measurement distorts.** Goodhart's Law is structural. What gets measured gets gamed.

- **Measurement violates.** Inner life is sacred terrain. Making it visible to institutions with power over careers creates risks that may exceed benefits.

- **Measurement reduces.** Human beings are not dashboards. Quantifying experience can flatten what it purports to reveal.

The design principles that follow attempt to honor both sides. There is no resolution to this tension, only navigation.

Design Principles

Two principles are specific to this book. The first is to measure embodiment, not knowledge. Traditional tests assess cognitive skills about emotions, which AI can replicate. Assessments should be weighted toward aspects that require biological existence: physiological regulation, interpersonal synchrony, neural integration under pressure. The second principle is to treat contradictions as data. When behavioral patterns say one thing and physiology indicates another, the gap between them is the most important finding. The avoidant person with high HRV is not a measurement error; the gap itself is the diagnosis.

The remaining principles, privacy architecture, justice frameworks, human oversight, and transparency, have been argued in the preceding sections. They are not optional nor original to this book. What is original is the insistence that measurement of emotional intelligence must be grounded in the body, validated across multiple domains, and interpreted by humans who understand that the same pattern means different things in different lives.

The Three-Tier Model

Tier One: Personal Development (Maximum Privacy). Individual growth with no external stakes. All processing happens on the personal device. Results are visible only to the individual.

Tier Two: Organizational Aggregate (Differential Privacy). Contributing to team-level patterns without individual attribution. Individual identification is not possible.

Tier Three: High-Stakes Assessment (Explicit Consent, Human Review). Used only for consequential decisions. Combines multiple assessment methods, mandatory human review, and involves temporary processing with built in contestability.

TABLE 17: Implementation Tiers Summary

Tier	Purpose	Privacy Level	What's Measured	Who Sees Results
Tier 1	Individual growth	Maximum (edge processing)	HRV, sleep, stress, communication	Only on personal device
Tier 2	Systemic patterns	High (differential privacy)	Team patterns, safety, trust (anonymized)	Aggregates only
Tier 3	Consequential decisions	Contextual (consent, review)	Comprehensive multimodal	Panel access with individual input

What Not to Do

Never optimize for the measurement. The person who artificially inflates their HRV score through breathing techniques without building genuine regulation has fooled the number, not themselves. They will still collapse under real pressure.

Never forget who measurement serves. Numbers serve humans. The moment an organization cares more about the score than the person, the system has inverted.

Never mistake precision for justice. High-resolution data combined with unequal access to developmental environments creates sophisticated discrimination. Every measurement system must ask: Who was denied the opportunity to develop what we are measuring?

The Bridge to Justice

The dashboard dysfunction we opened with revealed how measurement systems can obscure rather than illuminate truth.

What should have been measured: HRV patterns showing which leaders never recover and which teams are in chronic stress. Communication analytics revealing who repairs after conflict and who avoids. Behavioral patterns across thousands of interactions showing whose emotional expression is valued and whose is policed. These are operational now. The technology described in this chapter could have surfaced what that dashboard concealed.

Measurement without accountability is just sophisticated observation of harm in progress.

The capabilities described in this chapter, behavioral analytics across millions of messages, bias detection systems, physiological pattern reconstruction, are operational.

The next chapter is a courtroom.

A father who sat in his car unable to face his family because of what his livelihood had taken from him. A daughter holding her mother's coin, testifying about what silence cost. A founder checking his phone during testimony about this woman's death. Measurement in action: 1.4 million messages analyzed, bias detection systems, pattern reconstruction.

What follows is emotional intelligence failing at scale, and justice accessing the tools at its disposal.

JUSTICE

> *"The experience of power destroys the skills that gain us power in the first place."*
> **Dacher Keltner,** *The Power Paradox*

THE INTERNATIONAL TRIBUNAL

Three and a half billion people go to work every day. For most adults, the workplace is where institutional power first carries economic consequences: what is tolerated, what is protected, and what happens when someone speaks up. Worker justice is not a labor issue. It is a civilizational one.

When workplaces permit harm, the damage radiates outward: into families who absorb the stress, into communities that normalize silence, into the next generation's understanding of what authority means.

This chapter shows how emotionally unintelligent leadership compounds harm. The harm and the concealment are the same system. Every society that calls itself progressive must eventually answer for what it allows that system to do.

The Architecture of Accountability

The international tribunal draws its jurisdictional framework from real directives that have established that corporations bear legal accountability when they harm human rights across their value chains. It has not solved for coordination: when employment contracts route through an international subsidiary, harms are distributed across continents. Borders fragment jurisdiction. Non-disclosure agreements block aggregation. Misaligned roles occur between labor boards and financial regulators. Accountability gaps open between civil and criminal enforcement. Patterns compound. This tribunal is overdue. The breakthrough is data. Modeled on highly regulated industry protocols, centralized, anonymized data lakes are already a reality. Private arbitration records, public filings, internal communication logs can be accessed simultaneously.

Regulators and digital forensics teams have the tools, they simply haven't scaled. Systems operating as a Tier Three assessment: explicit consent from complainants, human judicial review at every stage, contestability built into the process are all available.

In the past, corporations used privacy laws to hide patterns. This system used privacy technology to reveal them. By tokenizing identities while preserving behavioral patterns, it allowed the court to see the shape of the harm without exposing the victims until they chose to step forward. What used to take legal teams five years of discovery now can happen in milliseconds, with an accuracy rate that made human document review look negligent.

In the near future, four judges sit on the bench. Beside them, a screen displays output from LAW-12: the behavioral analytics described in Chapter Ten, scaled to judicial evidence. The same communication pattern analysis that could distinguish Manager A from Manager B across 10,000 interactions, now applied to 1.4 million messages across a decade. The same natural language processing (NLP) that tracked patterns such as acknowledgment rates, repair language, and linguistic markers of psychological safety, was now reconstructing what an organization's digital behavior revealed about its culture. LAW-12 does not assess guilt. It makes the invisible visible.

The LAW-12 interface sits on a podium at the center of the room, visible and accessible to all participants. In this tribunal, objections are no longer traditional interruptions—challenges to testimony, queries, and data review are submitted through the interface in real time, allowing witnesses to complete their accounts without legal barriers. The courtroom moved differently here: the focus was on seeing the patterns, not on arguing over every line of testimony.

THE THRESHOLD

Karan Iyer sat alone outside Courtroom Twelve.

He could leave. He could walk out the front doors, take the train home, and tell his wife it was too much. Three years of this, the exclusions, the manufactured documentation, the termination, and eleven months unemployed, earned him the right to walk away.

The termination was punitive. Designed to make sure it would leave a wound, not just a gap. He went to HR once, early on, believing the door was real.

What followed wasn't dramatic. It was administrative. Former colleagues who texted support in the first weeks went quiet, then vanished. Some watched his LinkedIn from a distance, close enough to monitor, too far to be associated. The false narratives moved faster than he could correct them: that was difficult, that the situation was more complicated than it appeared, that there were things people couldn't say. The company's culture communications and PR continued without interruption, celebrating inclusion initiatives built on the silence of the people they excluded. Friends who knew the truth said nothing publicly.

For eleven months he watched the story be reshaped by the people who wrote him out of it.

There wasn't a confrontation to document, no threat to investigate. But the erasure of a person's professional identity, reputation, and community through coordinated silence isn't a workplace dispute. It's institutional violence.

He earned the right to close the door. No one would've blamed him.

But there was a weight that wouldn't let him. In the months after his termination, he found them: the others. People who had reached out to him and recognized the pattern because they had lived it.

People still inside who described the same machinery in whispered conversations they would later deny. He could see the future clearly: more names, the same pattern, the same silence. All of it dismissed in the shorthand that makes institutional harm invisible: **it was just work.**

Magnus had stolen from him. Not metaphorically. Karan's commission structure had been "restructured" three times multiple times, erasing $350,000 into calculations he wasn't allowed to see. The money was the least of it. Magnus had stolen his presence. The stress had taken his capacity for joy, for lightness. He came home, but he wasn't home.

He thought about the all-hands meeting. He could still see Magnus's face. The slight smile as he delivered the insult. The way his eyes found Karan in the crowd and held there, just for a moment, making sure Karan knew the humiliation was specific.

Fifty people in that room. No one said anything. A few laughed nervously. Magnus was emboldened by years of impunity. He learned that people like Karan could be removed without consequence.

Karan's phone buzzed. His daughter: *Good luck today papa. You're brave.*

It wasn't bravery, just exhaustion. He straightened his tie and reminded himself that he was fighting because not fighting meant letting Magnus steal one last thing: his ability to look his daughter in the eye and tell her that when something is wrong, you stand up for what's right.

This is integration under pressure. Not a skill performed in a workshop. A father choosing courage over comfort because his values require it, while his body wants to run.

INSIDE THE COURTROOM

Karan's eyes traced the lines of output from LAW-12. He didn't fear it—if anything, he welcomed it. Finally, what had been erased and denied would be visible. Each line, each pattern, felt like a step closer to the reckoning he had been waiting for. The weight of the last few years pressed on him, but beneath it was a clarity he hadn't known in months: the truth could no longer be ignored.

At the defense table Magnus Vale and his three lawyers, all in expensive suits, commiserated as they watched the AI screen with the unease of men watching their own obsolescence.

In the gallery sat Magnus's daughter Emma, hands folded.

"We will begin," Judge Sloane said.

THE FIRST LAYER: THE TARGET

Karan took the stand.

"Mr. Iyer," the prosecutor, Margaret Reeves began, "describe the all-hands meeting of October 2022."

Karan looked directly at Magnus. "He was discussing 'cultural fit.' He stopped, looked at me, and said, *We need people who understand how things work here. Certain cultures understand corporate excellence better than others.'* He held eye contact with me for two seconds. Long enough for everyone to notice."

"What happened in the room?"

"A few people laughed. The nervous kind. Most looked away. I watched them decide, in real time, that they hadn't seen what they'd seen."

"And after?"

"I was erased. Removed from distribution lists. Meetings happened without me. If I complained, I sounded paranoid. 'You weren't on that project,' or 'Didn't you get the email?' Everything was deniable. It was obvious what was happening."

"Why are you here, Mr. Iyer?"

"Because Magnus believed he could do this forever. That confidence came from years of watching nothing happen. I'm here to be the thing that happens."

THE SECOND LAYER: THE FOUNDER'S GRIP

Dr. Annika Lee, the original CTO, appeared via video link. She had been silent for sixteen years.

"I left because I saw what Magnus was," she testified. "He contributed the least capital and had the weakest skills. He understood power. When we succeeded, he became threatened. When your only skill is politics, competence in others becomes a threat."

"Did you warn anyone?"

"Who? The board he hand-picked? I told myself I was just leaving a bad situation. I didn't understand yet that I was leaving people behind to face what I escaped." She looked at Karan. "I took my equity and built a new company. I'm sorry I wasn't braver."

Reeves asked: "In sixteen years, did you follow what happened at the company?"

"I saw names I recognized leave. I told myself it was normal turnover. Then I saw their replacements leave. Then I stopped looking." She paused. "Sixteen years was long enough to build an entire career pretending my silence was a clean break. It wasn't. I just got far enough away that I couldn't hear them."

Reeves turned to the screen. "Mr. Vale maintained control not through contribution, but through elimination. The company bears his name, but the intellectual property, the strategy, the architecture:

none of it is his. He remained because leaving would have exposed the truth: without the people whose work he claimed, Magnus Vale had nothing."

THE THIRD LAYER: THE MASK

Dr. Eva Wells, an organizational psychologist, took the stand.

"Dr. Wells, prior to convening this tribunal, you submitted an report to LAW-12 analyzing Mr. Vale's behavior. Can you summarize it for the court?"

"We analyzed Mr. Vale's behavioral patterns using company data. Mr. Vale shows a consistent physiological stress response to professional excellence in others. His nervous system treats competent colleagues as threats to be managed."

"So, in your assessment, what does that indicate about Mr. Vale?" the prosecutor asked.

"He lacks self-awareness," Dr. Wells explained. "He doesn't recognize his own emotional patterns or how they affect others. Instead, a system of projection has taken hold: his discomfort with other people's competence shows up as seeing them as threats, rather than recognizing his own shortcomings. Without that self-awareness, he can't correct himself. And without self-correction, the pattern just escalates."

"Does this connect to the framework you referenced in your report?"

"Yes. In the Three Pillars framework, what we call self-awareness has been actively replaced by projection in Mr. Vale's case."

She pointed to the LAW-12 output.

"He also disabled the company's bias detection software in 2022. When asked why, he wrote: 'It causes friction.' The system flagged his hiring recommendations seventeen times."

The data manipulation went further. Reeves displayed HR database records showing employees over sixty coded as 'expired' to bypass age discrimination flags in the reporting system. To the algorithm, they weren't terminated. They had simply died. The bias detection system was designed to surface exactly this kind of pattern. Mr. Vale disabled it because it was working.

Reeves checked her list. "I call Arthur Pendelton, former Chief Commercial Officer."

Arthur stood up in the gallery. He was fifty-nine, wearing a gray suit, looking tired but alert.

The screen above the witness stand flashed red.

STATUS: DECEASED.

Judge Sloane frowned. "Please clarify. Is the witness no longer alive?"

The AI voice was synthesized, flat. "Affirmative. Status: Deceased. Cause of death: end of life cycle."

The courtroom turned to look at Arthur, who was walking down the aisle, visibly breathing. The expired coding wasn't an abstraction on a screen. It was a living man declared dead by a system his employer had corrupted.

Reeves pulled up an email.

FROM: Magnus Vale **TO:** Legal **DATE:** Dec 3, 2023

"Doesn't the US treat their people like dogs? Can't we just get rid of them? Do we need a reason? What about being old? Ask legal on a different email trail."

Magnus's lead counsel rose smoothly, walked to the podium in the center of the room, and tapped the tribunal's interface. *Context: Mr. Vale often used hyperbolic language to vent frustration. This was clearly an expression of stress, not a directive to discriminate.*

Reeves didn't even look up. "LAW-12, cross-reference 'hyperbolic language' with employment outcomes."

The screen shifted instantly.

> **QUERY:** [Language: "Dogs", "Rid of them", "Old"] + [Outcome: Termination within 90 days]
>
> **RESULT:** 100% Correlation. **CASES:** 14.

The defense lawyer froze. In the old world, he could've argued "intent" for weeks. In this room, the data already closed the loop between word and deed. He sat down slowly. The old magic didn't work here.

"You wrote 'ask on a different email trail' because," Reeves said, "you knew what you were doing was wrong."

Magnus shifted. His hand went to his collar. He said nothing.

THE FOURTH LAYER: THE CAPTURE

Camila Martinez, former VP of HR, sat in the witness box, pale and trembling.

"Ms. Martinez, the record shows Maria Reyes filed a discrimination complaint at 9:47 a.m. At 10:41 a.m., you emailed Mr. Vale. By 4:15 p.m., a performance improvement plan was being drafted."

"Thirty-six minutes from worker protection to retaliation planning," Reeves noted. "Did you believe the complaint process was fair?"

Camila looked down. "No."

"Then why?"

"I knew what happened to complaints. It turned people into problems to be managed. I was protecting myself from becoming the next Maria."

"When did you learn?" Reeves asked.

"My first year. I escalated a complaint the way the handbook said to. Magnus called me into his office. He didn't raise his voice. He said, 'I need people in your role who understand how things actually work.' The person who filed the complaint was gone within a month. I wasn't. That was the lesson."

"Investigators interviewed former employees," Reeves added. "Every single one was threatened with legal action if they spoke."

"Standard separation language," Camila whispered.

"Standard silencing."

THE FIFTH LAYER: THE BYSTANDERS

John Schneider, Karan's former friend, spoke quietly.

"It happened before. Others were pushed out. But they were quieter, newer. You could tell yourself a story: maybe they weren't the right fit, maybe there was something you didn't see. Karan was different. Everyone liked him. His numbers were the best on the team. There was no story you could tell yourself. Everyone in that room knew exactly what it was."

"That's what made it a demonstration. The retaliation was so over the top. So public that it could only mean one thing: his excellence made leadership look bad, and they made an example of him. Not to solve a problem. To make sure everyone watching got the message."

"And it worked. That's what I'm here to tell you.
The demonstration worked."

He looked at the judges, then back at the floor.

"They called me in. Asked if I'd noticed Karan's 'attitude.' They
weren't investigating; they were shopping for dirt. They asked
me to choose between my friend and my job."

"And?"

"I chose my job. I went back to my desk and didn't warn him."

"How many people knew?"

"Everyone. That's what made it possible. We all made the same
calculation: stay quiet, stay employed. The laughter in those rooms
wasn't joy. It was fear wearing a smile."

John paused, looking at his hands.

"I didn't think of myself as doing something wrong. I thought I was
getting through another day. That's how it works. You don't decide
to become complicit. You just keep living your life. And in the space
between what you see and what you do about it, something starts
to die."

He looked up at the judges.

"Every Sunday, figuratively speaking, we all went to church.
We thought of ourselves as good people. We were good, in every
part of our lives except this one. And this one, we didn't look at."

Chapter Eight called this the failure of discomfort tolerance: the inability to stay present in difficulty when comfort is available. John did not lack the moral clarity to see what was wrong. He lacked the capacity to act on that clarity when acting would cost him. Fifty people in that room had the same moral clarity. All fifty chose comfort. That is not a collection of individual failures. It is a culture designed to make discomfort intolerable.

THE SIXTH LAYER: THE DESTRUCTION

A court officer opened the side door. A young woman of seventeen stepped through. Alina Reyes. She held a worn coin in her hand.

"Please state your relationship to the victim."

"She was my mother."

Alina didn't look at the lawyers. She looked at Magnus.

"My mother was contagious with happiness. She loved fearlessly. She didn't live different versions of herself. And she was destroyed."

She held up the coin. "St. Michael. *'Give us strength to defeat our fears.'* My mom carried it when her father was dying. I carried it when she was dying."

She paused. Her voice caught.

"Now I carry it alone."

"She hit every target. She had no idea anything was wrong until they stopped paying her. They said they couldn't afford it. They paid *him*." She pointed at Magnus. "And he just walked around taking credit for her work."

"You don't make all that drama—the problems, the lies, the whispering behind her back—just to save money. You only do that when something's really messed up."

"Here's what I don't get. If it was about money, you take the money and leave. You didn't leave. You kept going."

She leaned forward looking directly at Magnus, "You made it about her even after she was gone. That's not business. That's sick."

Alina wiped her face.

"I know work problems don't cause cancer. She stopped fighting. Something in her just... gave up."

"You know, it was the silence that hurt her. Not being fired. She could have fought that. It was the people that acted like they were decent, the ones she stayed late to help, who looked away when she only needed one person to say, '**This is wrong.**'"

"She won't see me graduate. She won't meet whoever I marry. She won't hold my kids. They took all of that when they took her will to fight."

"She died without ever hearing the truth. She died thinking she failed."

Alina stopped. Her mouth opened but nothing came. She pressed the coin into her palm until her hands ached.

"She felt sorry for Magnus. She thought he didn't realize his worth."

"And the last thing she said to me was, 'I'm sorry I couldn't stay longer.'"

In the gallery, a woman pressed her hand to her mouth. A man wiped his eyes with his sleeve, not hiding it.

"They called it surrender. It was grace."

Alina looked up. Her voice steadied.

"I am not as generous."

She pulled a folded paper from her pocket. "My mother kept a journal. Names. Dates. Conversations. I'm publishing all of it."

Magnus looked up from his phone.

"Go ahead," she said. "Try to stop me."

Judge Sloane watched Magnus checking his phone during testimony about a woman's death. She made a note. **Conduct is evidence.**

THE RECOGNITION

Judge Sloane looked up from a document. "The court received a written statement from Emma Vale, the defendant's daughter. She asked that it be read into the record."

The courtroom stilled. Magnus's head turned toward the gallery. Emma's seat was empty.

Judge Sloane read: "I have watched my father my whole life. The way he mimicked accents after dinner parties. The way he called employees 'dead weight.' I learned at a young age not to bring friends home. The warmth was performance. People were instruments."

"When I read the testimony about the fear in his office, I recognized it. I've been calculating that fear my whole life."

"Dr. Lee left because she saw what he was. I don't get to leave. But I can stop pretending."

"To Mr. Iyer: you were right to come. You were right to speak."

Judge Sloane set the document down. Magnus stared at the empty seat in the gallery where his daughter was sitting that morning.

> *"If you are neutral in situations of injustice,*
> *you have chosen the side of the oppressor."*
> **Desmond Tutu**

THE JUDGMENT

Three weeks later.

"Magnus Vale is liable for $40.5 million in damages," Judge Sloane read. "Criminal matters referred for prosecution."

"This tribunal cannot redesign every organization," she continued. "We can establish a precedent. LAW-12 surfaced the patterns, but the judgment remains human. Mr. Vale, you held power not through competence, but through the mythology that protected you. You used that power to destroy people whose excellence exposed your inadequacy."

"The tools to identify these patterns exist. The courage to act on them is a choice. We hope this case makes that choice easier for those who come after."

THE AFTERMATH

Six months later.

The legal profession felt the shift first. For decades, employment law operated through procedural friction: delay discovery, isolate complainants, exhaust resources until the truth became too expensive to pursue. When behavioral analytics made pattern reconstruction instantaneous, the calculus changed. The defense strategy of "isolate each claim and argue intent" collapsed against a system that could surface fourteen terminations correlated with a single phrase. The lawyers who adapted fastest were those who recognized what the new tools demanded: not evasion, but accountability architecture. Helping organizations build systems that surface problems before they compound, rather than concealing them after they do. The profession did not transform overnight. It began to.

Karan Iyer works at a tech company building these accountability systems. "We need people who tell the truth when it costs," the CEO told him.

Magnus Vale served eighteen months. The company was broken up. The divisions built on Karan's and Maria's architecture sold at premiums. Magnus's division sold at a 40% discount; due diligence cited "systematic underinvestment." The market had always known: he wasn't the source of value; he was the obstacle to it.

The "Vale Standard" became a global precedent. Companies began assessing leaders differently, not because they suddenly valued empathy, but because they learned that leaders without self-awareness create liability.

One evening, Karan's daughter asked him, "Papa, everyone said you would lose. Did you win?"

He thought about the lost years. The money that couldn't fix the past.

"Justice isn't revenge, sweetheart," he said. "It's clarity. The world finally sees things as they are."

He looked at her. "Yes. We won."

The technology described in this chapter exists. Behavioral analytics, sentiment analysis, and pattern reconstruction are deployed in other domains today. The model of centralized, anonymized data sharing is already the standard in international healthcare research. What is imagined is the coordination: the application of these tools to workplace accountability at scale. The characters are fictional. The harm is not. **Justice requires emotional intelligence. Emotional intelligence requires justice.**

THE WORK AHEAD

You did not read this book to become more effective at work.

Maybe that is what you told yourself. Maybe you were searching for emotional intelligence, for leadership, or for a competitive advantage in the age of AI. Those are respectable, rational reasons, and true as far as they go.

They are not why you stayed.

Perhaps you stayed because something in you recognized what is at stake. Your agency. Your capacity to feel what you feel and choose what you do about it. The relationships that matter most to you. The quiet recognition that convenience is eroding something you cannot name.

You stayed because you want to remain the author of your own life.

This book gave you a framework for that claim. Three pillars:

- Self-Awareness: the capacity to see yourself clearly.

- Self-Mastery: the capacity to stay present when everything in you wants to leave.

- Relational Mastery: the capacity to connect authentically with other people even when connection is difficult.

Together, they form something that cannot be outsourced, delegated, or simulated.

You are not finished becoming who you are. The capacities you have been developing are not professional skills bolted onto a fixed self. They are the architecture of a self still forming. Every time you pause before reacting, you become someone slightly more capable of choosing. Every time you repair a rupture instead of retreating, you become someone more capable of intimacy. Every time you hold complexity without collapsing into certainty, you become someone more capable of wisdom.

THE CHOICE

What makes this possible is how you are built. Neural pathways that fire together strengthen; those that go unused fade. Contemplative traditions discovered this through practice long before neuroscience named it, and both arrived at the same conclusion: **You can change.** The capacity for transformation is standard human equipment.

What our spiritual traditions understand through practice, neuroscience has now confirmed through evidence. What they transmitted through lineage, this book makes accessible as systematic discipline. None of them faced the specific pressure we face: an age that can simulate these capacities without possessing them. That simulation is clarifying. It reveals that much of what we measured as emotional intelligence was pattern recognition all along. The real capacity, the one that changes who you are and not just what you produce, was always embodied. It was developmental and more human than our instruments could detect. Now we have better instruments and we have the added pressure. What remains is the practice.

Atrophy is also standard equipment. It is what happens when we stop practicing because the systems around us make passivity easy and our lives fill with busy.

We value what we measure, fund what we value, and teach what we fund. Literacy became universal only when societies decided it mattered enough to build systems around it. Emotional intelligence is ready for the same transition because the science and the methods exist. What remains is the decision to treat these capacities as infrastructure rather than accessory.

THE RIPPLE

Leadership begins here. Before you can steady others, you must be able to sit with discomfort and fear while managing your own reactivity,.

Leaders who cannot regulate themselves will dysregulate everyone around them. Those who have not examined their own patterns will inflict those patterns on others and call it management.

This is what it looks like when self-regulation is absent. Silence in the hallway. Promotions at the expense of others. The slow erosion of trust when speaking up changes nothing except one's own standing. The Tribunal has made the cost clear.

This is what it looks like when it is present: a team that performs without burning out, a room that feels safe enough for truth, and people who leave a leader feeling grateful and grown.

The distance between those two realities is not talent or luck. It is development. It is the accumulated weight of choices made under pressure, year after year, until the capacity to hold complexity becomes part of who someone is.

What you do ripples further than you see. Regulate under pressure, and those around you regulate more easily. Stay present in difficulty, and you give permission to others to stay as well. These effects are not metaphor; they are measurable in the nervous systems of everyone in the room.

Repeat this across enough rooms and something shifts. Exceptional becomes expected while courage becomes culture. What started as one person's practice becomes the way things are done.

Individual practice matters. Systems that support or erode that practice matter just as much. A person with developed self-awareness can be destroyed by a workplace that punishes honesty. A master of repair can be broken by an institution that treats conflict as betrayal. Individual capacity is necessary. It is not sufficient. The people who build these capacities still need institutions willing to protect them.

THE FRONTIER

The tools at our disposal will grow more powerful, seeing more of us, anticipating more from us, and do more for us than any generation has experienced. They will simulate empathy and generate the language of care, mirroring the responses of a skilled listener.

They will not decide what any of it means.

What machines cannot do is hold emotion. They have no body to register threat, no nervous system to synchronize with another person's, no lived experience that makes a moment of courage different from a performance of one. The same tools that can surveil and sort can also protect and repair, but only if people like you stay awake at the controls. Progress is not just what we build. It is who we become while building.

Convenience is frictionless. Practice is not. For five thousand years, these skills could only be transmitted person to person, teacher to student, parent to child. For the first time, we have tools that could make emotional development visible and teachable at a scale no previous generation imagined. Whether we use them depends on a single decision: **that this intelligence matters enough to measure, to fund, and to protect.**

Woven into every chapter of this book is a fierce hope in our humanity. We should be humbled by how little we understand. We are still learning what we are capable of, and those limits expand with every generation that chooses discomfort over convenience and presence over performance. After years of research, I am **certain** we are connected far more than we are separate, and that our capacity to transform each other is the deepest form of transcendence we possess.

As we stand at the rise of AI inside our lives, we face a choice: **will we lead, or be led?** This book is my answer. These capacities are the bridge between who we are and who we are capable of becoming.

THE CALL

Somewhere ahead is a moment that will test you.

It will not announce itself. It may arrive as a conversation you want to avoid, a decision that costs you comfort, or a quiet chance to protect someone who is not in the room.

In that moment you will feel the familiar pull toward speed, toward defense, toward avoidance. You will also feel something else: a small space opening between what you feel and what you do.

That space is the territory this book has been mapping.

You can hand that space to the systems around you, or you can hold it yourself. You can notice your body, name what you feel, remember what you value, and choose the response that aligns with who you are becoming.

If you do this once, you will feel the difference. If you do it often, **you will become the difference.**

The age of AI will be remembered for its tools. It will also be remembered for the people who refused to surrender judgment, presence, or courage to anything they built. That choice does not belong to the machines.

It belongs to you.

The father who sat in his car, unable to go inside. He found his way back. Not through insight alone. Through practice. Through choosing, again and again, to be present when everything in him wanted to disappear.

He was never just a character in a book. He is everyone who has lost themselves and is finding their way home.

Including you.

Your practice is not private. It is civilization learning to steer.

ACKNOWLEDGMENTS

This book was shaped by many minds and many conversations.

I am grateful to the researchers, thinkers, and teachers whose work in spirituality, emotional intelligence, psychology, neuroscience, and human development formed the foundation of these ideas. Your scholarship made it possible to argue that emotional intelligence is not sentiment, but structure. Not softness, but strength.

I am thankful to the colleagues and early readers who challenged my thinking, asked better questions, and resisted easy answers. Your clarity sharpened this work.

Rocky Mountain AI Interest Group (RMAIIG) and its subgroups, thank you for building a serious community of inquiry. To Trident Booksellers and Café, thank you for lending me your table space for the long hours that allowed this manuscript to take final shape.

For those who felt like steady light throughout this process: Brittanne Blose Sciarretti, Christopher N.Q. Nguyen, Cortney Stauffer, Alison Rooney, Ann Travis, Jaime Tousignant, Morgan Wade, Debra Lodge, Carol O'Malley Marland, Yvonne Caravia, and my colleagues who continue to show their support and collaborate professionally. Lightyear's Match.

Milton Jaimes, for keeping our beautiful children first.

Ahmet Samsa, thank you for the disciplined and thoughtful interior design work and cover. Andrea Corley, comprehensive copy editing.

APPENDIX NAVIGATION

A re-entry map for practitioners returning to this toolkit.

APPENDIX A: MEASUREMENT AND REFERENCE

APPENDIX B: AI REFERENCE

MEASUREMENT AND REFERENCE

Measurement without ethics becomes surveillance. This appendix provides frameworks for understanding how emotional intelligence can be assessed, how to recognise development over time, and the principles that must govern any measurement system. The goal is insight that serves growth, not data that enables control.

TABLE A.1: Measurement Methods and Instruments

Method	Instruments	What It Measures	Strengths	Limitations
Self-Report	EQ-i 2.0 (Bar-On, 133 items) TEIQue (Petrides, 153) SSEIT (Schutte, 33) SEI (Six Seconds, 77)	Subjective perception of emotional capacity	Easy to administer; widely validated	Relies on self-awareness to assess self-awareness; can be gamed
Performance	MSCEIT (Mayer-Salovey-Caruso, 141 items)	Emotional reasoning and problem-solving	Objective scoring; resistant to self-deception	Measures knowledge, not embodied capacity; AI can replicate
360-Degree	ESCI (Goleman/Boyatzis, 68 items)	Behavioural evidence from observers	Ecologically valid; real-world impact	Depends on rater honesty; measures perception
Physiological	HRV (Oura, WHOOP), EEG, GSR	Autonomic flexibility, neural integration	Cannot be faked; continuous	Requires equipment; baselines vary
Behavioural	Communication pattern analysis, typing dynamics	Patterns across digital interactions	Hard to game at scale	Privacy concerns; cultural norms vary
Relational	HRV synchrony, hyperscanning EEG	Nervous system coordination between people	Measures attunement directly	Emerging technology; context required

Method	Instruments	What It Measures	Strengths	Limitations
AI-Driven	Voice/speech analytics, facial analysis, MER	Vocal tone, micro-expressions, body language	Real-time; scalable	Cultural bias; cannot infer meaning
Simulation	VR emotion scenarios	Emotional responses in controlled environments	Ecological validity	Expensive; emerging field

Emotional expression norms differ by culture. Baseline nervous system activation varies by individual. Scores should be interpreted relative to role, culture, and context, not against a single global ideal.

TABLE A.2: Pillar Performance Indicators

Skill	Early Signals	Developed Capacity	Regression Signs
Interoception	Locates tension during stress	Reads body signals before cognition	Numb to cues; acts before noticing
Emotional Literacy	3–5 emotion words	50+ terms; subtle distinctions	Returns to "fine," "stressed"
Meta-Awareness	Notices patterns after	Catches reactions before acting	Blind to triggers
Values Alignment	Names core values	Decisions match values consistently	Compromises under pressure
Self-Command	One regulation strategy	Multiple strategies; adapts	Hijacked by emotion
Discomfort Tolerance	Stays with mild discomfort	Reframes stress as energy	Avoids difficulty
Resilience	Recovers within days	Rapid baseline return; learns	Prolonged depletion
Empathy	Recognises obvious cues	Senses states before words	Misreads others
Communication	Listens without interrupting	Full presence; repairs	Formulates while "listening"
Conflict Navigation	Calm in mild disagreement	Regulated in heated exchanges	Escalates or avoids
Persuasiveness	Articulates clearly	Inspires voluntary commitment	Manipulates or coerces

TABLE A.3: Integrated Measurement Indicators (Tiered Measurement and Governance Model (Neural + Digital + Physiological + Behavioral combined)

Skill	Neural	Physiological	Digital/Behavioural
Interoception	Insula activation	Heartbeat detection 70%+	Pauses before responding
Emotional Literacy	Prefrontal activation during labelling	Reduced amygdala reactivity	50+ emotion terms used
Meta-Awareness	DMN–Executive coordination	Stable HRV during reflection	Self-corrections before sending
Values Alignment	vmPFC–emotion integration	Coherent values-aligned response	Calendar matches priorities
Self-Command	Prefrontal-limbic connectivity	HRV stability under load	Steady patterns in conflict
Discomfort Tolerance	Sustained prefrontal activation	Adaptive cortisol	Consistent response to difficulty
Resilience	Rapid neural baseline return	HRV recovery; sleep quality	Returns to baseline after setbacks
Empathy	Mirror neuron activation	Physiological synchrony	Empathic language in distress
Communication	Language–emotion integration	Neural coupling	Balanced turn-taking
Conflict Navigation	Maintained prefrontal function	HRV stability in disagreement	De-escalation patterns
Persuasiveness	Social cognition integration	Coherent state	"We" pronouns; no coercion

TABLE A.4: Tiered Measurement and Governance

Tier	Purpose	Data Processing	Consent	Governance
1: Personal	Growth	Edge; never leaves device	User-initiated; pause anytime	Self-governed
2: Aggregate	Patterns	Federated; differential privacy	Explicit opt-in	Third-party audit
3: High-Stakes	Decisions	Temporary; deleted after	Informed; right to decline	Human + external oversight

TABLE A.5: Ethics, Privacy, and AI Limits

Principle	Implementation	Why It Matters
User Control	You choose what, when, who sees it	Development, not surveillance
Privacy by Design	Edge processing; data stays on device	Architectural, not policy protection
Transparency	Clear explanation of methods	No black boxes
Contestability	Challenge assessments; provide context	Human judgment overrides algorithm
Justice	Accounts for unequal access	Measurement without justice is oppression
Human Review	Algorithm informs; humans decide	Context determines interpretation
AI Limits	Cannot understand embodiment, courage, integrity	Machines process; humans experience

TABLE A.6: Core Emotions and Body Expressions

Based on Plutchik's Wheel of Emotions and body mapping research.

Emotion	Related Feelings	Body Signals
Anger	Frustrated, annoyed, enraged, resentful	Heat in chest/face, clenched jaw, shoulder tension
Fear	Nervous, anxious, terrified, apprehensive	Chest tightness, shallow breathing, cold extremities
Joy	Happy, content, proud, excited, playful	Warmth in chest, relaxed muscles, open posture
Sadness	Lonely, disappointed, grief-stricken	Heaviness in chest, throat tightness, fatigue
Disgust	Disapproving, embarrassed, revolted	Nausea, throat constriction, pulling away
Surprise	Shocked, confused, amazed, startled	Sharp inhale, widened eyes, momentary stillness
Trust	Comfortable, secure, compassionate	Warmth in chest, relaxed breathing, steady heartbeat
Anticipation	Curious, hopeful, watchful, eager	Forward lean, quickened breath, core alertness

TABLE A.7: Recovery and Resilience Framework

Stage	Techniques	Research Foundation
Awareness	Journalling, body scanning, mindful observation	Interoception; mindfulness research
Acceptance	Compassion practice, peer support, self-permission	ACT (Hayes); trauma-informed models
Processing	Narrative work, cognitive reframing, therapy	CBT (Beck); narrative therapy
Release	Breathwork, movement, stress cycle completion	Polyvagal Theory (Porges); somatic experiencing
Restoration	Values work, goals, deliberate re-engagement	ACT values integration; resilience training
Integration	Life story work, identity reconstruction	Post-traumatic growth; narrative identity
Connection	Social support, group processes, co-regulation	Biopsychosocial models; attachment research

AI REFERENCE

Understanding what AI systems actually do, and what they cannot do, is essential for anyone navigating the integration of these tools into human systems.

TABLE B.1: Main Categories of AI

AI Category	What It Does	Relevance to EI
Machine Learning	Identifies statistical patterns in data through iterative training rather than explicit rules. Includes supervised, unsupervised, and deep learning methods.	Detects emotional patterns across text, voice, and behavior at population scale. Powers most emotion recognition tools.
Natural Language Processing (NLP)	Analyses and generates human language by modelling grammar, semantics, and pragmatic context. Includes sentiment analysis and text classification.	Identifies emotional tone, urgency, and relational dynamics in written and spoken communication.
Computer Vision	Extracts information from images and video using convolutional neural networks and object detection algorithms.	Recognizes facial action units (Ekman), gaze direction, posture, and gesture. Foundation of facial emotion recognition systems.
Affective Computing	Computing that relates to, arises from, or influences emotions (Picard, 1997). Integrates physiological sensing, expression analysis, and adaptive response.	The core discipline bridging AI and emotion. Encompasses emotion recognition, affective response, and emotionally intelligent interfaces.
Large Language Models (LLMs)	Transformer-based models trained on billions of text tokens that generate contextually appropriate language. Capable of in-context learning without retraining.	Score comparably to humans on standard EI assessments. This reveals what EI tests actually measure: pattern recognition, not embodied emotional capacity.
Reinforcement Learning	Agents that learn optimal behavior through trial, error, and reward signals within an environment. Adapts strategies based on outcomes.	Powers adaptive coaching systems and personalized feedback. Relevant to developing AI that adjusts to individual emotional development trajectories.

TABLE B.2: AI-Assisted Emotional Measurement Channels

Channel	What AI Analyzes	Emotional Signals	Privacy Risk
Voice	Pitch, tempo, volume, tremor, prosody	Stress, anxiety, confidence, deception	Always-on recording; consent
Text	Word choice, syntax, emoji, response time	Mood, personality, emotional state	Persistent records; context loss
Face	Action units, gaze, micro-expressions	Basic emotions, attention, engagement	Surveillance; cultural bias
Physiology	HRV, skin conductance, EEG, cortisol	Arousal, regulation, cognitive load	Intimate data; health inferences
Behavior	Typing patterns, app usage, movement	Stress, routine disruption, engagement	Pervasive tracking; profiling
Multimodal	Integrated video, audio, text, biometrics	Cross-channel emotional patterns	Aggregation risk; requires multiple signals

TABLE B.3: What AI Can Infer versus What Humans Must Decide

AI Infers	Humans Decide
Statistical patterns across large datasets	Whether patterns are meaningful in context
Correlations between behaviors and outcomes	Causation and ethical implications
Emotional signals from voice, text, face	What those signals mean for this person
Deviation from individual baseline	Whether deviation indicates problem or growth
Probability of emotional state	Appropriate response to that state
Comparison to population norms	Whether norms apply to this individual
Risk scores and predictions	How to weigh risks against dignity and autonomy

TABLE B.4: Bias and Error Sources in Emotional AI

Source	How It Manifests	Mitigation
Training Data	Models trained on WEIRD populations misread other cultures	Diverse datasets; cultural calibration
Labeling	Annotators' assumptions embedded in ground truth	Diverse teams; explicit protocols
Context Blindness	Same expression, different meaning in different settings	Human review; contextual metadata
Demographic Gaps	Lower accuracy for underrepresented groups	Targeted collection; group validation
False Precision	Confidence scores overstate certainty	Uncertainty quantification; calibration
Gaming	Users produce desired signals without genuine change	Multimodal; long-term patterns
Over-Reliance	Leaders treat algorithmic output as truth	Human judgment requirement; audit trails

TABLE B.5: Integration by Domain

Domain	Integration Challenge	Without EI	With EI
Education	Content + well-being + readiness + culture	Teaching to metrics; students disengage	Rigor with safety; learning environments
Healthcare	Data + narrative + compliance + quality of life	Diagnostic accuracy; missed patient context	Evidence with empathy; relational attunement
Leadership	Direction + capacity + pressure + culture	Performance; burnout	Sustainability; vision with execution
AI Development	Capability + ethics + impact + consequences	Metrics without misuse consideration	Innovation with responsibility

TABLE B.6: Key Researchers and Contributors

Foundational EI Frameworks	
Salovey & Mayer	Defined EI as measurable intelligence (1990). Four-branch model. Created the MSCEIT.
Daniel Goleman	EI in mainstream awareness (1995). Five-domain model for leadership performance.
Reuven Bar-On	Developed EQ-i (1997), first validated EI measure. Trait-based model.
Marc Brackett	RULER framework, Yale. Emotional granularity and school-based EI programs.

Neuroscience of Emotion	
Antonio Damasio	Somatic marker hypothesis. Emotion as foundational to reasoning. Descartes' Error (1994).
Lisa Feldman Barrett	Theory of Constructed Emotion. Brain constructs emotions from interoception, prediction, context.
A. D. (Bud) Craig	Traced interoceptive signals to anterior insula as substrate of subjective feeling.
Joseph LeDoux	Mapped amygdala's role in fear processing. The Emotional Brain (1996).
Matthew Lieberman	Affect labeling: naming emotions engages prefrontal cortex, reduces amygdala activation.
Richard Davidson	Neuroplasticity of emotion circuits. Contemplative practice changes brain structure.
Vinod Menon	Triple-network model (2011): Salience, Default Mode, Executive networks.
Randy L. Buckner	Default Mode Network structure; self-referential processing and meaning-making.
Horner & Kaplan	Emotion regulation predicts working memory (2025). 72% cognitive-emotional neural overlap.
Paul Ekman	Universal facial expressions and micro-expressions. Nonverbal emotional communication.

Social Neuroscience and Relational Capacity

Stephen Porges	Polyvagal Theory. Autonomic nervous system supports social engagement and co-regulation.
Giacomo Rizzolatti	Discovered mirror neurons (1996). Empathy, imitation, action-emotion representation.
Uri Hasson	Neural coupling: listener-speaker synchronisation during effective dialogue.
John Gottman	Research-based relationship science. 5:1 ratio, repair mechanisms, conflict prediction.
Louis Cozolino	Relationships shape brain development. The Neuroscience of Human Relationships (2014).
Amy Edmondson	Psychological safety in teams. Interpersonal risk-taking produces better outcomes.
Sara Konrath	48% decline in empathic concern (1979–2009). Evidence for the emotional recession.

Cognition, Regulation, and Development

Daniel Kahneman	Cognitive biases and dual-process thinking. System 1/System 2 interaction.
Jon Kabat-Zinn	MBSR. Contemplative practice in clinical settings with measurable regulation outcomes.
Daniel Siegel	Mindsight and neural integration as foundation of mental health and self-awareness.
Alia Crum	Stress mindset determines outcomes. Reappraising stress produces measurable differences.
Joshua Greene	Moral decision-making is emotion-first. fMRI of emotion-reason interaction in ethics.
Robin Dunbar	Social brain hypothesis. Brain size evolved for relational complexity, not abstraction.
Susan Fiske	Dehumanisation and neural-level bias preceding conscious awareness.
James Gross	Process model of emotion regulation. Framework for managing responses at different stages.
Killgore & Yurgelun-Todd	fMRI differentiating Ability and Trait EI through distinct neural activation patterns.
Barbey & Operskalski	Mapped EI to brain regions. Prefrontal-limbic integration and network coordination.

CITATIONS BY CHAPTER

All references organized by chapter location.

INTRODUCTION: THE PAUSE

1. Barrett, Lisa Feldman. *How Emotions Are Made: The Secret Life of the Brain*. Boston: Houghton Mifflin Harcourt, 2017.

2. Descartes, René. *Discourse on the Method*. 1637. Also: Damasio, Antonio. *Descartes' Error: Emotion, Reason, and the Human Brain*. New York: Putnam, 1994.

3. Mattingly, Victoria, and Kurt Kraiger. "Can Emotional Intelligence Be Trained? A Meta-Analytical Investigation." *Human Resource Management Review* 29, no. 2 (2019): 140–155.

4. Rizzolatti, Giacomo, and Laila Craighero. "The Mirror-Neuron System." *Annual Review of Neuroscience* 27 (2004): 169–192.

5. Salovey, Peter, and John D. Mayer. "Emotional Intelligence." *Imagination, Cognition and Personality* 9, no. 3 (1990): 185–211.

CHAPTER 1: WHAT MACHINES CANNOT BE

6. Barrett, Lisa Feldman. *How Emotions Are Made: The Secret Life of the Brain*. Boston: Houghton Mifflin Harcourt, 2017.

7. Carpenter, Malinda, Katharina Nagell, and Michael Tomasello. "Social Cognition, Joint Attention, and Communicative Competence." *Monographs of the Society for Research in Child Development* 63, no. 4 (1998): 1–143.

8. Damasio, Antonio. *Descartes' Error: Emotion, Reason, and the Human Brain*. New York: Putnam, 1994.

9. DeCasper, Anthony J., and William P. Fifer. "Of Human Bonding." *Science* 208, no. 4448 (1980): 1174–1176.

10. Descartes, René. *Discourse on the Method.* 1637.

11. European Data Protection Board, *Five European Data Protection Authorities Fined Clearview AI* (2022–2024).

12. noyb. "Criminal Complaint Filed Against Clearview AI." Press release, October 28, 2025.

13. Öhman, Arne, Anders Flykt, and Francisco Esteves. "Emotion Drives Attention: Detecting the Snake in the Grass." *Journal of Experimental Psychology: General* 130, no. 3 (2001): 466–478.

14. Privacy International, *Five European Data Protection Authorities Fined Clearview AI* (2024).

15. Rizzolatti, Giacomo, Leonardo Fadiga, Vittorio Gallese, and Luciano Fogassi. "Premotor Cortex and the Recognition of Motor Actions." *Cognitive Brain Research* 3, no. 2 (1996): 131–141.

16. Salti, Maya, Yair Bar-Haim, and Dominique Lamy. "The Time Course of Biased Competition." *Journal of Cognitive Neuroscience* 21, no. 6 (2009): 1277–1286.

17. Smith, Linda Tuhiwai. *Decolonizing Methodologies: Research and Indigenous Peoples.* 3rd ed. London: Zed Books, 2021.

18. Warneken, Felix, and Michael Tomasello. "Altruistic Helping in Human Infants and Young Chimpanzees." *Science* 311, no. 5765 (2006): 1301–1303.

19. Yu, Feiyang, Alex Moehring, Oishi Banerjee, Tobias Salz, Nikhil Agarwal, and Pranav Rajpurkar. "Heterogeneity and Predictors of the Effects of AI Assistance on Radiologists." *Nature Medicine* 30 (2024): 837–849.

CHAPTER 2: THE HAUNTED JOB APPLICATION

20. Bogen, Miranda, and Aaron Rieke. *Help Wanted*. New York: Upturn, 2018.

21. Bradberry, Travis, and Jean Greaves. *Emotional Intelligence 2.0*. San Diego: TalentSmart, 2009.

22. Capgemini Research Institute. *Emotional Intelligence: The Essential Skillset for the Age of AI*. Paris: Capgemini, 2019.

23. Cherniss, Cary. *The Business Case for Emotional Intelligence*. CREIO, 2003.

24. Cornerstone. *Global State of the Skills Economy 2024*. Santa Monica, CA: Cornerstone OnDemand, 2024.

25. Feist, Gregory J., and Frank Barron. "Emotional Intelligence and Academic Intelligence in Career and Life Success." Paper presented at the Annual Convention of the American Psychological Society, San Francisco, June 1996.

26. Feist, Gregory J., and Frank Barron. "Emotional Intelligence and Academic Intelligence in Career and Life Success." *Journal of Research in Personality* 37, no. 2 (2003): 62–88.

27. Goleman, Daniel. *Emotional Intelligence: Why It Can Matter More Than IQ*. New York: Bantam Books, 1995.

28. Goleman, Daniel. *Working with Emotional Intelligence*. New York: Bantam Books, 1998.

29. Raghavan, Manish, et al. "Mitigating Bias in Algorithmic Hiring." *In Proceedings of FAT* (2020): 469–481.

30. Spencer, Lyle M., David C. McClelland, and Allan Kelner. *Competency Assessment Methods.* Boston: Hay/McBer, 1997.

31. Spencer, Lyle M., and Signe M. Spencer. *Competence at Work.* New York: Wiley, 1993.

32. World Economic Forum. *The Future of Jobs Report 2025.* Geneva: World Economic Forum, 2025..

CHAPTER 3: A HISTORY OF HUMAN UNDERSTANDING

33. Abimbola, Wande. *Ifá: An Exposition of Ifá Literary Corpus.* Oxford: Oxford University Press, 1976.

34. Aristotle. *The Nicomachean Ethics.* Translated by David Ross. Oxford: Oxford University Press, 2009. (Originally c. 350 BCE).

35. Armstrong, Karen. *The Great Transformation: The Beginning of Our Religious Traditions.* New York: Knopf, 2006.

36. Aurelius, Marcus. *Meditations.* Translated by Gregory Hays. New York: Modern Library, 2002. (Originally 180 CE).

37. Bar-On, Reuven. *The Emotional Quotient Inventory (EQ-i): Technical Manual.* Toronto: Multi-Health Systems, 1997.

38. Davidson, Richard J., and Antoine Lutz. "Buddha's Brain: Neuroplasticity and Meditation." *IEEE Signal Processing Magazine* 25, no. 1 (2008): 176–184.

39. Durlak, Joseph A., Roger P. Weissberg, Allison B. Dymnicki, Rebecca D. Taylor, and Kriston B. Schellinger. "The Impact of Enhancing Students' Social and Emotional Learning: A Meta-Analysis of School-Based Universal Interventions." *Child Development* 82, no. 1 (2011): 405–432.

40. James, William. *The Principles of Psychology*. Vols. 1–2. New York: Henry Holt, 1890.

41. Jaspers, Karl. *The Origin and Goal of History*. New Haven: Yale University Press, 1953.

42. Jung, C. G. *Alchemical Studies* (Collected Works, Vol. 13). Princeton: Princeton University Press, 1967.

43. Metz, Thaddeus. "Ubuntu as a Moral Theory and Human Rights in South Africa." *African Human Rights Law Journal* 11, no. 2 (2011): 532–559.

44. Salovey, Peter, and John D. Mayer. "Emotional Intelligence." *Imagination, Cognition and Personality* 9, no. 3 (1990): 185–211.

45. UNESCO. *Ifá Divination System: Masterpiece of the Oral and Intangible Heritage of Humanity*. Paris: UNESCO, 2005.

CHAPTER 4: THE TRANSCENDENT ADVANTAGE

46. Baldwin, James, and William F. Buckley. "Is the American Dream at the Expense of the American Negro?" Debate, Cambridge Union Society, February 18, 1965. BBC.

47. Barrett, Lisa F. "The Theory of Constructed Emotion." *Social Cognitive and Affective Neuroscience* 12, no. 1 (2017): 1–23.

48. Buccola, Nicholas. *The Fire Is upon Us*. Princeton: Princeton University Press, 2019.

49. Buhle, Jason T., James L. Silvers, Kevin S. Wager, et al. "Cognitive Reappraisal of Emotion: A Meta-Analysis of Human Neuroimaging Studies." *Cerebral Cortex* 24, no. 11 (2014): 2981–2990.

50. Carpenter, Michelle, Kristi Nagell, and Michael Tomasello. *Social Cognition, Joint Attention, and Communicative Competence.* Monographs of the Society for Research in Child Development 63, no. 4 (1998): 1–143.

51. Craig, A. D. "How Do You Feel—Now? The Anterior Insula and Human Awareness." *Nature Reviews Neuroscience* 10, no. 1 (2009): 59–70

52. Dunbar, Robin I. M. "The Social Brain Hypothesis." *Evolutionary Anthropology* 6, no. 5 (1998): 178–190.

53. Gardner, Howard. *Frames of Mind: The Theory of Multiple Intelligences.* New York: Basic Books, 1983

54. Jung, Rex E., and Richard J. Haier. "The Parieto-Frontal Integration Theory (P-FIT) of Intelligence." *Behavioral and Brain Sciences* 30, no. 2 (2007): 135–154.

55. Perner, Josef, and Heinz Wimmer. "Do Children Understand the Representational Mind?" *Journal of Experimental Child Psychology* 39, no. 3 (1985): 437–471.

56. Tomasello, Michael. *Becoming Human: A Theory of Ontogeny.* Cambridge, MA: Harvard University Press, 2019.

CHAPTER 5: THE CRISIS OF PASSIVE ADOPTION

57. Kellerman, Barbara. *The End of Leadership*. New York: Harper Business, 2012.

58. Konrath, Sara H., Edward H. O'Brien, and Courtney Hsing. "Changes in Dispositional Empathy in American College Students over Time." *Personality and Social Psychology Review* 15, no. 2 (2011): 180–198.

59. Uhls, Yalda T., Adam C. Ellison, Joshua L. Caplan, et al. "Five Days at Outdoor Education Camp without Screens Improves Preteen Skills with Nonverbal Emotion Cues." *Computers in Human Behavior* 39 (2014): 387–392.

CHAPTER 6: THE CHOICE

No numbered citations; narrative chapter.

CHAPTER 7: SELF-AWARENESS

60. Barrett, Lisa F. *How Emotions Are Made: The Secret Life of the Brain*. Boston: Houghton Mifflin Harcourt, 2017.

61. Barrett, Lisa F. "The Theory of Constructed Emotion." *Social Cognitive and Affective Neuroscience* 12, no. 1 (2017): 1–23.

62. Beck, Aaron T. *Cognitive Therapy and the Emotional Disorders*. New York: International Universities Press, 1976.

63. Brackett, Marc A. *Permission to Feel*. New York: Celadon Books, 2019.

64. Brown, Brené. *Daring Greatly*. New York: Gotham Books, 2012.

65. Brown, Brené. *The Gifts of Imperfection*. Center City, MN: Hazelden, 2010.

66. Covey, Stephen R. *The Seven Habits of Highly Effective People*. New York: Free Press, 1989.

67. Craig, A. D. "How Do You Feel—Now? The Anterior Insula and Human Awareness." *Nature Reviews Neuroscience* 10, no. 1 (2009): 59–70.

68. Damasio, Antonio. *Descartes' Error: Emotion, Reason, and the Human Brain*. New York: Putnam, 1994.

69. Devlin, Jacob, Ming-Wei Chang, Kenton Lee, and Kristina Toutanova. "BERT: Pre-training of Deep Bidirectional Transformers for Language Understanding." arXiv:1810.04805, 2018.

70. Frankl, Viktor E. *Man's Search for Meaning*. Boston: Beacon Press, 1946/2006.

71. Gigerenzer, Gerd. *Gut Feelings: The Intelligence of the Unconscious*. New York: Viking, 2007.

72. Greene, Joshua D. *Moral Tribes: Emotion, Reason, and the Gap Between Us and Them*. New York: Penguin Press, 2013.

73. Haidt, Jonathan. *The Righteous Mind: Why Good People Are Divided by Politics and Religion*. New York: Vintage, 2012.

74. Hinton, Geoffrey E. "Reducing the Dimensionality of Data with Neural Networks." *Science* 313, no. 5786 (2006): 504–507.

75. Kabat-Zinn, Jon. *Full Catastrophe Living*. New York: Delacorte Press, 1990.

76. Kahneman, Daniel. *Thinking, Fast and Slow*. New York: Farrar, Straus and Giroux, 2011.

77. Lieberman, Matthew D. *Social: Why Our Brains Are Wired to Connect*. New York: Crown, 2013.

78. Lieberman, Matthew D., et al. "Putting Feelings into Words: Affect Labeling Disrupts Amygdala Activity." *Psychological Science* 18, no. 5 (2007): 421–428.

79. Litz, Brett T., et al. "Moral Injury and Moral Repair in War Veterans: A Review and Framework." *Clinical Psychology Review* 29, no. 8 (2009): 695–706.

80. Mikolov, Tomas, Kai Chen, Greg Corrado, and Jeffrey Dean. "Efficient Estimation of Word Representations in Vector Space." arXiv:1301.3781, 2013.

81. Nussbaum, Martha C. *Creating Capabilities: The Human Development Approach*. Cambridge, MA: Harvard University Press, 2011.

82. Rogers, Carl. *On Becoming a Person*. Boston: Houghton Mifflin, 1961.

83. Schwartz, Shalom H. "Universals in the Content and Structure of Values: Theoretical Advances and Empirical Tests in 20 Countries." *Advances in Experimental Social Psychology* 25 (1992): 1–65.

84. Sherrington, Charles S. *The Integrative Action of the Nervous System*. New Haven: Yale University Press, 1906.

85. Siegel, Daniel J. *Mindsight: The New Science of Personal Transformation*. New York: Bantam, 2010.

86. Simon, Herbert A. "What Is an 'Explanation' of Behavior?" *Psychological Science* 3, no. 3 (1992): 150–161.

87. Wittgenstein, Ludwig. *Tractatus Logico-Philosophicus.* Translated by C. K. Ogden. London: Routledge & Kegan Paul, 1922.

CHAPTER 8: SELF-MASTERY

88. Adler, A. B., & Castro, C. A. 2019. "Soldier Resilience: Psychological and Behavioral Factors." *Military Medicine* 184 (Supplement_1): 34–40.

89. Aston-Jones, G., & Cohen, J. D. 2005. "An Integrative Theory of Locus Coeruleus–Norepinephrine Function." *Annual Review of Neuroscience* 28: 403–450.

90. Campbell, J. 1949. *The Hero with a Thousand Faces.* Pantheon Books.

91. Crum, A. J., Salovey, P., & Achor, S. 2013. "Rethinking Stress: The Role of Mindsets in Determining the Stress Response." *Journal of Personality and Social Psychology* 104 (4): 716–733

92. Ekman, P. 1992. "An Argument for Basic Emotions." *Cognition & Emotion* 6 (3–4): 169–200.

93. Gross, J. J. 2015. "Emotion Regulation: Current Status and Future Prospects." *Psychological Inquiry* 26 (1): 1–26.

94. Huberman, A. Research on physiological sighs. Stanford University.

95. Ipsos. 2024. *World Mental Health Day 2024 Global Survey.* October 2024.

96. Jamieson, J. P., Nock, M. K., & Mendes, W. B. 2012. "Mind over Matter: Reappraising Arousal Improves Cardiovascular and Cognitive Responses to Stress." *Journal of Experimental Psychology: General* 141 (3): 417–422.

97. LeDoux, J. E. 1996. *The Emotional Brain*. Simon & Schuster.

98. Loehr, J. 1994. *Stress for Success*. Crown Business.

99. Loehr, J., & Schwartz, T. 2003. *The Power of Full Engagement*. Free Press.

100. Lyubomirsky, S. 2008. *The How of Happiness*. Penguin Press.

101. NATO Human Factors and Medicine Panel. 2021. *Integrating Cognitive Enhancement Technologies into Human Performance*. NATO Science and Technology Organization.

102. Robbins, M. 2017. *The 5 Second Rule*. Savio Republic.

103. Spike, K. Personal communication, performance coaching context.

104. Stanislavski, K. 1936. *An Actor Prepares*. Theatre Arts Books.

105. Strasberg, L. 1987. *A Dream of Passion*. Little, Brown.

106. U.S. Army Performance Enhancement and Resilience (PEAR) Program documentation. Multiple years. U.S. Army Center for Initial Military Training.

107. Yerkes, R. M., & Dodson, J. D. 1908. "The Relation of Strength of Stimulus to Rapidity of Habit-Formation." *Journal of Comparative Neurology and Psychology* 18 (5): 459–482.

CHAPTER 9: RELATIONAL MASTERY

108. Ahbez, E. 1948. "Nature Boy." Capitol Records.

109. Ambady, N., & Rosenthal, R. 1992. "Thin Slices of Expressive Behavior as Predictors of Interpersonal Consequences." *Psychological Bulletin* 111 (2): 256–274.

110. Amodio, D. M. 2014. "The Neuroscience of Prejudice and Stereotyping." *Nature Reviews Neuroscience* 15 (10): 670–682.

111. Buolamwini, J., & Gebru, T. 2018. "Gender Shades." *Proceedings of the 1st Conference on Fairness, Accountability and Transparency*, 77–91.

112. Cozolino, L. 2014. *The Neuroscience of Human Relationships.* 2nd ed. W. W. Norton.

113. Dumas, G., et al. 2010. "Inter-Brain Synchronization during Social Interaction." *PLoS ONE* 5 (8): e12166.

114. Edmondson, A. C. 1999. "Psychological Safety and Learning Behavior in Work Teams." *Administrative Science Quarterly* 44 (2): 350–383.

115. Einstein, A. (Attributed). "In the Middle of Difficulty Lies Opportunity."

116. Fiske, S. T. 2011. *Envy Up, Scorn Down.* Russell Sage Foundation.

117. French, J. R. P., & Raven, B. 1959. "The Bases of Social Power." In *Studies in Social Power*, edited by D. Cartwright, 150–167. Institute for Social Research.

118.   Goldstein, P., et al. 2017. "Brain-to-Brain Coupling during Handholding Is Associated with Pain Reduction." *Proceedings of the National Academy of Sciences* 114 (11): E2528–E2537.

119.   Gottman, J. M., & Silver, N. 1999. *The Seven Principles for Making Marriage Work*. Crown.

120.   Harris, L. T., & Fiske, S. T. 2006. "Dehumanizing the Lowest of the Low." *Psychological Science* 17 (10): 847–853.

121.   Hasson, U., et al. 2012. "Brain-to-Brain Coupling: A Mechanism for Creating and Sharing a Social World." *Trends in Cognitive Sciences* 16 (2): 114–121.

122.   Krznaric, R. 2014. *Empathy: Why It Matters, and How to Get It*. Perigee Books.

123.   Mehrabian, A. 1971. *Silent Messages: Implicit Communication of Emotions and Attitudes*. Wadsworth.

124.   O'Neil, C. 2016. *Weapons of Math Destruction*. Crown.

125.   Porges, S. W. 2011. *The Polyvagal Theory*. W. W. Norton.

126.   Sun Tzu. 5th century BCE/2003. *The Art of War*. Translated by L. Giles. Dover.

127.   U.S. Surgeon General. 2023. *Our Epidemic of Loneliness and Isolation*. U.S. Department of Health and Human Services.

128.   Waldinger, R. J., & Schulz, M. S. 2023. *The Good Life*. Simon & Schuster.

CHAPTER 10: MEASURING WHAT MATTERS

129.   Bar-On, R. 2006. "The Bar-On Model of Emotional-Social Intelligence." *Psicothema* 18: 13–25.

130.   Dwork, C., & Roth, A. 2014. "The Algorithmic Foundations of Differential Privacy." *Foundations and Trends in Theoretical Computer Science* 9 (3–4): 211–407.

131.   Goodhart, C. A. E. 1984. *Monetary Theory and Practice: The UK Experience.* Macmillan.

132.   Gould, S. J. 1981. *The Mismeasure of Man.* W. W. Norton.

133.   Mayer, J. D., Salovey, P., & Caruso, D. R. 2002. *Mayer-Salovey-Caruso Emotional Intelligence Test (MSCEIT) User's Manual.* Multi-Health Systems.

134.   Saberi, M., & Beyraghi, N. 2023. "Can GPT-4 Pass Emotional Intelligence Tests?" arXiv preprint arXiv:2303.01234.

135.   Thayer, J. F., & Lane, R. D. 2009. "Claude Bernard and the Heart-Brain Connection." *Neuroscience & Biobehavioral Reviews* 33 (2): 81–88.

CHAPTER 11: THE TRIBUNAL

Fictional narrative chapter; technology and patterns are drawn from published research cited throughout.

CHAPTER 12: THE WORK AHEAD

Synthesis chapter; no numbered citations.

BIBLIOGRAPHY

Complete alphabetical listing of all works cited.

Abimbola, Wande. *Ifá: An Exposition of Ifá Literary Corpus.* Oxford: Oxford University Press, 1976.

Adler, Adam B., and Charles A. Castro. "Soldier Resilience: Psychological and Behavioral Factors." *Military Medicine* 184, suppl. 1 (2019): 34–40.

Ahbez, Eden. "Nature Boy." Song. Capitol Records, 1948.

Ambady, Nalini, and Robert Rosenthal. "Thin Slices of Expressive Behavior as Predictors of Interpersonal Consequences." *Psychological Bulletin* 111, no. 2 (1992): 256–74.

Amodio, David M. "The Neuroscience of Prejudice and Stereotyping." *Nature Reviews Neuroscience* 15, no. 10 (2014): 670–82.

Amodio, David M., and Mina Cikara. "The Social Neuroscience of Prejudice." *Annual Review of Psychology* 72 (2021): 439–69.

Amodio, David M., Eddie Harmon-Jones, and Patricia G. Devine. "Individual Differences in the Activation and Control of Affective Race Bias." *Journal of Personality and Social Psychology* 84 (2003): 738–53.

Aristotle. *The Nicomachean Ethics.* Translated by David Ross. Oxford: Oxford University Press, 2009.

Armstrong, Karen. *The Great Transformation: The Beginning of Our Religious Traditions.* New York: Knopf, 2006.

Aston-Jones, Gary, and Jonathan D. Cohen. "An Integrative Theory of Locus Coeruleus–Norepinephrine Function: Adaptive Gain and Optimal Performance." *Annual Review of Neuroscience* 28 (2005): 403–50.

Aurelius, Marcus. *Meditations.* Translated by Gregory Hays. New York: Modern Library, 2002.

Baldwin, James, and William F. Buckley Jr. "Is the American Dream at the Expense of the American Negro?" Debate, Cambridge Union Society, United Kingdom, February 18, 1965. Broadcast by BBC.

Bar-On, Reuven. *The Emotional Quotient Inventory (EQ-i): Technical Manual.* Toronto: Multi-Health Systems, 1997.

Bar-On, Reuven. "The Bar-On Model of Emotional-Social Intelligence." *Psicothema* 18 (2006): 13–25.

Barrett, Lisa Feldman. *How Emotions Are Made: The Secret Life of the Brain.* Boston: Houghton Mifflin Harcourt, 2017.

Barrett, Lisa Feldman. "The Theory of Constructed Emotion." *Social Cognitive and Affective Neuroscience* 12, no. 1 (2017): 1–23.

Beck, Aaron T. *Cognitive Therapy and the Emotional Disorders.* New York: International Universities Press, 1976.

The Bhagavad Gita. Translated by Eknath Easwaran. Tomales, CA: Nilgiri Press, 2007.

Bogen, Miranda, and Aaron Rieke. *Help Wanted: An Examination of Hiring Algorithms, Equity, and Bias.* Washington, DC: Upturn, 2018.

Brackett, Marc A. *Permission to Feel: Unlocking the Power of Emotions to Help Our Kids, Ourselves, and Our Society Thrive*. New York: Celadon Books, 2019.

Bradberry, Travis, and Jean Greaves. *Emotional Intelligence 2.0*. San Diego, CA: TalentSmart, 2009.

Brown, Brené. *The Gifts of Imperfection*. Center City, MN: Hazelden, 2010.

Brown, Brené. *Daring Greatly: How the Courage to Be Vulnerable Transforms the Way We Live, Love, Parent, and Lead*. New York: Gotham Books, 2012.

Brown, Brené. *Atlas of the Heart: Mapping Meaningful Connection and the Language of Human Experience*. New York: Random House, 2021.

Buccola, Nicholas. *The Fire Is upon Us: James Baldwin, William F. Buckley Jr., and the Debate over Race in America*. Princeton, NJ: Princeton University Press, 2019.

Buhle, Jason T., Jared A. Silvers, Tor D. Wager, Reuben Lopez, Chinedu Onyemekwu, Hedy Kober, Jutta Weber, and Kevin N. Ochsner. "Cognitive Reappraisal of Emotion: A Meta-Analysis of Human Neuroimaging Studies." *Cerebral Cortex* 24, no. 11 (2014): 2981–90.

Buolamwini, Joy, and Timnit Gebru. "Gender Shades: Intersectional Accuracy Disparities in Commercial Gender Classification." In *Proceedings of the 1st Conference on Fairness, Accountability and Transparency*, 77–91, 2018.

Campbell, Joseph. *The Hero with a Thousand Faces*. New York: Pantheon Books, 1949.

Capgemini Research Institute. *Emotional Intelligence: The Essential Skillset for the Age of AI*. Paris: Capgemini, 2019.

Carpenter, Malinda, Katherine Nagell, and Michael Tomasello. "Social Cognition, Joint Attention, and Communicative Competence from 9 to 15 Months of Age." *Monographs of the Society for Research in Child Development* 63, no. 4 (1998): 1–143.

Chödrön, Pema. *The Places That Scare You: A Guide to Fearlessness in Difficult Times*. Boston: Shambhala, 2001.

Christian, Brian. *The Alignment Problem: Machine Learning and Human Values*. New York: W. W. Norton, 2020.

Confucius. *The Analects*. Translated by D. C. Lau. New York: Penguin Classics, 1979.

Cornerstone. *Global State of the Skills Economy 2024*. Santa Monica, CA: Cornerstone OnDemand, 2024.

Covey, Stephen R. *The Seven Habits of Highly Effective People*. New York: Free Press, 1989.

Cozolino, Louis. *The Neuroscience of Human Relationships: Attachment and the Developing Social Brain*. 2nd ed. New York: W. W. Norton, 2014.

Craig, A. D. (Bud). "How Do You Feel—Now? The Anterior Insula and Human Awareness." *Nature Reviews Neuroscience* 10, no. 1 (2009): 59–70.

Crawford, Kate. *Atlas of AI: Power, Politics, and the Planetary Costs of Artificial Intelligence*. New Haven, CT: Yale University Press, 2021.

Crum, Alia J., Peter Salovey, and Shawn Achor. "Rethinking Stress: The Role of Mindsets in Determining the Stress Response." *Journal of Personality and Social Psychology* 104, no. 4 (2013): 716–33.

Csikszentmihalyi, Mihaly. *Flow: The Psychology of Optimal Experience.* New York: Harper & Row, 1990.

Damasio, Antonio. *Descartes' Error: Emotion, Reason, and the Human Brain.* New York: Putnam, 1994.

Davidson, Richard J., and Antoine Lutz. "Buddha's Brain: Neuroplasticity and Meditation." *IEEE Signal Processing Magazine* 25, no. 1 (2008): 176–84.

DeCasper, Anthony J., and William P. Fifer. "Of Human Bonding: Newborns Prefer Their Mothers' Voices." *Science* 208, no. 4448 (1980): 1174–76.

Descartes, René. *Discourse on the Method.* Translated by Donald A. Cress. Indianapolis: Hackett, 1998.

Devlin, Jacob, Ming-Wei Chang, Kenton Lee, and Kristina Toutanova. "BERT: Pre-Training of Deep Bidirectional Transformers for Language Understanding." arXiv preprint arXiv:1810.04805, 2018.

The Dhammapada. Translated by Eknath Easwaran. Tomales, CA: Nilgiri Press, 2007.

Duckworth, Angela. *Grit: The Power of Passion and Perseverance.* New York: Scribner, 2016.

Dumas, Guillaume, Jacqueline Nadel, Roland Soussignan, Jacques Martinerie, and Laurent Garnero. "Inter-Brain Synchronization during Social Interaction." *PLoS ONE* 5, no. 8 (2010): e12166.

Dunbar, Robin I. M. "The Social Brain Hypothesis." *Evolutionary Anthropology* 6, no. 5 (1998): 178–90.

Durlak, Joseph A., Roger P. Weissberg, Allison B. Dymnicki, Rebecca D. Taylor, and Kriston B. Schellinger. "The Impact of Enhancing Students' Social and Emotional Learning: A Meta-Analysis of School-Based Universal Interventions." *Child Development* 82, no. 1 (2011): 405–32.

Dwork, Cynthia, and Aaron Roth. *The Algorithmic Foundations of Differential Privacy. Foundations and Trends in Theoretical Computer Science* 9, nos. 3–4 (2014): 211–407.

Edmondson, Amy C. "Psychological Safety and Learning Behavior in Work Teams." *Administrative Science Quarterly* 44, no. 2 (1999): 350–83.

Edmondson, Amy C. *The Fearless Organization: Creating Psychological Safety in the Workplace for Learning, Innovation, and Growth.* Hoboken, NJ: Wiley, 2018.

Ekman, Paul. "An Argument for Basic Emotions." *Cognition & Emotion* 6, nos. 3–4 (1992): 169–200.

Elyoseph, Ziv, Dalia Hadar-Shoval, Kfir Asraf, and Michael Lvovsky. "ChatGPT Outperforms Humans in Emotional Awareness Evaluations." *Frontiers in Psychology* 14 (2023): 1199058.

Eubanks, Virginia. *Automating Inequality: How High-Tech Tools Profile, Police, and Punish the Poor.* New York: St. Martin's Press, 2018.

Feist, Gregory J., and Frank Barron. "Emotional Intelligence and Academic Intelligence in Career and Life Success." Paper presented at the Annual Convention of the American Psychological Society, San Francisco, CA, June 1996.

Feist, Gregory J., and Frank Barron. "Predicting Creativity from Early to Late Adulthood: Intellect, Potential, and Personality." *Journal of Research in Personality* 37, no. 2 (2003): 62–88.

Fiske, Susan T. *Envy Up, Scorn Down: How Status Divides Us*. New York: Russell Sage Foundation, 2011.

Fiske, Susan T., Amy J. Cuddy, Peter Glick, and Jun Xu. "A Model of (Often Mixed) Stereotype Content." *Journal of Personality and Social Psychology* 82, no. 6 (2002): 878–902.

Frankl, Viktor E. *Man's Search for Meaning*. Boston: Beacon Press, 2006.

French, John R. P., and Bertram Raven. "The Bases of Social Power." In *Studies in Social Power*, edited by Dorwin Cartwright, 150–67. Ann Arbor, MI: Institute for Social Research, 1959.

Gardner, Howard. *Frames of Mind: The Theory of Multiple Intelligences*. New York: Basic Books, 1983.

Gigerenzer, Gerd. *Gut Feelings: The Intelligence of the Unconscious*. New York: Viking, 2007.

Goldstein, Patrick, Inbal Weissman-Fogel, Guillaume Dumas, and Simone G. Shamay-Tsoory. "Brain-to-Brain Coupling during Handholding Is Associated with Pain Reduction." *Proceedings of the National Academy of Sciences* 114, no. 11 (2017): E2528–E2537.

Goleman, Daniel. *Emotional Intelligence: Why It Can Matter More Than IQ*. New York: Bantam Books, 1995.

Goleman, Daniel. *Working with Emotional Intelligence*. New York: Bantam Books, 1998.

Goleman, Daniel, and Richard J. Davidson. *Altered Traits: Science Reveals How Meditation Changes Your Mind, Brain, and Body*. New York: Avery, 2017.

Goodhart, Charles A. E. *Monetary Theory and Practice: The UK Experience*. London: Macmillan, 1984.

Gottman, John M., and Nan Silver. *The Seven Principles for Making Marriage Work*. New York: Crown, 1999.

Gould, Stephen Jay. *The Mismeasure of Man*. New York: W. W. Norton, 1981.

Grant, Adam. *Think Again: The Power of Knowing What You Don't Know*. New York: Viking, 2021.

Greene, Joshua D. *Moral Tribes: Emotion, Reason, and the Gap Between Us and Them*. New York: Penguin Press, 2013.

Gross, James J. "Emotion Regulation: Current Status and Future Prospects." *Psychological Inquiry* 26, no. 1 (2015): 1–26.

Haidt, Jonathan. *The Righteous Mind: Why Good People Are Divided by Politics and Religion*. New York: Vintage, 2012.

Hanh, Thich Nhat. *The Miracle of Mindfulness*. Boston: Beacon Press, 1975.

Hanson, Rick. *Hardwiring Happiness: The New Brain Science of Contentment, Calm, and Confidence*. New York: Harmony, 2013.

Harris, Leah T., and Susan T. Fiske. "Dehumanizing the Lowest of the Low: Neuroimaging Responses to Extreme Out-Groups." *Psychological Science* 17, no. 10 (2006): 847–53.

Hasson, Uri, Arash A. Ghazanfar, Bruno Galantucci, Steven Garrod, and Christian Keysers. "Brain-to-Brain Coupling: A Mechanism for Creating and Sharing a Social World." *Trends in Cognitive Sciences* 16, no. 2 (2012): 114–21.

Heifetz, Ronald A., and Marty Linsky. *Leadership on the Line: Staying Alive Through the Dangers of Leading*. Boston: Harvard Business School Press, 2002.

Hinton, Geoffrey E., and Ruslan R. Salakhutdinov. "Reducing the Dimensionality of Data with Neural Networks." *Science* 313, no. 5786 (2006): 504–7.

Hooks, Bell. *All About Love: New Visions*. New York: William Morrow, 2000.

Ipsos. *World Mental Health Day 2024 Global Survey*. Paris: Ipsos, October 2024.

James, William. *The Principles of Psychology*. Vols. 1–2. New York: Henry Holt, 1890.

Jamieson, Jeremy P., Matthew K. Nock, and Wendy B. Mendes. "Mind over Matter: Reappraising Arousal Improves Cardiovascular and Cognitive Responses to Stress." *Journal of Experimental Psychology: General* 141, no. 3 (2012): 417–22.

Jaspers, Karl. *The Origin and Goal of History*. New Haven, CT: Yale University Press, 1953.

Jung, Carl G. *Alchemical Studies*. Collected Works, Vol. 13. Princeton, NJ: Princeton University Press, 1967.

Jung, Rex E., and Richard J. Haier. "The Parieto-Frontal Integration Theory (P-FIT) of Intelligence." *Behavioral and Brain Sciences* 30, no. 2 (2007): 135–54.

Kabat-Zinn, Jon. *Full Catastrophe Living: Using the Wisdom of Your Body and Mind to Face Stress, Pain, and Illness*. New York: Delacorte Press, 1990.

Kahneman, Daniel. *Thinking, Fast and Slow*. New York: Farrar, Straus and Giroux, 2011.

Kellerman, Barbara. *The End of Leadership*. New York: Harper Business, 2012.

Konrath, Sara H., Edward H. O'Brien, and Courtney Hsing. "Changes in Dispositional Empathy in American College Students over Time." *Personality and Social Psychology Review* 15, no. 2 (2011): 180–98.

Kross, Ethan. *Chatter: The Voice in Our Head, Why It Matters, and How to Harness It*. New York: Crown, 2021.

Krznaric, Roman. *Empathy: Why It Matters, and How to Get It*. New York: Perigee Books, 2014.

Lao Tzu. *Tao Te Ching*. Translated by Stephen Mitchell. New York: Harper & Row, 1988.

LeDoux, Joseph E. *The Emotional Brain: The Mysterious Underpinnings of Emotional Life*. New York: Simon & Schuster, 1996.

Lembke, Anna. *Dopamine Nation: Finding Balance in the Age of Indulgence*. New York: Dutton, 2021.

Lieberman, Matthew D. *Social: Why Our Brains Are Wired to Connect*. New York: Crown, 2013.

Lieberman, Matthew D., Naomi I. Eisenberger, Michael J. Crockett, Stephanie M. Tom, Jennifer H. Pfeifer, and Brandon M. Way. "Putting Feelings into Words: Affect Labeling Disrupts Amygdala Activity in Response to Affective Stimuli." *Psychological Science* 18, no. 5 (2007): 421–28.

Linehan, Marsha M. *DBT Skills Training Manual*. 2nd ed. New York: Guilford Press, 2015.

Litz, Brett T., Nathan Stein, Eric Delaney, Lori Lebowitz, William P. Nash, Christina Silva, and Shira Maguen. "Moral Injury and Moral Repair in War Veterans." *Clinical Psychology Review* 29, no. 8 (2009): 695–706.

Loehr, Jim. *Stress for Success*. New York: Crown Business, 1994.

Loehr, Jim, and Tony Schwartz. *The Power of Full Engagement*. New York: Free Press, 2003.

Lyubomirsky, Sonja. *The How of Happiness: A Scientific Approach to Getting the Life You Want*. New York: Penguin Press, 2008.

Mattingly, Victoria, and Katherine Kraiger. "Can Emotional Intelligence Be Trained? A Meta-Analytical Investigation." *Human Resource Management Review* 29, no. 2 (2019): 140–55.

Mayer, John D., Peter Salovey, and David R. Caruso. *Mayer-Salovey-Caruso Emotional Intelligence Test (MSCEIT) User's Manual*. Toronto: Multi-Health Systems, 2002.

McGilchrist, Iain. *The Master and His Emissary: The Divided Brain and the Making of the Western World*. New Haven, CT: Yale University Press, 2009.

Meadows, Donella H. *Thinking in Systems: A Primer*. White River Junction, VT: Chelsea Green Publishing, 2008.

Mehrabian, Albert. *Silent Messages: Implicit Communication of Emotions and Attitudes*. Belmont, CA: Wadsworth, 1971.

Merton, Thomas. *New Seeds of Contemplation*. New York: New Directions, 1961.

Metz, Thaddeus. "Ubuntu as a Moral Theory and Human Rights in South Africa." *African Human Rights Law Journal* 11, no. 2 (2011): 532–59.

Mikolov, Tomas, Kai Chen, Greg Corrado, and Jeffrey Dean. "Efficient Estimation of Word Representations in Vector Space." arXiv preprint arXiv:1301.3781, 2013.

Nagoski, Emily, and Amelia Nagoski. *Burnout: The Secret to Unlocking the Stress Cycle*. New York: Ballantine Books, 2019.

NATO Human Factors and Medicine Panel. *Integrating Cognitive Enhancement Technologies into Human Performance*. Brussels: NATO Science and Technology Organization, 2021.

Newport, Cal. *Digital Minimalism: Choosing a Focused Life in a Noisy World*. New York: Portfolio, 2019.

Noble, Safiya U. *Algorithms of Oppression: How Search Engines Reinforce Racism*. New York: NYU Press, 2018.

noyb. "Criminal Complaint Filed against Clearview AI" [Press release]. October 28, 2025.

Nussbaum, Martha C. *Creating Capabilities: The Human Development Approach*. Cambridge, MA: Harvard University Press, 2011.

Öhman, Arne, Andreas Flykt, and Francisco Esteves. "Emotion Drives Attention: Detecting the Snake in the Grass." *Journal of Experimental Psychology: General* 130, no. 3 (2001): 466–78.

O'Neil, Cathy. *Weapons of Math Destruction: How Big Data Increases Inequality and Threatens Democracy*. New York: Crown, 2016.

Patterson, Kerry, Joseph Grenny, Ron McMillan, and Al Switzler. *Crucial Conversations: Tools for Talking When Stakes Are High*. 2nd ed. New York: McGraw-Hill, 2012.

Perner, Josef, and Heinz Wimmer. "John Thinks That Mary Thinks That…: Attribution of Second-Order Beliefs." *Journal of Experimental Child Psychology* 39, no. 3 (1985): 437–71.

Pessoa, Luiz. "To What Extent Are Emotional Visual Stimuli Processed without Attention and Awareness?" *Current Opinion in Neurobiology* 15, no. 2 (2005): 188–96.

Porges, Stephen W. *The Polyvagal Theory: Neurophysiological Foundations of Emotions, Attachment, Communication, and Self-Regulation.* New York: W. W. Norton, 2011.

Privacy International. *Clearview AI: A Case Study in Mass Surveillance* [Report]. London: Privacy International, 2024.

Raghavan, Manish, Solon Barocas, Jon Kleinberg, and Kate Levy. "Mitigating Bias in Algorithmic Hiring: Evaluating Claims and Practices." In *Proceedings of the 2020 Conference on Fairness, Accountability, and Transparency,* 469–81. New York: ACM, 2020.

Rizzolatti, Giacomo, and Laila Craighero. "The Mirror-Neuron System." *Annual Review of Neuroscience* 27 (2004): 169–92.

Rizzolatti, Giacomo, Luciano Fadiga, Vittorio Gallese, and Leonardo Fogassi. "Premotor Cortex and the Recognition of Motor Actions." *Cognitive Brain Research* 3, no. 2 (1996): 131–41.

Robbins, Mel. *The 5 Second Rule: Transform Your Life, Work, and Confidence with Everyday Courage.* New York: Savio Republic, 2017.

Rogers, Carl. *On Becoming a Person: A Therapist's View of Psychotherapy.* Boston: Houghton Mifflin, 1961.

Rosenberg, Marshall B. *Nonviolent Communication: A Language of Life.* 3rd ed. Encinitas, CA: PuddleDancer Press, 2015.

Rumi, Jalal al-Din. *The Essential Rumi.* Translated by Coleman Barks. San Francisco: HarperOne, 1995.

Russell, Stuart. *Human Compatible: Artificial Intelligence and the Problem of Control.* New York: Viking, 2019.

Salovey, Peter, and John D. Mayer. "Emotional Intelligence." *Imagination, Cognition and Personality* 9, no. 3 (1990): 185–211.

Salti, Maya, Yair Bar-Haim, and Dalit Lamy. "The Time Course
of Biased Competition." *Journal of Cognitive Neuroscience* 21, no. 6
(2009): 1277–86.

Sandberg, Sheryl, and Adam Grant. *Option B: Facing Adversity, Building
Resilience, and Finding Joy.* New York: Knopf, 2017.

Schwartz, Shalom H. "Universals in the Content and Structure
of Values." *Advances in Experimental Social Psychology* 25
(1992): 1–65.

Seligman, Martin E. P. *Flourish: A Visionary New Understanding
of Happiness and Well-Being.* New York: Free Press, 2011.

Senge, Peter M. *The Fifth Discipline: The Art and Practice of the Learning
Organization.* New York: Doubleday, 1990.

Sherrington, Charles S. *The Integrative Action of the Nervous System.*
New Haven, CT: Yale University Press, 1906.

Siegel, Daniel J. *Mindsight: The New Science of Personal Transformation.*
New York: Bantam, 2010.

Simon, Herbert A. "What Is an 'Explanation' of Behavior?" *Psychological
Science* 3, no. 3 (1992): 150–61.

Smith, Linda Tuhiwai. *Decolonizing Methodologies: Research
and Indigenous Peoples.* 3rd ed. London: Zed Books, 1999/2021.

Spencer, Lyle M., and Signe M. Spencer. *Competence at Work: Models
for Superior Performance.* New York: Wiley, 1993.

Spencer, Lyle M., David C. McClelland, and Allan Kelner. *Competency
Assessment Methods: History and State of the Art.* Boston: Hay/
McBer, 1997.

Stanislavski, Konstantin. *An Actor Prepares*. New York: Theatre Arts Books, 1936.

Stevenson, Bryan. *Just Mercy: A Story of Justice and Redemption*. New York: Spiegel & Grau, 2014.

Stone, Douglas, Bruce Patton, and Sheila Heen. *Difficult Conversations: How to Discuss What Matters Most*. 2nd ed. New York: Penguin, 2010.

Strasberg, Lee. *A Dream of Passion: The Development of the Method*. Boston: Little, Brown, 1987.

Suleyman, Mustafa, and Manish Bhaskar. *The Coming Wave: Technology, Power, and the Twenty-First Century's Greatest Dilemma*. New York: Crown, 2023.

Sun Tzu. *The Art of War. Translated by Lionel Giles*. Mineola, NY: Dover Publications, 2003.

Tegmark, Max. *Life 3.0: Being Human in the Age of Artificial Intelligence*. New York: Knopf, 2017.

Thayer, Julian F., and Richard D. Lane. "Claude Bernard and the Heart-Brain Connection: Further Elaboration of a Model of Neurovisceral Integration." *Neuroscience & Biobehavioral Reviews* 33, no. 2 (2009): 81–88.

Tomasello, Michael. *Becoming Human: A Theory of Ontogeny*. Cambridge, MA: Harvard University Press, 2019.

Turkle, Sherry. *Alone Together: Why We Expect More from Technology and Less from Each Other*. New York: Basic Books, 2011.

Turkle, Sherry. *Reclaiming Conversation: The Power of Talk in a Digital Age*. New York: Penguin Press, 2015.

Uhls, Yalda T., Marina Michikyan, Jennifer Morris, Daniel Garcia, Gary W. Small, Eleni Zgourou, and Patricia M. Greenfield. "Five Days at Outdoor Education Camp without Screens Improves Preteen Skills with Nonverbal Emotion Cues." *Computers in Human Behavior* 39 (2014): 387–92.

UNESCO. *Ifá Divination System: Masterpiece of the Oral and Intangible Heritage of Humanity*. Paris: UNESCO, 2005.

Ury, William. 2015. *Getting to Yes with Yourself: And Other Worthy Opponents*. HarperOne.

U.S. Army Center for Initial Military Training. Multiple years. *Performance Enhancement and Resilience (PEAR) Program Documentation*.

U.S. Department of Health and Human Services, Office of the Surgeon General. 2023. *Our Epidemic of Loneliness and Isolation: The U.S. Surgeon General's Advisory on the Healing Effects of Social Connection and Community.*

Waldinger, Robert J., and Marc S. Schulz. 2023. *The Good Life: Lessons from the World's Longest Scientific Study of Happiness*. Simon & Schuster.

Walker, Matthew. 2017. *Why We Sleep: Unlocking the Power of Sleep and Dreams*. Scribner.

Warneken, Felix, and Michael Tomasello. 2006. "Altruistic Helping in Human Infants and Young Chimpanzees." *Science* 311 (5765): 1301–1303.

Wellman, Henry M., David Cross, and Jacqueline Watson. 2001. "Meta-Analysis of Theory-of-Mind Development: The Truth about False Belief." *Child Development* 72 (3): 655–684.

Wiener, Norbert. 1950. *The Human Use of Human Beings: Cybernetics and Society.* Houghton Mifflin.

Wilkerson, Isabel. 2020. *Caste: The Origins of Our Discontents.* Random House.

Wittgenstein, Ludwig. 1922. *Tractatus Logico-Philosophicus.* Translated by C. K. Ogden. Routledge & Kegan Paul.

World Economic Forum. 2025. *The Future of Jobs Report 2025.* Geneva: World Economic Forum.

Yerkes, Robert M., and John D. Dodson. 1908. "The Relation of Strength of Stimulus to Rapidity of Habit-Formation." *Journal of Comparative Neurology and Psychology* 18 (5): 459–482.

Yu, Fang, et al. 2024. "Impact of Artificial Intelligence Assistance on Radiologist Diagnostic Performance." *Nature Medicine* 30: 1034–1042.

Zaki, Jamil. 2019. *The War for Kindness: Building Empathy in a Fractured World.* Crown.

Zuboff, Shoshana. 2019. *The Age of Surveillance Capitalism: The Fight for a Human Future at the New Frontier of Power.* PublicAffairs.

RECOMMENDED READING

Organized by the Three Pillars framework to support continued learning and practice.

FOUNDATIONAL WORKS

These texts provide essential background for understanding emotional intelligence as a field.

Bar-On, R. 1997. *The Emotional Quotient Inventory (EQ-i): Technical Manual.* Multi-Health Systems. Foundational assessment work that shaped how emotional intelligence is measured.

Barrett, L. F. 2017. *How Emotions Are Made: The Secret Life of the Brain.* Houghton Mifflin Harcourt. Rewrites the science of emotion, showing how the brain constructs feelings from bodily signals, context, and prediction.

Damasio, A. 1994. *Descartes' Error: Emotion, Reason, and the Human Brain.* Putnam. The neuroscientific classic proving emotion and reason are inseparable, foundational to understanding why EI matters biologically. Goleman, D. 1995. *Emotional Intelligence: Why It Can Matter More Than IQ.* Bantam Books. The landmark book that brought emotional intelligence into mainstream consciousness and established its importance in personal and professional success.

Goleman, D. 1998. *Working with Emotional Intelligence.* Bantam Books. Extends the framework to workplace applications, demonstrating how emotional competencies drive professional performance across 200 organisations.

Lieberman, M. D. 2013. *Social: Why Our Brains Are Wired to Connect*. Crown Demonstrates that social connection is as fundamental to survival as food and shelter, with neural evidence for why relationships shape performance.

McGilchrist, I. 2009. *The Master and His Emissary: The Divided Brain and the Making of the Western World*. Yale University Press. How different modes of attention shape human experience and why integration matters for emotional intelligence.

Salovey, P., and J. D. Mayer. 1990. "Emotional Intelligence." *Imagination, Cognition and Personality* 9 (3): 185–211. The original academic article that defined emotional intelligence as a measurable form of intelligence.

PART 1: THE HUMAN IMPERATIVE

Understanding the AI Context

Christian, B. 2020. *The Alignment Problem: Machine Learning and Human Values*. W. W. Norton. How AI systems learn and why human values must guide their development.

Crawford, K. 2021. *Atlas of AI: Power, Politics, and the Planetary Costs of Artificial Intelligence*. Yale University Press. Critical examination of AI's social and human costs.

Kissinger, H., E. Schmidt, and D. Huttenlocher. 2021. *The Age of AI: And Our Human Future*. Little, Brown. How AI reshapes cognition, security, and human identity at the civilizational level.

Mitchell, M. 2019. *Artificial Intelligence: A Guide for Thinking Humans*. Farrar, Straus and Giroux. Clear-eyed assessment of what AI can and cannot do, illuminating the gap between machine optimization and human understanding.

Russell, S. 2019. *Human Compatible: Artificial Intelligence and the Problem of Control.* Viking. Essential framework for understanding AI alignment and why human judgment remains necessary.

Suleyman, M., and M. Bhaskar. 2023. *The Coming Wave: Technology, Power, and the Twenty-First Century's Greatest Dilemma.* Crown. Current analysis of AI's transformative impact on human capacity and the containment problem.

Tegmark, M. 2017. *Life 3.0: Being Human in the Age of Artificial Intelligence.* Knopf. Explores what makes human intelligence distinct and worth preserving.

The Case for Human Capacity

Gopnik, A. 2009. *The Philosophical Baby: What Children's Minds Tell Us About Truth, Love, and the Meaning of Life.* Farrar, Straus and Giroux. How infants and young children are the most sophisticated learners on the planet, with innate capacities for empathy, moral reasoning, and social cognition that get trained or neglected.

Haidt, J. 2024. *The Anxious Generation: How the Great Rewiring of Childhood Is Causing an Epidemic of Mental Illness.* Penguin Press. Data on how smartphone culture reshapes emotional development, with direct relevance to the emotional recession described in Chapter 5.

Murthy, V. H. 2020. *Together: The Healing Power of Human Connection in a Sometimes Lonely World.* Harper. The former Surgeon General's case for connection as public health imperative.

Newport, C. 2019. *Digital Minimalism: Choosing a Focused Life in a Noisy World.* Portfolio. Practical framework for maintaining human capacity in digital environments.

Turkle, S. 2011. *Alone Together: Why We Expect More from Technology and Less from Each Other*. Basic Books. Documents the erosion of relational capacity through technology.

Turkle, S. 2015. *Reclaiming Conversation: The Power of Talk in a Digital Age*. Penguin Press. The case for face-to-face connection and its irreplaceable value.

Historical and Cross-Cultural Foundations

Armstrong, K. 2006. *The Great Transformation: The Beginning of Our Religious Traditions*. Knopf. The Axial Age and humanity's first systematic development of emotional wisdom.

Baldwin, J. 1963. *The Fire Next Time*. Vintage International. Two essays on what it costs to see clearly in a society that rewards not seeing. Baldwin's work is emotional intelligence under pressure: reading a room, holding composure while speaking truth, moral courage as embodied practice.

Henrich, J. 2020. *The WEIRDest People in the World: How the West Became Psychologically Peculiar and Particularly Prosperous*. Farrar, Straus and Giroux. Why psychological research drawn primarily from Western populations distorts our understanding of universal human capacities.

Jaspers, K. 1953. *The Origin and Goal of History*. Yale University Press. The philosophical framework for understanding cross-cultural convergence in human development.

Nussbaum, M. C. 2011. *Creating Capabilities: The Human Development Approach*. Harvard University Press. Universal human needs as foundations for dignity and flourishing.

Smith, L. T. 1999/2021. *Decolonizing Methodologies: Research and Indigenous Peoples* (3rd ed.). Zed Books. Essential reading on how knowledge systems are shaped by power, and why emotional intelligence frameworks must account for colonial epistemology.

Tutu, D. 1999. *No Future Without Forgiveness*. Doubleday. Ubuntu in action through the Truth and Reconciliation Commission. Demonstrates the emotional intelligence required for restorative justice: the capacity to hold pain without retaliation, to see the humanity in those who caused harm, and to choose accountability over vengeance.

PART 2: FROM INSIGHT TO ACTION

Self-Awareness (Pillar 1)

Beck, A. T. 1976. *Cognitive Therapy and the Emotional Disorders*. International Universities Press. The foundations of cognitive behavioural therapy and metacognition.

Brackett, M. 2019. *Permission to Feel: Unlocking the Power of Emotions to Help Our Kids, Ourselves, and Our Society Thrive*. Celadon Books. The RULER framework for emotional literacy from Yale's Center for Emotional Intelligence.

Brown, B. 2021. *Atlas of the Heart: Mapping Meaningful Connection and the Language of Human Experience*. Random House. Maps eighty-seven distinct emotions with stories and research to build emotional vocabulary.

Frankl, V. E. 1946/2006. *Man's Search for Meaning*. Beacon Press. Finding purpose in adversity and the space between stimulus and response.

Kabat-Zinn, J. 1990. *Full Catastrophe Living: Using the Wisdom of Your Body and Mind to Face Stress, Pain, and Illness.* Delacorte Press. The foundational text on mindfulness-based stress reduction.

Kahneman, D. 2011. *Thinking, Fast and Slow.* Farrar, Straus and Giroux. The definitive guide to cognitive biases and how to recognize them.

Johnson, R. A. 1991. *Owning Your Own Shadow: Understanding the Dark Side of the Psyche.* HarperOne. A concise, practical guide to Jungian shadow work: recognizing the parts of yourself you have rejected and integrating them into conscious awareness.

Jung, C. G. 1959/1969. *The Archetypes and the Collective Unconscious* (Collected Works, Vol. 9i). Princeton University Press. The primary source on shadow, anima/animus, and the Self. Foundational for understanding the psychological structures that shape emotional patterns beneath conscious awareness.

Kross, E. 2021. *Chatter: The Voice in Our Head, Why It Matters, and How to Harness It.* Crown. Research on managing internal dialogue and the tools that help us gain distance from our own rumination.

Seth, A. 2021. *Being You: A New Science of Consciousness.* Faber & Faber. How the brain constructs our experience of reality from prediction and perception, extending Barrett's work into consciousness itself.

Siegel, D. J. 2010. *Mindsight: The New Science of Personal Transformation.* Bantam. Neural integration and the observer self as foundations of self-awareness.

Van der Kolk, B. 2014. *The Body Keeps the Score: Brain, Mind, and Body in the Healing of Trauma.* Viking. The definitive account of how emotional experience lives in the body, essential for understanding interoception and embodied intelligence.

Self-Mastery (Pillar 2)

Csikszentmihalyi, M. 1990. *Flow: The Psychology of Optimal Experience.* Harper & Row. The state of complete engagement and its role in mastery.

Crum, A. J., P. Salovey, and S. Achor. 2013. "Rethinking Stress: The Role of Mindsets in Determining the Stress Response." *Journal of Personality and Social Psychology* 104, no. 4: 716–733. Research on stress mindset and reappraisal.

Duckworth, A. 2016. *Grit: The Power of Passion and Perseverance. Scribner.* The psychology of sustained effort and resilience.

Goleman, D., and R. J. Davidson. 2017. *Altered Traits: Science Reveals How Meditation Changes Your Mind, Brain, and Body.* Avery. How contemplative practice builds neural infrastructure for regulation.

Hanson, R. 2013. *Hardwiring Happiness: The New Brain Science of Contentment, Calm, and Confidence.* Harmony. Building resilience through neuroplasticity.

Huberman, A. 2025. *Protocols: An Operating Manual for the Human Body.* Avery. Evidence-based tools for regulating stress, focus, and recovery, grounded in neuroscience.

LeDoux, J. E. 1996. *The Emotional Brain: The Mysterious Underpinnings of Emotional Life.* Simon & Schuster. How fear and emotion work in the brain, foundational for understanding emotional regulation.

Lembke, A. 2021. *Dopamine Nation: Finding Balance in the Age of Indulgence.* Dutton. Neuroscience of pleasure, pain, and emotional balance.

Loehr, J., and T. Schwartz. 2003. *The Power of Full Engagement.* Free Press. Energy management and sustainable high performance.

Nagoski, E., and A. Nagoski. 2019. *Burnout: The Secret to Unlocking the Stress Cycle*. Ballantine Books. Completing the stress cycle and sustainable performance.

Nestor, J. 2020. *Breath: The New Science of a Lost Art*. Riverhead Books. How breathing patterns shape emotional regulation, stress response, and nervous system function. Connects ancient breathing practices to modern pulmonary science.

Seligman, M. E. P. 2011. *Flourish: A Visionary New Understanding of Happiness and Well-being*. Free Press. Positive psychology framework for resilience and thriving.

Walker, M. 2017. *Why We Sleep: Unlocking the Power of Sleep and Dreams*. Scribner. Sleep's essential role in emotional regulation and recovery.

Relational Mastery (Pillar 3)

Barks, C., trans. 1995. *The Essential Rumi*. HarperOne. The definitive English translation of Jalāl ad-Dīn Muhammad Rūmī, the thirteenth-century Sufi poet whose work illuminates the territory where self-knowledge meets love, loss, and the courage to remain open. Poetry as emotional intelligence in its purest form.

Capra, F. 1975/2010. *The Tao of Physics*: An Exploration of the Parallels Between Modern Physics and Eastern Mysticism. Shambhala. The classic that revealed how quantum physics confirms what contemplative traditions have long taught: interconnection is not metaphor but the fundamental structure of reality. See also The Web of Life (1996) for the systems theory extension.

Cozolino, L. 2014. *The Neuroscience of Human Relationships: Attachment and the Developing Social Brain*. W. W. Norton. How the brain is built for connection.

Edmondson, A. C. 2018. *The Fearless Organization: Creating Psychological Safety in the Workplace for Learning, Innovation, and Growth*. Wiley. Building environments where people can speak up and take risks.

Gottman, J., and N. Silver. 2015. *The Seven Principles for Making Marriage Work*. Crown. Research-based relationship patterns including the five-to-one ratio and repair.

Heen, S., and D. Stone. 2014. *Thanks for the Feedback: The Science and Art of Receiving Feedback Well*. Viking. How to learn from criticism, coaching, and evaluation without being derailed by emotional reactivity.

Krznaric, R. 2014. *Empathy: Why It Matters, and How to Get It*. Perigee Books. Practical guide to developing empathy across difference.

Patterson, K., J. Grenny, R. McMillan, and A. Switzler. 2012. *Crucial Conversations: Tools for Talking When Stakes Are High* (2nd ed.). McGraw-Hill. Practical methods for dialogue under pressure.

Porges, S. 2011. *The Polyvagal Theory: Neurophysiological Foundations of Emotions, Attachment, Communication, and Self-regulation*. W. W. Norton. The biological basis of social engagement and co-regulation.

Rovelli, C. 2021. *Helgoland: Making Sense of the Quantum Revolution*. Riverhead Books. A luminous argument that reality itself is relational: nothing exists independently, only in interaction. The "relational interpretation" of quantum mechanics mirrors the book's core claim that identity is formed through connection, not isolation.

Rosenberg, M. B. 2015. *Nonviolent Communication: A Language of Life* (3rd ed.). PuddleDancer Press. Framework for expressing needs and hearing others without judgment.

Stone, D., B. Patton, and S. Heen. 2010. *Difficult Conversations: How to Discuss What Matters Most* (2nd ed.). Penguin. Framework for navigating high-stakes communication.

Ury, W. 2015. *Getting to Yes with Yourself: And Other Worthy Opponents.* HarperOne. Internal preparation for effective negotiation.

Waldinger, R. J., and M. S. Schulz. 2023. *The Good Life: Lessons from the World's Longest Scientific Study of Happiness.* Simon & Schuster. Findings from the over eighty-year Harvard Study of Adult Development.

Zaki, J. 2019. *The War for Kindness: Building Empathy in a Fractured World.* Crown. Empathy as a developable skill with practical strategies. Porges, Stephen. *The Polyvagal Theory: Neurophysiological Foundations of Emotions, Attachment, Communication, and Self-regulation* (2011). The biological basis of social engagement and co-regulation.

PART 3: SCALING HUMAN WISDOM

Organizational and Systems Applications

Chamorro-Premuzic, T. 2019. *Why Do So Many Incompetent Men Become Leaders? (And How to Fix It).* Harvard Business Review Press. Data-driven analysis of why emotional intelligence predicts leadership effectiveness better than confidence or charisma.

Coyle, D. 2018. *The Culture Code: The Secrets of Highly Successful Groups.* Bantam. How safety, vulnerability, and shared purpose create high-performing teams.

Divine, M. 2013. *The Way of the SEAL: Think Like an Elite Warrior to Lead and Succeed.* Scribner. Mental segmentation, box breathing, and emotional redirection under extreme pressure. Demonstrates how elite military training develops the same regulation capacities described in this book.

Falconer, D. 2000. *First Into Action: A Dramatic Personal Account of Life in the SBS*. Headline. Presence in ambiguity, emotional neutrality in chaos, and sustained composure during high-stakes operations. A first-hand account of how self-mastery operates when the stakes are life and death.

Grant, A. 2021. *Think Again: The Power of Knowing What You Don't Know*. Viking. Intellectual humility and revising assumptions in organizations.

Heifetz, R., and M. Linsky. 2002. *Leadership on the Line: Staying Alive Through the Dangers of Leading*. Harvard Business School Press. Adaptive leadership and managing organizational change.

Kellerman, B. 2012. *The End of Leadership*. Harper Business. Critical examination of leadership development and its failures.

Meadows, D. H. 2008. *Thinking in Systems: A Primer*. Chelsea Green Publishing. Essential introduction to systems dynamics and leverage points.

Muller, J. Z. 2018. *The Tyranny of Metrics*. Princeton University Press. How measurement fixation corrupts institutions across healthcare, education, policing, and business. A book-length treatment of Goodhart's Law with case studies showing the measurement paradox explored in Chapter Ten.

Sandberg, S., and A. Grant. 2017. *Option B: Facing Adversity, Building Resilience, and Finding Joy*. Knopf. Organizational and personal resilience after loss.

Senge, P. 1990. *The Fifth Discipline: The Art and Practice of the Learning Organization*. Doubleday. Systems thinking and organizational learning.

Justice, Ethics, and Accountability

Benjamin, R. 2019. *Race after Technology: Abolitionist Tools for the New Jim Code*. Polity. How technology encodes racial inequality and what design justice looks like in practice.

Broussard, M. 2023. *More than a Glitch: Confronting Race, Gender, and Ability Bias in Tech*. MIT Press. Argues that tech bias is not a bug to be fixed but a feature of systems built without diverse emotional and ethical intelligence.

Crawford, K., and V. Joler. 2023. *Calculating Empires: A Genealogy of Technology and Power, 1500–2025*. Self-published. A sweeping visual research project mapping how communication and computation systems have been used to classify, control, and commodify humans across five centuries.

Eubanks, V. 2018. *Automating Inequality: How High-Tech Tools Profile, Police, and Punish the Poor*. St. Martin's Press. The human cost of algorithmic decision-making.

Kak, A., ed. 2023. *Regulating AI: Critical Issues*. AI Now Institute. Policy-focused collection on AI governance frameworks, accountability structures, and the institutional design required to ensure technology serves human dignity.

Noble, S. U. 2018. *Algorithms of Oppression: How Search Engines Reinforce Racism*. NYU Press. Critical analysis of bias in AI systems.

O'Neil, C. 2016. *Weapons of Math Destruction: How Big Data Increases Inequality and Threatens Democracy*. Crown. How algorithms can perpetuate bias and harm.

Stevenson, B. 2014. *Just Mercy: A Story of Justice and Redemption*. Spiegel & Grau. The relationship between justice, mercy, and human dignity.

Wilkerson, I. 2020. *Caste: The Origins of Our Discontents*. Random House. How invisible hierarchies shape human experience and organizational life.

Zuboff, S. 2019. *The Age of Surveillance Capitalism: The Fight for a Human Future at the New Frontier of Power*. PublicAffairs. How data extraction threatens human autonomy. Stevenson, Bryan. *Just Mercy: A Story of Justice and Redemption* (2014). The relationship between justice, mercy, and human dignity.

CONTEMPLATIVE AND WISDOM TRADITIONS

Chödrön, P. 2001. The *Places That Scare You: A Guide to Fearlessness in Difficult Times*. Shambhala. Buddhist approach to working with fear and uncertainty.

Hanh, T. N. 1975. *The Miracle of Mindfulness*. Beacon Press. Accessible introduction to mindfulness in daily life.

hooks, b. 2000. *All About Love: New Visions*. William Morrow. Love as practice and its role in personal and social transformation.

Linehan, M. M. 2015. *DBT Skills Training Manual* (2nd ed.). Guilford Press. Dialectical behavior therapy's practical emotional regulation techniques.

Merton, T. 1961. *New Seeds of Contemplation*. New Directions. Christian contemplative practice and inner development.

Palmer, P. J. 2004. *A Hidden Wholeness: The Journey Toward an Undivided Life*. Jossey-Bass. How to close the gap between inner truth and outer action, with frameworks for integrity in professional life.

Rogers, C. 1961. *On Becoming a Person: A Therapist's View of Psychotherapy*. Houghton Mifflin. The foundations of humanistic psychology and authentic development.

RECENT ADVANCES (2022-2026)

Selected research and reports reflecting the most current developments in emotional intelligence, neuroscience, and AI.

Bender, E. M., T. Gebru, et al. 2021. "On the Dangers of Stochastic Parrots: Can Language Models Be Too Big?" *Proceedings of the 2021 ACM Conference on Fairness, Accountability, and Transparency (FAccT).* The foundational paper that sparked the AI ethics reckoning, raising questions about what large language models understand versus what they merely reproduce.

Buhle, J. T., et al. 2014. "Cognitive Reappraisal of Emotion: A Meta-Analysis of Human Neuroimaging Studies." *Cerebral Cortex* 24 (11): 2981–2990. Landmark meta-analysis confirming shared neural infrastructure between emotion regulation and working memory.

Durlak, J. A., et al. 2011. "The Impact of Enhancing Students' Social and Emotional Learning." *Child Development* 82 (1): 405–432. Meta-analysis of SEL programmes across 50 countries confirming the trainability of emotional intelligence at scale.

Haidt, J. 2024. *The Anxious Generation.* Penguin Press. Comprehensive data on how smartphone and social media culture is reshaping emotional development in young people.

Huberman, A. 2025. *Protocols: An Operating Manual for the Human Body.* Avery. Peer-reviewed neuroscience translated into actionable tools for stress regulation, focus, and recovery.

U.S. Surgeon General. 2023. *Our Epidemic of Loneliness and Isolation.* U.S. Department of Health and Human Services. Public health framework for understanding the connection crisis and its consequences.

World Economic Forum. 2025. *Future of Jobs Report 2025*. World Economic Forum. Current data showing seven of the top ten workforce skills are emotional intelligence competencies. Published January 2025.Cornerstone. *Global State of the Skills Economy 2024* (2024). Data showing employer demand for human skills now exceeds demand for digital skills.

GLOSSARY OF KEY TERMS

Terms are organized alphabetically for easy reference. Chapter numbers indicate primary discussions.

Active Listening: The practice of fully concentrating on a speaker, understanding their message, and responding thoughtfully. Requires redirecting attention from internal dialogue to genuinely track another person's words, tone, and emotions. (Chapter 9)

Affect Labeling: The neuroscientific term for naming emotions. Research shows that putting feelings into words activates the prefrontal cortex and reduces amygdala activation, creating an immediate regulatory effect. The mechanism behind "name it to tame it." (Chapter 7)

Affective Empathy: The capacity to share and resonate with another person's emotional experience. Distinguished from cognitive empathy by its felt, embodied quality. Also called emotional empathy or empathic resonance. (Chapter 9)

Amygdala: A brain structure central to processing emotions, particularly fear and threat detection. Often called the brain's "alarm system." Can be modulated through affect labeling and regulation practices. (Chapters 1, 7, 8)

Anterior Cingulate Cortex (ACC): Brain region that monitors conflict between competing signals and demands resolution. Registers the discomfort when analytical conclusions contradict intuitive sense. (Chapter 4)

Anterior Insula: The brain region where interoceptive signals converge, creating the foundation for subjective feeling and self-awareness. Central to Bud Craig's research on embodied emotion. (Chapter 7)

Attunement: The ability to read others accurately without projecting your own emotional patterns. A foundational empathy skill that operates through nervous system-to-nervous system communication. (Chapter 9)

Autonomic Nervous System: The body's automatic regulatory system, comprising sympathetic (activation/arousal) and parasympathetic (rest/recovery) branches. Central to Polyvagal Theory and emotional regulation. (Chapters 7, 8, 9)

Axial Age: The period roughly 800 to 200 BCE when major philosophical and spiritual traditions emerged independently across civilisations. Karl Jaspers' term for this unprecedented convergence in human development of emotional and ethical wisdom. (Chapter 3)

Bias (Neural): Fear-driven automatic categorization that precedes conscious thought. Neuroscience shows the amygdala fires within milliseconds of exposure to difference, before deliberate judgment occurs. Distinct from prejudice (rationalized beliefs) though often connected. (Chapter 9)

Box Breathing: A regulation technique using equal counts for inhale, hold, exhale, and hold (typically four seconds for each). Used by military, athletes, and performers to calibrate nervous system activation. (Chapter 8)

Cartesian Logic: The framework derived from René Descartes that separates mind from body and elevates reason above emotion. Modern neuroscience has corrected this error, showing emotion and cognition are biologically integrated. ()

Cognitive Behavioral Therapy (CBT): A therapeutic approach developed by Aaron Beck that addresses the relationship between thoughts, emotions, and behaviors. Emphasises metacognition and identifying cognitive distortions. (Chapter 7)

Cognitive Empathy: The ability to understand another person's perspective intellectually without necessarily sharing their emotional state. Also called perspective-taking or theory of mind. (Chapter 9)

Compassion: The feeling that arises when witnessing suffering, combined with motivation to help relieve it. Distinguished from empathy by its action orientation and activation of different neural circuits. (Chapter 9)

Coregulation: The process by which one person's nervous system helps regulate another's. A calm presence can steady an activated person through mirror neurons and physiological synchrony. Foundation of relational safety. (Chapters 7, 9)

Default Mode Network: Brain network active during rest, self-reflection, and mind-wandering. Associated with rumination but also with self-awareness and meaning-making when engaged intentionally. (Chapter 7)

De-escalation: Skills for reducing emotional activation when tensions rise. Builds on self-command and discomfort tolerance to remain grounded while helping others regulate. (Chapter 9)

Discomfort Tolerance: The ability to sustain action, focus, and growth across periods of challenge by connecting difficulty to purpose. Distinguished from mere endurance by its use of meaning as fuel. Second self-mastery skill. (Chapter 8)

Dual Consciousness: The capacity to experience intense physical and emotional states without being consumed by them. Maintaining witness awareness even in crisis. Essential for peak performance under pressure. (Chapter 8)

Embodiment: The quality of being grounded in physical, felt experience rather than operating purely from abstract cognition. Central to this book's argument about what distinguishes human from artificial intelligence. (Chapters 1, 4, 7)

Emotional Embedding: A structured, retrievable imprint of emotional experience with context and meaning. Over time, the mind builds a detailed map of emotional experiences through naming and differentiation. (Chapter 7)

Emotional Granularity: The ability to make fine-grained distinctions between emotional states. High granularity means distinguishing between related emotions (irritation versus frustration versus anger) rather than experiencing them as undifferentiated "bad." Trainable through vocabulary expansion. (Chapter 7)

Emotional Intelligence (EI): The ability to perceive, understand, manage, and use emotions to guide thinking and behavior. As defined in this book: embodied capacity that integrates self-awareness, self-mastery, and relational mastery. (Introduction, throughout)

Emotional Literacy: The ability to identify, name, and understand emotions with precision. Second foundational self-awareness skill. Transforms raw sensation into usable information through language. (Chapter 7)

Emotional Memory: Stanislavski's technique of deliberately recalling personal experiences to generate authentic emotion. Foundation of Method Acting and applicable to intentional state generation. (Chapter 8)

Emotional Recession: A systemic decline in emotional capacity, including empathy, presence, and relational skill, triggered not by trauma but by neglect. Skills we stop practicing begin to atrophy. (Chapter 5)

Emotional Self-Command: The trained ability to access, generate, and direct emotional states with intention. First self-mastery skill. Distinguished from suppression by its purposeful direction of emotion rather than elimination. (Chapter 8)

Emotional Valuation: The brain's continuous process of assigning felt significance to competing inputs. Determines what to amplify, suppress, or act on first. The mechanism that enables integration across brain networks. (Chapter 4)

Empathy: The ability to discern and appreciate another person's perspective or emotional state while remaining grounded in your own. First relational mastery skill. Comprises attunement, resonance, and moral awareness. (Chapter 9)

Fight/Flight/Freeze/Fawn: The four primary stress responses mediated by the autonomic nervous system. Understanding one's default response patterns is essential for self-awareness and regulation. (Chapters 7, 8)

Flow State: The experience of complete absorption in an activity, characterized by loss of self-consciousness and optimal performance. Related to the optimal arousal zone of the Yerkes-Dodson law. (Chapter 8)

Frontoparietal Control Network: Brain network that coordinates attention, working memory, and cognitive control. Shared infrastructure for both cognitive tasks and emotional regulation, explaining why emotional flooding impairs thinking. (Chapter 4)

Goodhart's Law: "When a measure becomes a target, it ceases to be a good measure." Applied to emotional intelligence, explains why assessment must serve development rather than compliance. (Chapter 10)

Heart Rate Variability (HRV): The variation between heartbeats, indicating autonomic flexibility. High HRV signals a nervous system that can shift fluidly between activation and recovery. Measurable marker of regulation capacity. (Chapters 8, 10)

Hedonic Adaptation Prevention: Sonja Lyubomirsky's term for practices that prevent taking achievements for granted. Conscious cultivation of appreciation that sustains motivation and prevents burnout. (Chapter 8)

Interoception: The brain's ability to sense, interpret, and integrate signals from inside the body: heartbeat, breath, temperature, tension. First self-awareness skill. The raw data of emotional experience. (Chapter 7)

Intuition: Rapid pattern recognition developed through experience, reflection, and feedback. Herbert Simon defined it as "nothing more and nothing less than recognition." Emerges from trained interoception and meta-awareness. (Chapter 7)

Limbic System: Brain structures including the amygdala, hippocampus, and cingulate cortex that process emotion, memory, and motivation. Often contrasted with the prefrontal cortex in discussions of emotional regulation. (Chapters 1, 7)

Ma'at: The ancient Egyptian principle of truth, balance, justice, and harmony. Practiced as a way of living that integrated personal virtue with cosmic order. Predates Axial Age developments by over a millennium. (Chapter 3)

Meta-Awareness: The ability to observe your own mental processes: to think about your thinking and notice your patterns. Third self-awareness skill. Creates the space between stimulus and response. (Chapter 7)

Micro-expressions: Brief, involuntary facial expressions that reveal genuine emotion. The nervous system detects these in as little as seventeen milliseconds, before conscious recognition. (Chapters 1, 7)

Mindfulness: Nonjudgmental, moment-to-moment awareness of present experience. Jon Kabat-Zinn's MBSR program demonstrated its clinical effectiveness. Foundational practice for developing meta-awareness. (Chapter 7)

Mindfulness-Based Stress Reduction (MBSR): The eight-week program developed by Jon Kabat-Zinn that brought contemplative practice into clinical settings. Demonstrates the trainability of attention and regulation. (Chapter 7)

Mirror Neurons: Neurons that fire both when performing an action and when observing others perform it. First discovered by Giacomo Rizzolatti. Foundation for understanding empathy, imitation, and social learning. (Chapters 1, 4)

Moral Awareness: The recognition of how choices and behaviors affect others, combined with decision to act in ways that protect dignity and well-being. Transforms empathy from sentiment into ethical responsibility. (Chapter 9)

Moral Injury: Psychological damage from perpetrating, witnessing, or failing to prevent acts that violate fundamental beliefs about right and wrong. Distinct from trauma (threat to physical safety). Activates different neural pathways than post-traumatic stress disorder (PTSD). (Chapter 7)

Myelination: The process by which neural pathways become coated with myelin, increasing transmission speed and efficiency. Relevant to skill development: practiced pathways literally become faster. (Chapter 7)

Name It to Tame It: Dan Siegel's phrase for the regulatory effect of affect labeling. Naming emotions integrates different brain regions and reduces their intensity. (Chapter 7)

Neural Coupling: Uri Hasson's finding that during effective communication, speaker and listener brain activity synchronizes. Deep listening shows anticipation of speaker's brain activity. (Chapter 9)

Neural Integration: The coordination of different brain regions and networks to produce unified, adaptive responses. Central to this book's definition of emotional intelligence as integration capacity. (Chapters 1, 4)

Neuroplasticity: The brain's capacity to reorganize itself by forming new neural connections throughout life. Scientific basis for the trainability of emotional intelligence. (Chapters 3, 7)

Parasympathetic Nervous System: The "rest and digest" branch of the autonomic nervous system. Activated during recovery, relaxation, and social engagement. Central to Polyvagal Theory. (Chapters 7, 8, 9)

Passive Adoption: The delegation of judgment to systems without asking what human capacities atrophy, what wisdom is lost, or what happens when systems fail. A form of slow anaesthesia. (Chapter 5)

Pattern Recognition: The ability to identify regularities and meaningful configurations in experience. Distinguished from mere data processing by its reliance on accumulated lived experience. What intuition is built from. (Chapters 4, 7)

Persuasiveness: The ability to inspire voluntary change through ethical influence, shared purpose, and mutual benefit. Fourth relational mastery skill. Distinguished from manipulation by transparency and consent. (Chapter 9)

Polyvagal Theory: Stephen Porges' framework explaining how the autonomic nervous system supports social engagement. Describes three states: social engagement (ventral vagal), fight/flight (sympathetic), and freeze (dorsal vagal). (Chapter 9)

Prefrontal Cortex: Brain region associated with executive functions including planning, decision-making, and impulse control. Activated during affect labeling and deliberate regulation. Can be "offline" during emotional flooding. (Chapters 1, 7, 8)

Psychological Flexibility: The ability to be present, open up to difficult experiences, and take values-directed action. Related to but broader than emotional regulation. (Chapter 7)

Psychological Safety: Amy Edmondson's concept describing environments where people feel safe to take interpersonal risks: speaking up, making mistakes, and asking questions, without fear of punishment or humiliation. (Chapters 9, 11)

Referent Power: Influence derived from respect rather than position. Built through consistent integrity and values alignment over time. Contrasted with coercive or positional power. (Chapter 9)

Repair: The process of rebuilding connection after rupture in relationships. Requires awareness, mastery, and relational skill to acknowledge impact, take responsibility, make amends, and change behavior. (Chapter 9)

Resilience: The capacity to recover from difficulty and transform adversity into renewed strength. Third self-mastery skill. Distinguished from mere endurance by its alchemical quality: converting challenge into growth. (Chapter 8)

Resonance: The empathy subskill of sharing another person's emotional experience, allowing their inner world to echo within you while maintaining separate awareness. Creates the feeling of being truly understood. (Chapter 9)

RULER Framework: Marc Brackett's emotional literacy system: Recognizing, Understanding, Labeling, Expressing, and Regulating emotions. Developed at Yale Center for Emotional Intelligence. (Chapter 7)

Self-Awareness: The first pillar of emotional intelligence. The capacity to recognize and understand your own emotional states, patterns, and values. Comprises interoception, emotional literacy, meta-awareness, and values alignment. (Chapter 7)

Self-Mastery: The second pillar of emotional intelligence. The capacity to regulate emotional states, sustain effort through difficulty, and recover from challenge. Comprises emotional self-command, discomfort tolerance, and resilience. (Chapter 8)

Social Engagement System: In Polyvagal Theory, the neural platform that supports connection through facial expression, vocalization, and listening. Requires safety and activates the ventral vagal complex. (Chapter 9)

Somatic Marker Hypothesis: Antonio Damasio's theory that emotions create bodily sensations that guide decision-making, often before conscious reasoning. Positions emotion as essential to, not separate from, rational choice. (Chapter 7)

Stress Inoculation: The process of building resilience through progressive exposure to manageable stressors. Explains how deliberate engagement with difficulty increases tolerance and capacity. (Chapter 8)

Stress Reappraisal: The technique of reframing stress as performance-enhancing rather than debilitating. Alia Crum's research shows this interpretation shift produces measurable differences in health and performance outcomes. (Chapter 8)

Sympathetic Nervous System: The "fight or flight" branch of the autonomic nervous system. Mobilizes energy for action but can become chronically activated under prolonged stress. (Chapters 7, 8)

Three Pillars Framework: This book's organizing structure for emotional intelligence: Self-Awareness (the foundation), Self-Mastery (choosing skillfully), and Relational Mastery (connecting meaningfully). (Introduction, Part 2)

Transcendence: The capacity to let experience change who you are in ways that widen your circle of concern and deepen your alignment with what matters beyond yourself. Distinguished from mere skill improvement by its transformative quality. (Chapter 4)

Ubuntu: African philosophy meaning "I am because we are." Recognizes identity as formed through relationship and individual well-being as inseparable from collective flourishing. (Chapter 3)

Vagal Tone: The strength and flexibility of vagus nerve function, reflecting parasympathetic capacity. High vagal tone is associated with better emotional regulation, social connection, and stress recovery. Related to HRV. (Chapters 7, 8, 9)

Values Alignment: The practice of making choices that reflect your deepest principles, especially when uncomfortable. Fourth self-awareness skill. Creates integrity between inner conviction and outer action. (Chapter 7)

Ventral Vagal Complex: In Polyvagal Theory, the evolutionarily newest branch of the vagus nerve that supports social engagement, connection, and calm alertness. Active when we feel safe. (Chapter 9)

Window of Tolerance: The zone of optimal arousal where a person can process information, feel emotions, and respond effectively. Outside this window (hyper- or hypo-aroused), functioning degrades. (Chapter 8)

Yerkes-Dodson Law: The principle that performance increases with arousal to a point, then decreases, creating an inverted-U curve. Peak performance occurs at moderate stress levels. (Chapter 8)

WHO THIS BOOK IS FOR

This book is for leaders, technologists, educators, and practitioners responsible for human systems in an age of artificial intelligence. If you design teams, shape culture, implement AI, or develop people, you will find here an operating manual for building measurable emotional intelligence into how you decide, design, and lead. If you are navigating your own development, you will find a framework grounded in science and practice. The principles apply whether you lead an organization, a classroom, a family, or yourself.